Intellectual Property

Intellectual Property

The Many Faces of the Public Domain

Edited by

Charlotte Waelde

University of Edinburgh, UK

Hector MacQueen

University of Edinburgh, UK

Edward Elgar
Cheltenham, UK • Northampton, MA, USA

Published by
Edward Elgar Publishing Limited
The Lypiatts
15 Lansdown Road
Cheltenham
Glos GL50 2JA
UK

Edward Elgar Publishing, Inc.
William Pratt House
9 Dewey Court
Northampton
Massachusetts 01060
USA

A catalogue record for this book
is available from the British Library

ISBN 978 1 84542 874 7

Typeset by Manton Typesetters, Louth, Lincolnshire, UK

Contents

Contributors

Toby Bainton is Secretary of SCONUL, the Standing Conference of National and University Libraries.

Ann Bruce is a research fellow at ESRC Innogen Centre, University of Edinburgh.

John Cahir practises as an intellectual property lawyer in Dublin and was previously a research scholar at the Queen Mary Intellectual Property Research Institute, University of London, where he completed a doctoral thesis about the evolution of property concepts in the Internet environment.

Gillian Davies is a practising barrister at Hogarth Chambers, 5 New Square, Lincoln's Inn. She is a senior editor of *Copinger and Skone James on Copyright*, 15th edition (Sweet and Maxwell, 2005) and a former Chairman of a Technical Board of Appeal and Member of the Enlarged Board at the European Patent Office in Munich.

Ronan Deazley is a Reader in the Law School at the University of Birmingham. He is the author of *On the Origin of the Right to Copy: Charting the Movement of Copyright Law in Eighteenth Century Britain (1695–1775)* (Oxford: Hart, 2004).

Graham Dutfield is Herchel Smith Senior Research Fellow at the Queen Mary Intellectual Property Research Institute, Queen Mary, University of London.

Johanna Gibson is a Reader in intellectual property law at the Queen Mary Intellectual Property Research Institute, Queen Mary, University of London.

F. Willem Grosheide is Professor of Private Law and Intellectual Property Law at the Molengraaff Institute for Private Law/Centre for Intellectual Property Law (CIER), Utrecht University.

John Howkins is Executive Chairman of Tornado Productions Ltd, which provides webcasting to corporate and media clients. He is also a director of ITR

Ltd, Equator Group plc, Television Investments Ltd and World Learning Network Ltd. He chaired the committee that produced the Royal Society of Arts Adelphi Charter on Creativity, Innovation and Intellectual Property.

Manfredi M.A. La Manna is a Reader in the School of Economics at the University of St Andrews.

Fiona Macmillan is a Professor in the School of Law at Birkbeck, University of London, and Convenor of the AHRC Research Network to Consider New Directions in Copyright, Birkbeck, University of London.

Hector MacQueen is Professor of Private Law and Director of the AHRC Research Centre for Studies in Intellectual Property Law and Technology at the School of Law, University of Edinburgh. He was a member of the committee that produced the Royal Society of Arts Adelphi Charter on Creativity, Innovation and Intellectual Property, and has been a member of the UK Cabinet Office Advisory Panel on Public Sector Information since 2004.

Sue Mayer is Executive Director of GeneWatch, UK. She is an honorary research fellow at the University of Lancaster, a trustee of Vetwork UK (an animal welfare charity) and a member of the Government's Agriculture and Environment Biotechnology Commission.

Richard Susskind OBE is an Honorary Professor, Gresham College, London; Professor (part-time), Centre for Law, Computers and Technology, University of Strathclyde; IT Adviser to the Lord Chief Justice of England and Chairman of the UK Cabinet Office Advisory Panel on Public Sector Information

Antony Taubman is Director (a/g) and Head, Traditional Knowledge (Global Intellectual Property Issues) Division, WIPO, and Senior Lecturer (on leave), College of Law, Australian National University.

Bill Thompson is a journalist, commentator and technology critic and a regular commentator on the BBC World Service programme *Go Digital*.

Charlotte Waelde is a senior lecturer and co-director of the AHRC Research Centre for Studies in Intellectual Property and Technology Law at the School of Law, University of Edinburgh.

Helen Wallace is Deputy Director of GeneWatch UK. She has worked as an environmental scientist in academia and industry and as Senior Scientist at Greenpeace UK, where she was responsible for science and policy work on a range of issues.

Introduction: the many faces of the public domain

Hector MacQueen and Charlotte Waelde

This volume is part of the output from the Arts and Humanities Research Council (AHRC) Research Centre for Studies in Intellectual Property and Technology Law at Edinburgh University Law School, under one of its three anchor research themes: 'Intellectual Property, Cultural Heritage and the Public Domain'.

Among the aims of the projects being carried out under this theme are the examination of the history, role and function of the public domain in relation to all areas of intellectual property, together with consideration of the extent to which the public domain may be diminishing with the expansion of intellectual property right claims, and the effect this may have on cultural and scientific production. In particular, there is to be exploration of the implications of digitisation of public domain material for use on the Internet, with particular reference to issues about access, reproduction, commercial exploitation and privacy.

From the beginning of the Centre in 2002 an inter-disciplinary approach to this investigation was thought to be essential. A working group with participants drawn from many different backgrounds met in March 2003 to identify areas crossing over between concepts of public domain and scientific and cultural heritage. The choice of topics for discussion in this book owes much to the deliberations of the working group, and indeed many of the contributors were among the participants on that occasion. One other follow-up to the 2003 meeting was a further meeting, held in September 2004, with another multi-disciplinary group to discuss 'An IP-Free World in Higher Education'.[1] This meeting produced some more of the topics of and contributors to this book, work for which began in earnest shortly afterwards.

The importance of the idea of the 'public domain' in the cultural and scientific contexts is that it is a body of knowledge and information to which there is general access for use for purposes such as education (formal and informal) and

---

[1] A note summarising the discussion and tentative conclusions reached at that meeting is available on the AHRC Centre's website, http://www.law.ed.ac.uk/ahrb.

the further development of knowledge, understanding, creativity and inventiveness. Great names of the past may be quoted in support of its value: for example, Samuel Taylor Coleridge's version of a famous metaphor, 'The dwarf sees farther than the giant, when he has the giant's shoulder to mount on.'[2] A more down-to-earth metaphor is provided in the present collection by Bill Thompson, speaking on behalf of creative writers, whether of fiction or non-fiction: 'For a writer the "public domain" is ... the mulch on the forest floor of creativity through which we chew our way.' A well-stocked and healthy public domain is therefore crucial, it is said, to ongoing innovation in both the cultural and scientific arenas, at least standing alongside intellectual property's incentive of exclusivity and potential financial reward in pursuit of the same general goal. The arrival of the Internet has given new potency to this idea of a public domain, by making available to all with access to the network an extraordinary array of material in a variety of forms – not quite the sum of human knowledge and experience available at the click of a mouse, but much nearer to that than at any time in history, and meanwhile continuing to grow at an exponential rate.

If the public domain is so important, it becomes as important to identify what it is, and what its continued well-being requires, as it is to promote the development and enforcement of intellectual property rights. For lawyers such as our contributors Gillian Davies and Fiona Macmillan, the natural starting point in thinking about ideas of public domain in relation to cultural and scientific knowledge is the law of intellectual property. Indeed, as Willem Grosheide observes, in the medieval and early modern world before intellectual property, the concept of a general public domain was barely thinkable. The great Renaissance scholar Erasmus of Rotterdam might say around 1500 that 'friends hold all things in common', but the circle of friends in a world before printing, mass literacy and readily accessible communications technology was a very limited one. One of the earliest appearances of the phrase 'public domain' in a legal setting is found in Article 18 of the Berne Convention for the Protection of Literary and Artistic Works 1886, referring to the position of works the copyright in which has expired. Public domain analysis in law really begins from the identification of whatever it is that lies unprotected by intellectual property rights and so is free for use by all engaged in intellectual endeavours of whatever kind, being incapable of that exclusivity which is the core of legal conceptualisations of ownership.

Other forms of property right may also be relevant, or even more important in practical terms: for example, private ownership of personal papers or works of art may be all that is needed to keep such material out of any form of public view or use, regardless of whether or not intellectual property rights are also

---

[2]   *The Friend*, vol. 1, essay 8 (1818).

involved. However, as another contributor, Antony Taubman, points out, since property and intellectual property laws are fundamentally territorial, varying from jurisdiction to jurisdiction, this means at least that the scope and content of the public domain so defined is also fundamentally contingent upon the facts of legal geography, and not everywhere the same. The starting point for further analysis may therefore be James Boyle's perceptive observation, made in an earlier colloquium on the subject at Duke University in the USA, that we have not one but many public domains;[3] or, perhaps, that the public domain has many different faces according to the place from which it is viewed.

On the evidence of this volume, however, the lawyer's initial perception of the public domain as the opposite of property is often shared by those working in other disciplinary contexts. Thus, from the perspective of creative writers and librarians respectively, Bill Thompson and Toby Bainton see copyright as the key determinant of the public domain. Economists, says Manfredi La Manna, are ill at ease with concepts of the public domain because their most trusted points of reference, such as, well-defined property rights and individual incentives, are missing. In the scientific world Helen Wallace and Susan Mayer see the research agenda as increasingly driven by the pursuit of patents and what is patentable, rather than by global needs in terms of health and food security, particularly those of poor and disadvantaged populations. This does at least point to a different, possibly more political than legal, approach to the public domain, a theme taken up by Ann Bruce when she argues, referring in particular to the GM crops debate, that 'public domain' in relation to science means greater public engagement with, and control of, scientific research, reducing the 'private domain' of scientists and expert advisory groups in this area. Bruce sees this form of the public domain expanding now and in the future.

To define the public domain as everything not subject to the claims of property is, however, potentially a serious over-simplification, as Ronan Deazley reminds us in his contribution. It is not, for example, an abuse of language to think of something as being in the public domain which, whatever its intellectual property status, is merely published or even just publicised. Dan Brown's celebrated (or reviled, according to taste) novel *The Da Vinci Code* is as surely in the public domain as it is in copyright. The sale, gift and loan of millions of copies around the world, together with a major film adaptation and coverage across the media of a sensational court case in London,[4] have ensured that much of the book's

---

[3] Boyle, J. (2003), 'The Second Enclosure Movement and the Construction of the Public Domain', 66 *Law and Contemporary Problems* 33.

[4] *Baigent v Random House Group Ltd* [2006] EWHC 719 (Ch). The case also demonstrates the extent to which Dan Brown (and his wife) relied upon what the judge found to be the public domain elements of other copyright works in composing *The Da Vinci Code*.

story line, incident and underpinning ideas can be the subject of water-cooler discussions among people around the world, including those who find the whole phenomenon offensive or shocking and as a result refuse to read the book. Even the most aggressive corporate lawyer will recognise that no copyright can stop me, prompted by the curiosity sparked by publicity, idly glancing through, absorbing or confirming knowledge of the contents of, but not buying, *The Da Vinci Code* in an airport bookshop while awaiting the calling of my flight. In another realm of intellectual property, one of the points of a patent is the public disclosure of the invention for others to use in their own inventive work even while the patent is still live. James Boyle himself pointed out that such dedications of material to the public domain as the General Public Licence for open-source software and, more generally, Creative Commons licences, nonetheless gain their binding quality from the underpinnings of intellectual property rights in the subject matter.[5]

Further, free use does not necessarily mean simply use for free; or, as Richard Stallman famously put it, free is often better understood as in free speech (or, indeed, freedom) rather than as in free beer.[6] Gillian Davies refers to, although only to reject, the concept of the 'paying public domain', under which there is a continuing obligation to pay for the use of works after copyright expires, the royalties being collected for the general benefit of living authors or for other cultural purposes. Another possible but different example of this kind of free but paid for use may arise from new European laws requiring public bodies to allow the re-use of information gathered by them in the discharge of their public function. But, as explained here by Richard Susskind, Chair of the United Kingdom Cabinet Office Advisory Panel on Public Sector Information,[7] the copyright which public bodies enjoy in the material they produce allows them a discretion on whether or not to charge, so long as they do so on fair, transparent and equal terms. Antony Taubman shows that a somewhat similar approach is taken by international bodies such as the United Nations with regard to the treaty texts of which they are guardians, and Davies discusses UNESCO policy guidelines on the development and promotion of governmental information, issued in 2004, that accept such use of public body intellectual property rights while also encouraging permissive licences or waivers.[8] There is, of course, an important contrast here with the position in the United States, where publicly produced information (such as mapping and weather data) is outside copyright

---

[5]   Boyle (2003), 'Second Enclosure Movement', 44–9, 64–6.
[6]   See the GNU website, at http://www.gnu.org/philosophy/free-sw.html (last visited 2 July 2006).
[7]   See for the Advisory Panel its website: http://www.appsi.gov.uk/ (last visited 2 July 2006).
[8]   Available at http://unesdoc.unesco.org/images/0013/001373/137363eo.pdf.

and freely available (in all senses) for re-use by anyone wishing to do so; public domain, in other words, in the fullest possible way.

Most of our contributors, however, see the public domain as indeed under threat as a result of the modern development of intellectual property law, especially copyright, and agree that this is not for the good. From the European perspective, the evidence includes the extension of copyright terms in the 1990s, which not only lengthened the protection of works already in copyright but also brought back into copyright works whose protection had lapsed within the previous 20 years. The *sui generis* database right is seen as extending legal protection to facts and information, and not just the way in which those facts are expressed. In patent law, the scope of protection for the products of biotechnology and the software industry has expanded significantly despite the apparent limitations of the European Patent Convention 1973, although there has been so far successful resistance to the United States extension of patentability to business methods. There may be anxiety, apparent in the contributions by Macmillan and by Wallace and Mayer in particular, that as a result of these and other developments the public domain is being appropriated by commercial and corporate interests whose care is only for present profit and not the general good.

A number of contributors also take note of the way in which copyright law now lends support to the technological protection measures (TPMs) and digital rights management (DRM) systems with which right-holders and producers surround their digital and Internet products, to ensure that would-be users pay for their use. This appears to be at least a threat to the public domain, in as much as TPMs and DRM may bar free uses which copyright law would allow – reproduction which is fair dealing for purposes of non-commercial research or private study, for example – or even the use of material no longer or never in copyright. So the public domain possibilities of the Internet are, or may be, stunted and even cut off.

So, if the public domain is a good thing but under threat of diminution or even extinction in places, what is to be done about it? Discussion in the United States has called for an affirmative approach to the public domain: that, instead of defining it principally by reference to what it is not, the concept should be given a positive role in the law.[9] At its simplest, this might amount to saying that everything is in the public domain save that which is covered by claims of individual or intellectual property. While that might not seem to change very much, it would support arguments that where new intellectual property rights

---

[9]   See generally the proceedings of the Duke University Conference on the Public Domain (2003) published in 66 *Law and Contemporary Problems*; see also Lange, D. (1981), 'Recognizing the Public Domain', 44 *Law and Contemporary Problems* 147; Litman, J. (1990), 'The Public Domain', 39 *Emory LJ* 965.

were under discussion the burden of proof of benefit should lie on the proponents of the new rights. It might mean that rules currently allowing reproduction for certain kinds of fair dealing in relation to such public goods as education, research and news reporting could be transformed from 'copyright exceptions and limitations', useful only as defences to claims of infringement, into user rights, capable of enforcement against those who might deny them through contracts made with the help of TPMs or DRM. And proposals for the solution of practical difficulties often created by the existence of uncertain intellectual property rights – for example, the problem of 'orphan works', discussed by Bainton – would be shaped by a presumption of policy that favoured the easiest possible transition of the material into the public domain.

Some of this reflects the approach of the Royal Society of Arts Adelphi Charter on Creativity, Innovation and Intellectual Property which was launched in London in October 2005.[10] John Howkins, who chaired the group which produced the Charter, argues here that the fundamental goal of policy should be the promotion of what he calls the creative economy: not just the creative industries, but all players in creativity and invention.[11] In this view, intellectual property law has its place as a means of *regulating* the creative economy, with three factors being taken into account: access, use and reward. Laws on intellectual property should be seen as means of achieving these social, cultural and economic goals. Human rights such as the rights to health, education and free expression, as Macmillan too argues, also have a major role to play in reshaping, if not the public domain itself, the ways in which we approach and understand it. Macmillan, following the earlier work of Carol Rose,[12] and supported in the concluding chapter by Charlotte Waelde, also finds potential models for a multi-layered public domain in the perhaps unexpected source of Roman law. Concepts of *res publicae, res universitatis, res communes, res nullius* and *res divini juris* as forms of non-exclusive property go some way towards meeting the challenge for notions of public domain presented by the 'tragedy of the commons' thesis (that the absence of private property entails over-use and under-investment of the subject matter[13]).

Attractive though all this may sound, there are still pitfalls. As Waelde notes, it seems unlikely that Latin rhetoric will sway modern policy-makers, legislators

---

[10]   Available at http://www.adelphicharter.org/adelphi_charter.asp (last checked 2 July 2006).

[11]   See also Howkins, John (2001), *The Creative Economy: How People Make Money from Ideas*, London: Penguin Books.

[12]   Rose, C.M. (2003), 'Romans, Roads, and Romantic Creators: Traditions of Public Property in the Information Age', 66 *Law and Contemporary Problems* 89.

[13]   Famously stated in Hardin, G. (1968), 'The Tragedy of the Commons', *Science*, 13 December, 1243.

or industry, creative or otherwise. Thompson reminds us of another fundamental, also forcefully brought to our attention at the initial seminar from which this collection springs: that not all professional writers are salaried academics; like most other creators, such writers rely on copyright for their living and do not want everything they create to be in the public domain. John Cahir cautions against too ready a use of rights language in relation to the public domain, which, he argues, following Hohfeld's famous analysis, is best expressed in terms of liberties; the public domain is a land of no rights and should remain so. Claims that citizens are being starved of information or having their freedom of expression rights violated as a consequence of copyright and TPMs or DRM are virtually unsupported by even hearsay evidence. On the contrary, the Internet and digital technology more generally have unleashed a flood of high- (and low-) quality information, seemingly impervious to the supposed threats of copyright law allied with self-help exclusionary measures. Graham Dutfield imagines a world without intellectual property rights, deploying counterfactual techniques to analyse historical events. He finds that, although certain developments in pharmaceuticals would have occurred in the absence of patents, there would have been less than we now have. Abolition of drug patents is difficult to argue for realistically, given the high costs of research and development. Likewise copyright reflects something of the way authors see themselves as individuals, and abolition of copyright would be in diminution of that sense of self. Dutfield suggests that we cease to oppose 'rights' and 'no-rights' models, and ask instead what rights we need and what rights we should have.

A particularly telling critique is provided by Johanna Gibson, who discusses the problems which the concept of public domain rights presents for the indigenous knowledge of local and traditional communities around the world (a matter also touched upon by Taubman). This 'traditional knowledge' (TK) was, and to an extent continues to be, interpreted within the discourse of the common heritage of mankind, or public domain; yet this amounts to a justification for appropriation, often directly against the wishes of the community and its perception of its needs and entitlements. For Macmillan, TK may be best seen as *res universitatis* within the public domain: that is, as a regime bounded by property rights, with a type of limited public domain (or commons) inside those boundaries. But nonetheless the issue shows how culturally specific notions of public domain may cut across or undermine diversity and the identity and cultural integrity of different communities.

The public domain thus does indeed have at least many faces, if it is not in fact plural and diverse; and we are far from understanding what the implications may be for law or policy. But this volume does at least offer a further step towards coming to grips with these questions and defining the boundaries within which debate should be taking place. In so far as the concept aims to support innovation, creativity and invention, it appears to have the same objectives as intellectual property rights; and their mutual recognition is therefore surely not out of reach. Perhaps too in this process we need to think a little less of rights and a little more of liberties, freedom and respect for human dignity. Somewhere in that mix we may begin to get the balance a little better and enable the Internet to realise its awesome potential.

1. In search of the public domain during the prehistory of copyright law

F. Willem Grosheide

Everyone has thoughts. Some may turn them into ideas.
Even fewer will be able to give them form and colour.
And who is doing this, constantly will hear:
Just what I thought. Yes, indeed, except context, colour,
shadows, i.e. except very much. (Multatuli, 1862)[1]

1 PRELIMINARY OBSERVATIONS

Between the years 1862 and 1877 the Dutch author Multatuli compiled seven
bundles of what he called *ideeën* (ideas), in which he gave his anachronistically
radical views on a wide range of societal and paradigmatic issues, running from
education to feminism, or from religion to roulette. In the idea which has been
placed as the motto above this account of early views on the public domain
during the prehistory of copyright law, Multatuli, referring to the common and
the individual parts in human communication, hints at some form of crediting,
social or legal, to the originator of the expressed idea.[2] When he wrote, the
Netherlands, like other Western European countries, already recognised a ru-

---

[1]   Multatuli, the pseudonym of Eduard Douwes Dekker (1820–87), is one of the
greatest Dutch authors whose radical opinions and freshness of style managed to escape
from the middle of the road, self-satisfied, bourgeois Dutch literature of the mid-19th
century.

[2]   As is well known, Multatuli was not the only European writer, or rather intellectual, who at the time was striving for social and legal recognition. For example,
Honoré de Balzac in France raised his voice against the 'barbarian' law that protects
'the land' and 'the home of the working-class man' but 'confiscates the work of the
poet who has thoughts' ('Lettre adressée aux écrivains français du XIXème siècle',
La Revue de Paris 1834, vol. II, 64–5). The characterisation of the early days of copyright law as its 'prehistory' is taken from Strömholm, S. (1966–73), *Le droit moral de
l'auteur en droit Allemand, Français et Scandinave (I, II, III)*, Stockholm: P.A. Norstedt
& Söners.

dimentary form of what in retrospect may be called copyright law *avant la lettre*, that is, a form of legal protection for authors of works.[3] Indeed, in the last quarter of the 19th century the societal and paradigmatic state of affairs in the then civilised world, that is, Western Europe, was getting ready for the coming into existence of copyright law as we know it today.[4] In fact, it was Multatuli's French fellow-*artiste* Victor Hugo who laid the foundations of the Association Littéraire et Artistique Internationale (ALAI) in 1882, the organisation that, following the spirit of an international awakening, paved the way for the establishment of the Berne Convention (BC) 1886 on the international legal protection of works of authorship.[5] Seen in that light, modern copyright law is really an invention of the 19th century.[6]

---

[3]   See e.g. French Copyright Act 1793; Dutch Copyright Act 1817; Prussian Copyright Act 1834. Germany, during that period in time, was still far from being the national state that came into existence in 1806/15. The Holy Roman Empire, where hundreds of principalities exercised more or less autonomous jurisdiction over trade in their respective domains, did not have any uniform copyright statute.

[4]   The view that creating an international copyright law regime is an act of civilisation can be found in the works of many legal scholars writing at the end of the 19th century. See De Beaufort, H.L. (1909[1993]), *Het auteursrecht*, Utrecht, p. 309. Compare Sherman, B. and Bently, L. (1999), *The Making of Modern Intellectual Property Law*, Cambridge: Cambridge University Press.

[5]   I refer to Victor Hugo as a fellow-*artiste* (instead of a fellow-*author* or fellow-*writer*) since during his lifetime as a writer it became fashionable in France to use the term *artiste* as a generic indication for all who were involved in the art of creation. See Heinich, N. (2005), *L'élite artiste – Excellence et singularité en regime démocratique*, Paris: Gallimard, p. 177: 'Lorsqu' un "Jeune-France" choisit de se dire "artiste" et non pas "écrivain", il manifeste une volonté d'appartenir à un collectif plus large que celui des hommes de lettres, englobant les créateurs d'oeuvres plastiques et musicales.' This is interesting, since not much earlier the French writer Etienne Pivert de Sinancour preferred the term *écrivain* instead of *hommes de lettres*, since the first term was associated with working in a guild (*la profession*), the second with following a mission (*une vocation*). See Heinrich, p. 79, referring to Bémichou, P. (1966), *Le Sacre de l'Écrivain 1750–1830*, Paris: Gallimard, p. 207. The expression 'international awakening' is used by Ploman, Edward W., and Clark, Hamilton L. (1980), *Copyright – Intellectual Property in the Information Age*, London: Routledge & Kegan Paul. See, on the history of the BC, Cavalli, J. (1986), *La Génèse de la Convention de Berne pour la Protection des Oeuvres Littéraires et Artistiques du 9 Septembre 1886*, Lausanne: Imprimeries Réunies; Ricketson, S. (1987), *The Berne Convention for the Protection of Literary and Artistic Works: 1886–1986*, London: Centre for Commercial Studies and Deventer: Kluwer.

[6]   I have elaborated on the thesis of modern copyright law as a 19th century invention in Grosheide, F.W. (1986), *Auteursrecht op maat*, Deventer: Kluwer, Chapter II, section 2.2. Van Horn Melton, J. (2001), *The Rise of the Public in Enlightenment Europe*, Cambridge: Cambridge University Press, p. 147, refers to the 'invention of copyright' already in the 18th century.

It follows that in the light of the theme of this chapter it is appropriate to investigate whether and, if so, in what way the public domain as a concept was already known before 1886,[7] particularly during the late Middle Ages and the Renaissance.[8] Such an investigation cannot be carried out without taking into account the intellectual history that lies at the basis of the introduction of the BC. Further, in respect of what follows and in order to avoid any possible misunderstanding, it seems to be appropriate, in addition – taking account of the necessarily generalising approach of the theme of this chapter – to make some clarifying observations in relation to some notions and terms already used and to be used again below.

First, and following on from what has already been said, the unreflective use of the notion and the term 'copyright (law)' may lead to confusion, since the various existing models that protect authors and works operate differently in many ways. For that reason, in the next section I will use the term 'copyright (law)' as a common denominator for either the civil law or the common law model for the protection of (works of) authorship, although the term copyright (law) *stricto sensu* refers to the common law model of copyright (law).

---

[7] Although the BC 1886 clearly bears a civil law, i.e. *a droit d'auteur*, stamp, its gist is that it unified, to a large extent, that one model with the common law, i.e. the copyright law *stricto sensu*. It is of note that this did become possible owing to the common cultural roots of the civil law system and the common law system: copyright law seen as a certain variant of legal regulation of human communication originating solely within the framework of Western culture, serving mainly to safeguard the exploitation of cultural information upon its dissemination. It should be underlined that – as a consequence thereof – the copyright law regime of the early BC only related to the exploitation of works of authorship, i.e. the economic aspect (Grosheide (1986), Chapter 6). I am well aware that, by referring to 'cultural information' as the object of communication in a generic sense, I am using a concept that has been developed in the context of early modern print culture.

[8] For present purposes it seems not to be necessary to distinguish between the various copyright systems that have evolved in the course of time in the Western world and to emphasise the common roots of these systems in a historical perspective. See on various copyright systems Strömholm, S., Chapter 2 ('Copyright – National and International Development') and Chapter 5 ('Copyright – Comparison of Laws'), in F.K. Beier and G. Schricker, (1983–90) *Copyright and Industrial Property*, Mohr: Nijhoff Publishers. See also Bappert, W. (1962), *Wege zum Urheberrecht*, Frankfurt am Main: Klostermann; Ströwel, A. (1993), *Droit d'Auteur et Copyright*, Bruxelles: Bruylant, including the German *Urheberrecht* in the *droit d'auteur*-model; Edelman, B. (2001), *Le Combat du Droit d'Auteur*, Paris: Les Impressions Nouvelles. See, on the relationship between French and American copyright law, Ginsburg, J.C. (1990), 'A Tale of Two Copyrights: Literary Property in Revolution France and America', 64 *Tulane Law Review* (5), reprinted in Sherman, B. and Ströwel, A. (1994), *Of Authors and Origins*, Oxford: Clarendon Press, p. 131.

Second, it should be stressed that notions and terms such as 'author' and 'work' have been given their proper meaning as social, cultural and legal terms over the course of time. In a historical perspective, an author, in the strict sense of the term, is 'someone acknowledged as responsible for a printed (or sometimes written) work; that is, authorship is taken to be a matter of attribution by others, not of self-election'.[9] As Woodmansee rightly observes, the 'author' in its modern sense is a relatively recent invention.[10] Interestingly, this socially and culturally determined notion of the author refers to what in the years to come would legally be articulated as the personal (or rather moral) interests of the author. It does not refer to the legal regime that emerged with the invention of the printing press in order to regulate the book trade. That so-called pre-copyright law focused on the work as a commodity; it was concerned with censorship and competition. At issue here, in fact, is the juxtaposition of what in later years would be indicated as the two basic forms of copyright law protection: on the one hand, protection against plagiarism; on the other, protection against piracy.[11] In addition, and since the notion and the term 'author' have in the course of time become generic indicators for the subject of copyright protection, I will use that notion/term indiscriminately for the writer, composer, painter, architect or whoever may be called an individual creator in today's

---

[9]   Johns, A. (1998), *The Nature of the Book*, Chicago: The University of Chicago Press, p. xxi.

[10]   Woodmansee, M. (1984), 'The Genius and the Copyright: Economics and Legal Conditions of the Emergence of the "Author"', *Eighteenth-Century Studies*, **17** (4), 425–48, ('author' in its modern sense is the product of the rise in the 18th century of a new group of individuals: writers who sought to earn their livelihood from the sale of their writings to the new and rapidly expanding reading public). See also Grosheide (1986), pp. 169–266 (Chapter IV); Rose, M. (1993), *Authors and Owners: The Invention of Copyright*, Cambridge, MA: Harvard University Press. With regard to a copyright law concerned with an author's rights the term 'authorial copyright' – used by Loewenstein, J. (2002), *The Author's Due*, Chicago: The University of Chicago Press, Chapter 7, p. 192, for the emergence of attribution of works to authors in 17th century England – seems appropriate here.

[11]   Johns (1998), p. xx, states that the term 'piracy' in a historical perspective is controversial. He argues that in the 17th century the most common term used to describe an offence against literary propriety was not piracy or plagiarism but 'usurpation' (p. 461). In the text the terms 'piracy' and 'plagiarism' are used in their actual legal meaning. Piracy is the infringement of copyright as a property right; plagiarism is the infringement of copyright as a personality right. The first takes a free ride on exploitation; the second fails to give credit. So, for example, piracy is publishing a book without the permission of the right owner, plagiarism is passing off the work of a writer as one's own work. Put in other words: by forbidding piracy copyright law grants control over the (exploitation of the) form of a work; but it does not grant control over the content (information, ideas) of that work.

copyright-speak. The notion/term *writer* is used in the vernacular sense to refer to the author *stricto sensu*.[12]

Third, the notion or term 'public domain' also needs clarification. It should be underlined that we can view the public domain from an external and an internal legal perspective, while also realising that the public domain is a modern concept used in order to describe the origins and development of an actual state of affairs. In fact, the notion of the public domain is an abstraction which can be applied to a society's institutions only when the appropriation or privatisation of information (that is, the monopolisation of knowledge) becomes legally possible.[13] Further, it is already noteworthy at this stage of the discussion that the public domain does not necessarily coincide with the public interest. But what, then, legally speaking, is the public domain? Obviously, this chapter cannot do without at least a working definition of that notion/term. However, it appears that the question posed is not easy to answer and that any definition is – as Lange has put it – 'a function of perspective and agenda'.[14] That may be so, but, while an in-depth analysis of the public domain is beyond the scope

---

[12]   Johns (1998), p. xxi, uses the term writer for the one 'who composes a printed (or at least written) work; he may or may not attain authorship'.

[13]   Compare Rose, M. (2003), 'Nine-tenths of the Law: the English Copyright Debate and the Rhetoric of the Public Domain', 66 *Law & Contemporary Problems*, 75–87: 'Copyright and the public domain were born together. They were formed in the course of the long social process that Jürgen Habermas identifies as the emergence of the "public sphere". This process involves the circulation of cultural products as commodities rather than as displays of aristocratic magnificence and it involves a sense of civil society as a collectivity distinct from either the private realm of the family or the public realm of the state.'

[14]   How correct this observation is is evidenced by the many varying definitions of the public domain that can be found in the legal literature. See above all Lange, D. (2003), 'Reimaging the Public Domain', 66 *Law & Contemporary Problems* 463–83. Lange's paper is a response to James Boyle's introduction, 'The Second Enclosure Movement and the Construction of the Public Domain', to the 2001 Duke Law School Conference on the Public Domain, in which Boyle questioned an earlier paper by Lange (1981), 'Recognizing the Public Domain', 44 *Law & Contemporary Problems* 147, in which Lange concluded that the public domain in itself contains a set of individual intellectual property rights. 'But what does this mean?' Boyle asks. 'What is the nature of these individual rights in "the public domain"? Who holds them? Indeed, what is the public domain?' Referring to his early paper as a sort of pre-stage for his actual thoughts (the public domain as 'a place of refuge for creative expression' (p. 470)), Lange answers Boyle's question by saying that a better metaphor for the public domain than that of a 'place, a wilderness, a commons, a sanctuary, a home' (p. 474); is the 'status … that arises from the exercise of the creative imagination, thus to confer entitlements, privileges and immunities in the service of that exercise' (p. 474). A full account of the Duke Law School conference and the related interesting papers is to be found at www.law.duke. edu/pd/papers.html.

of this chapter, this does not detract from the need for a working definition as suggested.[15]

Following Lange and taking account of the additional relevant literature, particularly Litman's study of the subject, at least three different approaches to the public domain can be distinguished:

- the public domain seen as the state of affairs that obtains if the term of the legal protection of some informational product has lapsed
- the public domain seen as the whole of intellectual contributions that do not meet any agreed standard of originality set by the law
- the public domain seen as a common and freely accessible reservoir for authors to use for the making of works.[16]

In what follows, the focus will be on the third approach. The originality criterion and the term of protection both being creations of positive law after the prehistory of copyright law ended, the first and second approaches are not at issue here. So, the stage having been set in this way, the remainder of this chapter is structured in the following order. Section 2 provides a brief account of the shared historical roots of the civil law and the common law copyright systems in the late Middle Ages and the Renaissance, and the role of the public domain in that perspective. Section 3 reflects upon the legal regulation of dissemination of, and access to, cultural information after the introduction of the printing press. Finally, section 4 offers an evaluation of the legal status of the public domain in the period under discussion.

---

[15]   An in-depth analysis of the public domain can be found in the Duke Law School papers mentioned in note 14.

[16]   Litman, J. (1990), 'The Public Domain', 39, *Emory Law Journal* (4). See also Belder, L. (2005), 'Public Domain', paper presented at an AHRC Conference in London, June (published in (2006), *New Directions in Copyright Law: Vol 2*, Cheltenham: Edward Elgar), arguing that '[t]he idea of the intellectual commons as a positive community, refers to a public domain where all objects have equal status as non-property, or at least as freely accessible.' The common denominator of the three approaches to the public domain is of course the state of non-protection. But the reasons why protection is not granted may and do differ. In the text I refer indiscriminately to informational products, intellectual contributions and works, since I consider those terms as synonyms for the purpose of this chapter. I use the term 'making' instead of 'creating' in order to avoid connotations such as the author as a God-like *creator ex nihilo*.

2   THE PREHISTORY OF COPYRIGHT LAW

If it is true that the history of modern copyright law starts in the last quarter of the 19th century, then it is equally true that its prehistory begins in the transition period from the Middle Ages to the Renaissance in (Western) Europe.[17] For it was during this period that this part of the world underwent the societal and paradigmatic changes which eventually led to what Boorstin calls 'widening the communities of knowledge'.[18] In the context of this chapter, two particularly connecting developments are of interest here: the shift in communication technologies and the internationalisation of commerce, both of them contributing to the trade in books.[19]

The printing press redefined the way in which human beings organised knowledge: from oral and script culture to print culture. It changed – as Rifkin states – the nature of human consciousness.[20] Before the print medium, knowl-

---

[17]   Strömholm, S. (1983), 'Droit Moral – The International and Comparative Scene from a Scandinavian view point', *IIC* 1983, 1 et seq. : 'Nevertheless it was not until well into the 19th century that it could clearly be seen that the prehistory of the institution had ended and its history had begun.' See also Loewenstein (2002). It should be stressed in this respect that this so-called prehistory of copyright law concerns only acts of creativity that can be communicated in written or printed texts: acts of creativity which in today's society will be ascribed to 'intellectuals'.

[18]   Boorstin, D.J. (1983), *The Discoverers – A History of Man's Search to Know His World and Himself*, New York: Random House, Part Thirteen, p. 480 et seq.

[19]   With reference to Habermas, J. (1962), *The Structural Transformation of the Public Sphere (Strukturwandel der Öffentlichkeit: Untersuchungen zur einen Kategorie der bürgerlichen Gesellschaft)*, Luchterhand: Darmstadt & Neuwied, Van Horn Melton (2001), pp. 4–6, observes that the indicated developments – the rise of modern nation states dating from the late Middle Ages (connected to the emergence of society as a realm distinct from the state) and the rise of (mercantile) capitalism – strip the noble family or, as the case may be, the household of the functions as a unit of production and as the sphere of domination. See also Boorstin (1983), Part Six, 'Doubling the World', p. 146 et seq.

[20]   Rifkin, J. (2000), *The Age of Access – How the Shift from Ownership to Access is Transforming Modern Life*, London: Penguin Books, p. 204. See generally Eisenstein, E.L. (1979), *The Printing Press as an Agent of Change – Communications and Cultural Transformation in Early Modern Europe* (arguing that print culture is primarily characterised by making texts subject to standardisation, dissemination and fixity, and as a consequence of the possibility of mass reproduction of precisely the same text contributing to the stability of languages and laws), Cambridge: Cambridge University Press, contested by Johns (1998), p. 30 (print culture did not arrive with movable type but rather slowly took shape in the centuries following the establishment of printing presses throughout Europe. Eisenstein's print culture never existed. One should distinguish instead between different print cultures in particular historical circumstances). For present purposes there is no need to elaborate upon the Eisenstein/Johns debate.

edge of whatever kind was preserved primarily by memorising. Medieval scholars did not consider memorising merely as a practical skill, but rather as a virtue. It followed from the feudal structure of medieval society that the preservation of knowledge by memorising was exercised by those privileged to belong to a classified group such as that of priests, musicians or lawyers. Preservation by memory in classified groups at the same time made it possible to keep the respective bodies of knowledge secret, commonly known only by those who belonged to a certain profession. 'Secret' coincides with 'sacral' here, since the manuscript book was a kind of sacred object, an aid to religious and legal rituals.[21] Understandably, the learned community warned that print would lead to the popularisation of books and, as a consequence thereof, to the vulgarisation of learning and knowing. The existence of this so-called 'Empire of the Learned' (Boorstin) was also due to a great extent to the fact that it was held together by the use of Latin as the language of its inhabitants. Obviously, practising Latin as the vehicle of communicating knowledge at the same time functioned as a barrier between the learned and ordinary people.[22]

With regard to the internationalisation of trade, it is of interest to note that, measured by the standards of previous ages, owing to ever better transportation systems, the world's economy grew very rapidly between 1450 and 1800. In fact, in Western Europe no public authority was able to halt the continuing commercialisation which was a consequence of this growth. Understandably, the internationalisation of commerce meant internationalisation of communication, that is, the exchange of (and trade in!) information, crucially again favoured by the invention of the printing press.[23]

In addition it should be noted that – as is well documented – during this period of time Europe was characterised by the feudal organisation of the state, that is, the same people simultaneously holding leading political and religious positions,

[21]   Boorstin (1983), pp. 401–8; 529–30. Boorstin, p. 483, quotes William Blackstone noting in 1765: 'Thus the British as well as the Gallic druids committed all their laws as well as learning to memory; and it is said of the primitive Saxons here, as well as their brethren on the continent, that *leges sola memoria et usu retinebant.*' See, for an account of the transition from memory to print, Boorstin, pp. 480–88: 'The printed book would be a new warehouse of Memory, superior in countless ways to the internal invisible warehouse in each person' (p. 485).
[22]   Boorstin (1983), p. 489. Johns (1998), pp. 49–50, refers to Francis Bacon's reservations with regard to 'open printing', insisting that his own ideas be known only to 'some fit and selected minds', and that state-produced knowledge (which he advocated) be similarly guarded.
[23]   McNeill, J.R. and McNeill, W.H. (2003), *The Human Web – a Bird's Eye-view of World History*, London/New York: N.W. Norton & Company, pp. 179–80; 201–2.

articulated in the societal institutions of censorship and the privilege system.[24,25] At the same time, and because of their contribution to the existing closed environment of learning and knowing, from a societal point of view the still dominant position of the guilds and the patronage system is important. In this respect the advent of the Reformation should also be mentioned, since it is indicated by some as a countervailing factor. For, so the argument goes, the availability of the Bible in one's own language and the emphasis on lay Bible-reading contributed to the explosion of literacy, that is, the de-secretising and de-sacralising of information.[26] However, as has been argued by Van Horn Melton, this supposed relationship between Protestant confession and literacy is controversial.[27]

---

[24]   Hesse, C. (2002), *The Rise of Intellectual Property, 700 BC – AD 2000: an idea in balance*, Daedalus, p. 29: 'It fell to God's agents upon the earth to determine how much of the knowledge putatively transmitted from God was actually divine in origin, as well as how widely and by whom such knowledge should be circulated within their kingdoms, empires and cities. Rulers forged alliances with religious authorities to control the production and circulation of ideas and information – both spiritual and technical – in their realms.' See also Boncompain, J. (2001), *La Révolution des Auteurs – Naissance de la propriété intellectuelle (1773–1815)*, Paris: Fayard, p. 29: 'La multiplication des livres, contemporaine de la Réforme, va contribuer puissamment à la diffusion d'idées politiques et réligieuses jusque-là circonscrites à quelques personnes, dans un mouvement qui n'est pas sans annoncer celui des Lumières. Dans un esprit de police et de respect de ce que nous appelons aujourd'hui les droits des consommateurs, les autorités civiles et réligieuses vont surveiller étroitement la composition et la mise en circulation des publications. Au même moment, l'imprimeur qui doit faire face à des investissements considérables, entend se prémunir contre la contrefaçon, naissante, dès lors qu'il supporte seul les frais d'achat du manuscrit de l'auteur.' See also Grosheide (1986), pp. 47–65.

[25]   See, for a broad account of this state of affairs in the Netherlands (with references to France, Great Britain and Germany), Schriks, C. (2004), *Het Kopijrecht*, Deventer: Walburg Pers–Kluwer. In fact censorship and the privilege system are early forms of what in today's legal terminology would be called limitation of the freedom of expression and competition law; see Grosheide (1986), Chapter II. It is of note that in this period in time only writers and performing artists relied upon the patronage system, living a life as a courtier, whereas painters and sculptors, being regarded as artisans and craftsmen, were organised in guilds. See Hauser, A. (1962), *The Social History of Art*, London: Routledge & Kegan Paul.

[26]   See e.g. Ginzburg, C. (1980), *The Cheese and the Worms – The Cosmos of a Sixteenth Century Writer*, London: Routledge & Kegan Paul, referring to the provocative stands of the central figure of the book: 'Printing enabled him to confront books with the oral tradition in which he had grown up and fed him to the world to release that tangle of ideas and fantasies he had within him. The Reformation gave him the courage to express his feelings to the parish priest, to his fellow villagers, to the inquisitors – even if he could not, as he wished, say them in person to the pope, to cardinals, and princes.'

[27]   Van Melton Horn (2001), pp. 83–6: 'Protestant reformers of the sixteenth century often expressed reservations about the indiscriminate promotion of Bible reading among the laity. The spread of radical sects like the Anabaptists convinced some protestant

Concerning this state of affairs, for present purposes the 15th and 16th centuries may be seen as an important, if not decisive, link in the chain of events that connects the scribal culture of the Middle Ages through the Renaissance to the full-grown print culture of Modernity. The life and work of Erasmus (1466–1536) can serve as an illustration of that argument.[28] For indeed, while he was writing mainly in Latin and depending on patronage and state-controlled publishers to disseminate his scholarly works, it may be said that during his lifetime the secret and sacral culture of the handmade manuscript was gradually replaced by the open and democratic culture of the printed book.[29] In that perspective it is of special interest for present purposes to consider whether Erasmus' writings provide evidence of any such notion as a public domain of learning and knowing.

3 FRIENDS HOLD ALL THINGS IN COMMON

In order to consider appropriately Erasmus' possible position towards a public domain, something more should first be said about the nature of the book in his day. A book, whether a handmade manuscript or printed, was generally seen as the physical carrier of a God-given content. The perception of knowledge as a gift from God consequently made it impossible either to own or sell. This does not mean that there was no trade in books. Obviously there was, and the invention of print and the spread of literacy – restricted by pre-publication censorship and state-licensed printing monopolies – increasingly contributed to that effect. However, what could be owned and sold was the carrier and not the content, illustrating that already in these days the notion of a 'book' had a double meaning.[30] In the words of Hesse:

---

leaders of the need to restrict and control lay Bible reading and to rely instead on oral catechistic instruction as a tool of religious instruction.' According to Hesse (2002), p. 30, the Reformation even spurred and intensified the state regulation of the printed word. As will be seen later, things changed dramatically from the 17th century onwards.

[28] *Erasmus (Gerhard Gerards) 1466–1469 (Rotterdam) – 1536 (Basel),* biography by Johan Huizinga, (Haarlem: Tjeenk Willink, 1924; Rotterdam: Ad Donker, 1988); idem, *Erasmus* (New York/London: Charles Scribner's Sons 1924).

[29] Boorstin (1983), pp. 515–16: 'During the first century of printing the scribes who were practicing the art of "natural" writing and the printers practicing the new art of "artificial" writing competed for the same customers. The printing press did not at once put the scribes out of business.' Ibid., p. 517: 'The triumph of the printed book soon brought the triumph of the languages of the marketplace, which became the languages of learning across Europe.'

[30] See, on the double meaning of the notion of a book, Edelman, B. (2004), *Le Sacre de l'Auteur*, Paris: Éditions du Seuil, p. 107: (referring to the doctrine of the *deux corps*

The author may lay claim to the manuscript he created, and the printer to the book reprinted, but neither could possess the contents that lay within it. The Renaissance elevated the poet, the inventor, and the artist to unprecedented heights, but their 'genius' was still understood to be divinely inspired rather than a mere product of their mental skills or worldly labors. (Hesse, 2002)[31]

So, if there were concerns about piracy in those days, the complaints came not from writers but mainly from publishers (printers, booksellers) who encountered unfair competition from unauthorised publishing. But at the time the whole concept of piracy was unclear. Condemned by some (the suppliers of original works) referring to their financial investments (buying manuscripts against outright fees and paying for printing privileges), it was defended by others (the counterfeiters), who claimed to promote the spread of literature and science. If writers such as Luther and Erasmus were concerned at all about piracy, it was not so much out of pecuniary interest, but because they worried about the integrity of their texts. Understandably, at that point concerns about piracy coincided with concerns about plagiarism. So it may be said that these concerns were of a moral rather than a legal character, since it was not false attribution that mattered in the first place, but respect for the work as written or printed text.[32]

---

du roi): 'd'un côté, on aurait le livre en tant qu'objet matériel, le volume, assimilable au corps mortel et périssable du roi; de l'autre côté, il y aurait la parole divine, inscrite dans le livre, impérissable et immortel comme la fonction royale.' Profit-making from the trade in their books was of course in the interest of writers also. They would aim to sell their works for an outright price to a licensed publisher. But their real material rewards came from royal or aristocratic patronage. See, on profit-making, Boncompain (2001), pp. 23–7.

[31] Hesse (2002), p. 28. At p. 27 Hesse stipulates that a review of all great civilisations of the pre-modern world 'reveals a striking absence of any notion of human ownership of ideas or their expressions.' Compare Rifkin (2000), p. 205: 'Print also made important the idea of authorship. While individual authors were previously recognized they were few in number. Manuscript writing was often anonymous and the result of the collective contribution of many scribes over long periods of time. The notion of authorship elevated the individual to a unique status, separating him or her from the collective voice of the community.' Edelman (2004), p. 92, referring to Kantorowicz, E. (1984), 'La Souveraineté de l'Artiste', in *Mourir pour la Patrie*, PUF, p. 51, (in medieval thinking) 'le travail de l'auteur procède de la même source que la création du monde, c'est-à-dire le verbe: Dieu a créé le monde par la force de sa parole, tout comme l'auteur invente et compose son livre par la virtu de la seule écriture.' According to Edelman this implied that the sovereignty of the writer would lead, in the course of time, to thinking about the book in terms of property.

[32] Johns (1998), Chapter 7, 'Piracy and Usurpation', pp. 444–52; Schriks (2004), Chapter 1 (English summary). In a historical perspective piracy particularly concerned printed books and their original printers. This kind of piracy is in fact a corollary of the invention of the printing press. It would even become an epidemic in the 18th century

There was yet another reason why the content of a book could not be owned in the vernacular sense of the term, let alone in any legal sense. For, still in Erasmus' time, written as well as printed texts *per se* lacked authority of their own, since they were far from fixed and stable. This was first due to the fact that particularly cultural texts (such as songs) had a content that was open to elaboration and adaptation by their communicators, who were not perceived as their authors.[33] Second, unreliability followed from the existence of different opinions about the correct production of books.[34] This is not surprising in a world that still stuck to imitation as the standard for creative activities.[35]

Where does Erasmus fit in all this? If one were asked to write his biography in a few lines, the following characterisation would be appropriate: one of Europe's leading Renaissance intellectuals, living in the transition period of the 15th to the 16th century; in spite of his clerical background, a founding father of Humanism, the *auctor intellectualis* of an impressive and influential scholarly opus, written in Latin and dealing with a great variety of societal and paradigmatic issues; relying on patronage for most of his life; a true cosmopolitan, that is, a European *avant la lettre*. And, although as a consequence Erasmus moved

---

with the increase in literacy and, as a consequence thereof, the spread of reading and the growth of the book trade. Plagiarism, on the other hand, is not related to any form of communication or distribution technology.

[33]   Edelman (2004), p. 75: (stating that texts were often anonymous): 'À cet anonymat de l'auteur correspond une nature très particulière du texte, qui apparait comme une sorte de bien collectif, une valeur commune que chacun peut s'approprier librement. Le texte comme 'œuvre' n'a pas beaucoup de sens : il est un matériau soit verbal, soit écrit, que chacun remodèle a sa guise et s'autorise à modifier.'

[34]   Johns (1998), p. 5: 'If an early modern reader picked up a printed book ... then he or she could not be immediately certain that it was what it claimed to be, and its proper use might not be so self-evident. Piracy was again one reason: illicit uses of the press threatened the credibility of all printed products. More broadly, ideas about the correct ways to make and use books varied markedly from place to place and time to time.' Compare Boorstin (1983), Book Four, Chapter 65, 'Transforming the Book', pp. 525–26: (reflecting upon the roll as the carrier of manuscripts): 'We cannot be surprised that quotations in early literature are so variant and so inaccurate. We, too, would naturally rely on our memory rather than unwind a long roll to search for the desired passage. Since every manuscript was unique, there were no numbered pages, no index, and nothing like the modern title page. The name of the "author" was seldom attached to a roll.'

[35]   Strömholm (1983), p. 6, stating that 'both in antiquity and in the Middle Ages it was a matter, on the one hand, of the private reactions of writers and artists and, on the other – in élite circles – of evaluations which lay entirely in the area of tact, good taste, or at the highest level, ethics.' According to Orgel, S. (1981), 'The Renaissance Artist as Plagiarist', in *English Language History*, **48**, 476–95, for many Renaissance artists, including writers, invention was 'deeply involved with copying' (p. 479), and 'a great deal of Renaissance art offered its patrons precisely the pleasures of recognition' (p. 480).

for most of his life in élite circles, that is, those of courts, clergymen and intellectuals, he felt, as his works show, an immense responsibility for developments in the society of his time.

One of the works that particularly expresses this sense of social responsibility is the *Adagia*.[36] This book was published for the first time in 1500 under the title *Adagiorum Collectanea* as a small collection of approximately 800 adages. But Erasmus kept adding to the collection during the following 25 years. So, when he died in 1536, the number of adages had in the meantime grown to more than 4000. The opening *adagium* of the latest edition of the collection reads as follows: '*Amicorum communia omnia*', or 'Friends hold all things in common'. The *adagium* has not always had that prominent position. Erasmus only promoted the adage to that first place in 1508 when he republished the book under the new title *Adagiorium Chiliades*. The adage has served since then as the proclamatory starting point of the whole collection. According to Erasmus' own introduction in the *Prologomena* to the book, he based this *adagium* on classic Greek philosophy, particularly that of Pythagoras, in which the connection between friendship and common property can already be found. Referring also to the Christian faith and particularly to the teachings of Augustinus, Erasmus argued that no one can deny that common property amongst friends contributes to their well-being.

The prominent place given to the adage about friendship and property in later editions of the *Adagia* underscores the central message of the book. The collection, in itself already a bundling of common knowledge and wisdom, reflects and exposes this characteristic feature of communality even more by anchoring it in friendship.[37] Although at first sight it may seem that by compiling the *Adagia* Erasmus had already taken common knowledge and wisdom from the public domain in order to enclose it in the private domain of friends, upon second reading it appears that his aim was rather to expand the access to the intellectual heritage of mankind.[38]

---

[36] Desiderii Erasmi Roterodami, (1962), *Opera Omnia*, Amsterdam: North Holland, published according to the 1700 edition by Paula Koning; see also www.let.leidenuniv.nl/dutch/latijn/ErasmusAdagia.html. The translation from the Latin original of the *adagium* is used as the heading of this section.

[37] The same idea can be found in Plato (R*es Publica, Leges*), Aristotle (*Politeia*) and Cicero (*De Legibus, De Officiis*). A similar understanding can also be found in Rule 3 of Augustine, reading in English as follows: 'Call nothing your own, but let everything be yours in common …'. Somewhat later Spinoza would express himself in the same way in his correspondence with Henry Oldenburg of the Royal Society.

[38] Huizinga (1924), pp. 57–8: 'Erasmus maakte de klassieke geest courant. … Niet onder alle mensen, want door het Latijn beperkte hij zijn directe invloed tot de groep van de beschaafden, dat wil zeggen de hogere standen. … Het humanisme hield op, een monopolie van enkelen te zijn. Volgens Beatus Rhenanus had de schrijver toen hij de

Recently, Erasmus' view on friendship and property has been elegantly studied by Eden.[39] She places Erasmus' connection between the two emphatically in the key area of positive law, and she even argues that this is an early sign of the breakthrough of the idea of shared intellectual property, that is, common ownership of *immaterialia.* Eden's book has been described by critics as original, intelligent and thought-provoking, but not convincing. According to Emmett, for example, Eden fails to indicate that the *Adagia* fits into a literary tradition; she overlooks the point that Erasmus' reference to property is just a metaphor and that the book was written for the sole purpose of making money.[40] This may be so, but such critics certainly do not deny that, even when used metaphorically, the idea of a proprietarian common domain of knowledge and wisdom for the benefit of one's friends is rather remarkable.

In section 5 below I will reflect upon the possible implications for the development of the (legal) concept of the public domain, placed in the context of the leading societal and paradigmatic state of affairs in Erasmus' time. But before doing so, first, in the next section, another issue related to that of commonly held knowledge and wisdom will be analysed, set off against the memorising culture of the day.

4   ORGANISING INFORMATION: THE COMMONPLACE BOOK

Indeed, the example of Erasmus' *Adagia* may also serve to introduce another 15th century phenomenon which is intriguing with regard to the perception of the public domain at that period: the commonplace book. Commonplace books were the learned world's response to what was already being experienced as an information overload.[41,42] In that respect the commonplace book functioned

---

Adagia ging uitgeven, van sommigen moeten horen: Erasmus, gij verklapt onze mysteriën'. [Erasmus made the classical spirit current. ... Not amongst all people, since by using Latin, he limited his direct influence to the civilized, that is, the higher classes. ... Humanism ceased to be a monopoly of a few. According to Beatus Rhenamus, after hearing that he planned to publish the Adagia, some should have said to him: Erasmus, you are giving away our mysteries.] (Translation FWG.)

[39]   Eden, K. (2001), *Friends Hold All Things in Common*, New Haven: Yale University Press.

[40]   Emmett, L. and Bryn, M. (2002), *Classical Review*, 15 August.

[41]   See, about the early modern information overload, the collection of articles in (2003) *Journal of the History of Ideas*, **64** (1).

[42]   With regard to its use for a person's own writing, the commonplace book has been compared to what today may be called 'headings'. The collected notes allowed the writer to select the kind of information which was most appropriate for insertion in their own

as a *trait d'union* between printing and the memorising practices referred to in section 1. In addition to collecting more books and exercising selective judgment concerning their reading, scholars began to devise short-cuts (sometimes based upon medieval antecedents) as an aid to their reading. These short-cuts, being generally a way of compiling knowledge, would consist of alphabetical indices, reference books or listings of abbreviations. Essentially, these *aides-mémoire* were 'the personal and printed collections of sayings and examples that once promised to provide writers with a storehouse of materials to use in compositions of their own making'.[43] Commonplace books are an intriguing phenomenon from the perspective of the public domain since by their very nature they consist of cultural information taken from many sources. Besides, it is of interest that they appear to function as an interface between the manuscript culture and the print culture in which they seem to decline.[44]

The function of the commonplace books as *aides-mémoire* underlines the way in which, before the printing press existed, knowledge was preserved: by the sheer act of memorising. As Boorstin points out, this was true for every kind of knowledge that was considered to be beneficial for a society. Laws, for example, were preserved by memory before they were documented. The same was true for liturgies and related items of interest for religious services. The memorising of all this immense quantity of a society's vital knowledge had a price. How to master the act of memorising had been elaborated, however, in countless systems. The printed book destroyed these 'invisible cathedrals of memory' (Boorstin); they formed new databases, the collective memory of society.[45]

But, apart from being incorporations of a society's collective memory as organisers for study and teaching by scholars and students, commonplace books had a more intimate function as collections of personal notes about individual

---

speeches or letters. See Dyck, P. (Winter 1997), 'Reading and Writing the Commonplace: Literary, Culture Then and Now', *(Re) Soundings*.

[43] Eichhorn, K. (2003), 'Digital Analogues: Writing Histories and the Future of Writing in the Commonplace-book, New Histories of Writing IV – Forms and Rhetorics', MMLA Meeting, Chicago, 8 November, p. 13; Moss, A. (1996), *Printed Commonplace-books and the Structuring of Renaissance Thought*, Oxford: Clarendon Press, VI, speaks of 'an information retrieval system'.

[44] Rhodes, N. and Sawday, J. (2000), *The Renaissance Computer: Knowledge Technology in the First Age of Print*, London: Routledge & Kegan Paul, speaking of 'the overlap, or continuity, between different technological regimes', characterising the commonplace book as an attempt to cope with the disorder that print caused, providing 'a way for bite-sized pieces of information (to be) manipulated and rearranged.'

[45] Boorstin (1983), pp. 480–81: 'After Gutenberg, realms of everyday life once ruled and served by Memory would be governed by the printed page. In the late Middle Ages for the small literate class, manuscript books had provided an aid and sometimes a substitute for Memory.' See also note 23.

experiences, used for private reading and writing. In that second function the
commonplace book is similar to the diary. Commonplace books are *per saldo*
of a hybrid nature: on the one hand, sources of public knowledge; on the other,
repositories of private experiences.[46] If one follows Eichhorn in her account of
the development of the commonplace book throughout the Renaissance and into
the Enlightenment, an intriguing ambiguity appears. On the one hand, the fact
that commonplace books are in print, making it possible to refer to title pages,
the date and place of publication, and pagination, causes a shift from citing authorities (as in the case of manuscripts) to citing documents. On the other hand,
in the course of time there is apparent a growing attempt to ensure that borrowed
textual fragments could be traced back to specific authors and even specific
editions of texts, indicating a growing preoccupation with originality, authorial
intent, and ownership of ideas and words. By its ambiguous character the commonplace book clearly illustrates that the late Medieval and Renaissance period
may indeed be called one of transition.[47]

It appears that again Erasmus is an exemplary figure in this respect, characterising the commonplace book as the storehouse of the mind, to assist the reader
in mastering all knowledge. Using the metaphor of the beehive, which serves
its owner in transforming the stored honey into any product of its own making,
he applies the word 'hive' to describe a place where readers might store their
intellectual honey in order to use it later in their own works. This shows that
Erasmus understood the works of other writers as being inextricably linked to
a reader's own writings. It follows that he apparently considered the works of
others to be freely accessible and retrievable, that is, in the public domain.[48] In
fact, it was the function of the commonplace book as an information retrieval
system that really mattered for Erasmus.[49]

---

[46] Eichhorn (2003), p. 5; Eichhorn (like others) compares the commonplace book
culture with the modern Internet web logs: 'it is worth noting that many of the websites
that describe themselves as digital or electronic commonplace-books or evoke the concept to identity the context of one or more of their features also identify as blogs'
(p. 6).
[47] Eichhorn (2003), p. 8 (with notable references to Erasmus).
[48] Erasmus, Desiderius, *De Copia* (Collected Works of Erasmus, 2, Toronto: University of Toronto Press, p. 192). Eichhorn (2003), p. 3, observes that Erasmus in fact
used the metaphor of the beehive in a dual sense: as a sort of database for cultural information and as a physical place to read and write. This last meaning raises questions about
whether common readers in Erasmus' time were able to retreat to private places: questions, one may say, about the private sphere (e.g. studies) and the public sphere (e.g.
libraries).
[49] Eichhorn (2003), p. 7: 'This is both due to the fact that discourses on the keeping
and use of commonplace book(s) provided a forum in which to explore and rework traditional imitative modes of rhetorical production and to debate the distinction between
common and private forms of intellectual property in response to developing print cul-

The state of affairs just described raises the question as to whether Erasmus' enthusiasm for building databases of knowledge consisting of information collected and stored out of many sources was generally accepted in his time. In the absence of any actual developed notion of copyright law, and imitation during this period still being valued as part of the curriculum, the commonplace book indeed appears to have raised concerns about piracy and plagiarism. Such concerns were even greater in the 17th and 18th centuries. Was Erasmus himself aware of this creeping possibility of piracy and plagiarism? According to Eichhorn, he might indeed have taken this possibility into account, given his repeated attempts to distinguish his use of commonplace books from the ancient practice of patchwork.[50] He specifically expressed his anxieties in an attack on writers who merely 'scrape up a few phrases from here and there, producing nothing more than a patchwork or a mosaic'.[51] Eichhorn suggests that this kind of observation provides evidence of Erasmus' recognition that his proposed discursive method was already somewhat incompatible with the new views on subjectivity and authorship that had emerged in the developing print culture.[52]

The commonplace book in its function as a database of knowledge in the 16th and 17th centuries ensured that the collected and stored information could be traced back to specific authors and even specific editions of texts. This may be so, but does not refute the fact that in Erasmus' time there was tension between, on the one hand, a firm belief in cultural continuity and the need for wide and unhampered access to the reservoir of human knowledge at least within and between particular epistemic communities, and, on the other hand, a growing awareness – favoured by the print culture which made this actually possible – that reliability and fairness require correct attribution of texts to their authors.

5 TRIUMPH OF THE COMMONS?

As the referenced source materials allow one to conclude, neither in the Middle Ages nor in the Renaissance did Western European (legal) culture recognise a general concept of the public domain in any of the senses indicated in section 1.

---

tures.' Eichhorn refers to Crane, M.T. (1993), *Framing Authority: Sayings, Self and Society in Sixteenth-Century England*, New Jersey: Princeton University Press. See also Kewes, P. (ed.) (2003), *Plagiarism in Early Modern England*, New York: Palgrave Macmillan; Orgel (1981).

[50] Eichhorn (2003), p. 7.

[51] Ibid.

[52] Ibid., p. 8. According to Eichhorn also, other Renaissance writers adopted the stand promoted by Erasmus.

This is also true for the concept of the public domain as a common and freely accessible reservoir for authors to use for the making of works, which lies at the heart of this chapter. If one can find occasional traces of communality and free access, these are invariably within special interest groups such as that of scholars. Taking account of the reported *acta et facta*, this situation was largely due to the concurrence of, above all, the following societal and paradigmatic factors that were characteristic of the transition period from a scribal to a print culture:

- the absence of a separation of powers between the church and the state in combination with the lack of a clear distinction between public law and private law, resulting in the systems of privilege and censorship;
- the existing class-structure of society, widespread illiteracy, and Latin being the language of knowledge;
- the absence of a developed public sphere, the household being the nucleus of society.

As a consequence of these factors, society was divided into various personal circles (such as the nobility, commoners, the patronised) and professional circles (such as the clergy, legal profession, guilds), all of them building and sharing their specific knowledge, keeping it secret from the outside world (and sometimes considering it sacral at the same time). This factual information monopoly, however, had no legal corollary: writers did not have property rights in their products. Besides, this factual information monopoly failed to exist from the moment that writers sold their manuscripts to publishers (printers, booksellers). From that moment onwards the exploiters of printed texts, by virtue of private law ownership and public law privilege, obtained the factual and legal power over the copy of any printed book they published.[53] Understandably, seen from the perspective of the exploiters, promoting the concept of the public domain was not in their commercial interest. All this may explain why scholars like Erasmus, subject to the actual societal and paradigmatic state of affairs, shared their knowledge solely amongst friends.[54]

---

[53]   According to Johns (1998), p. 446 (writing about the Stationers in England), this property right applied both to the text as a commodity and to the interpretation of the actual sheets being reproduced: 'They were now free to produce as many editions as they thought fit, along with the epitomes, abridgements, and translations prohibited to other's by Stationers' Company protocol.' Edelman (2004), Chapitre 1, 'Un Auteur dépossédé', pp. 115–29: 'Pis en tenailles entre le mécénat et le corporatisme, entre une légitimité symbolique et une dépossession matérielle de son œuvre, l'auteur n'a qu'une existence "déléguée". Non seulement sa souveraineté lui est octroyée, non seulement son discours, une fois publié, lui échappe, mais encore auqune régle juridique ne le protège.'

[54]   Loewenstein (2002), p. 123, gives an interesting picture of how blurred the situation was in these days: 'That there is a general logic of opposition between print and

However, it should not be overlooked that the introduction of the print culture had also reverse, albeit paradoxical, effects. This is particularly true for the involvement of the law in the production and dissemination of cultural information. As a consequence thereof it is also indicative of the then concept of the public domain.[55] In that respect, it is worth noting that the exponential growth in the book trade in this period was as much due to the invention of print as to the availability of content in modern, domestic languages. Print served the convenience of readers in various ways. It introduced the standardisation of the book as a commodity, ready for mass-market selling.[56] Consequently, '[b]ooks go public' (Boorstin), a development marked not only by a regular increase in the numbers of copies of each edition but also by the advent of public libraries.[57] Publication of books in one's native tongue was the second decisive factor that accounted for the explosive book trade in the indicated period. Boorstin characterises this state of affairs as follows:

> The triumph of the printed book soon brought the triumph of the languages of the marketplace, which became the languages of learning across Europe. Vernacular literatures in print shaped thinking in two quite disparate ways. They democratized but they also provincialized. When works of science now appeared not only in Latin but in English, French, Italian, Spanish, German and Dutch ... knowledge tended to become national or regional.[58]

Indeed, knowledge became de-secretised and de-sacralised, the marketplace breaking through the monitoring of publishing, that is, the dissemination of information by church and state. However, in close conjunction with print, its twin-sister piracy became more virulent than ever. This may have furthered the emergence of a factual, subversive 'creative commons'; a reaction could not

---

monopoly is easy enough to see. The press had pioneered in the development of protected production, having substantially elaborated the older protectionism long associated with artisanal 'mystic'. But the press was also an ideal sphere for the competitive erosion of the new form of industrial property. The expertise requisite for the printing of a primer was no longer dazzling: the expertise requisite for the counterfeiting of a privileged edition was every bit as unremarkable. Agent of novelty, the press was also an agent of technical dissemination, of industrial demystification.'

[55] For further reading see above all Steinberg, S.H. (1996), *Five Hundred Years of Printing*, New Castle, DE: Oak Knoll Press – first edn, 1955.

[56] Johns (1998), p. 36, however, is more sceptical on this point: 'I do not question that print enabled the stabilization of texts, to some extent; although fixity was far rarer and harder to discern in early modern Europe than most historians assume. I do, however, question the character of the link between the two.'

[57] Boorstin (1983), Chapter 64 ('Communities in the Vernacular'), pp. 517–24; Chapter 65 ('Transforming the Book'), pp. 524–32; Chapter 66 ('Books Go Public'), pp. 533–8.

[58] Boorstin (1983), p. 517.

stay away. And so it happened that print's triumphant expansion went hand in hand with legal regulation of the book trade. The powers that were – alarmed by this development – answered by intensifying the already existing systems of censorship and privilege. It is true that society would gradually develop towards a greater appreciation of religious tolerance and intellectual freedom. But, in Catholic and Protestant Europe alike, religious and intellectual censorship continued to be powerful between 1650 and 1750, that is, until well into the Enlightenment period. It appears that all across Europe unacceptable views were suppressed and publishers (printers and booksellers), as well as writers of illicit books, were prosecuted. The extent to which censorship was executed differed, however, from country to country, depending mainly on how strong the linkage was between church and state. In France, where the Roman Catholic Church was still influential, book burnings were frequent. But even in the Dutch Republic and England radical writers were often profoundly influenced by censorship.[59]

As far as piracy is concerned, in the course of time public authorities grew more and more concerned about how to maintain the monopolistic privilege system from which they benefited against the developing opposition thereto. Particularly in France and Britain, book piracy escalated in the 18th century in response to the monopolistic control of the book market by a small group of licensed publishers.[60] So in the end it may well be said that the prehistory of copyright law did not recognise any general – societal or legal – concept of the public domain.

[59] Israel, J.J. (2001), *Radical Enlightenment*, Oxford: Oxford University Press, Chapter 5 ('Censorship and Culture'), pp. 98–118: 'The history of European censorship between 1650 and 1750 thus clearly demonstrates that the moderate Enlightenment, however far-reaching institutionally and intellectually the changes it brought about, largely rejected freedom of thought, the principle of "*libertas philosophandi*" (freedom to philosophize), which Spinoza, in contrast to Hobbes, Locke and the official stance of the Encyclopédie, proclaimed as one of his chief objectives' (pp. 116–17).
[60] Johns (1998), pp. 105, 159, 311, 355; Van Horn Melton (2001), pp. 141–43.

2. Copyright's public domain

Ronan Deazley

1 INTRODUCING THE PUBLIC DOMAIN

When we first heard Julie Andrews sing that immortal phrase, 'Let's start at the very beginning, it's a very good place to start', intuitively we knew she was right, that in almost all endeavours in life, whether reading or singing, swinging from trees or fashioning play-suits from old curtains, the place to start is indeed at the beginning. When the particular endeavour at hand is a commentary upon the concept of the public domain within the context of intellectual property doctrine, most would agree that the origins of contemporary scholarship upon the public domain lie with the publication of David Lange's seminal work 'Recognizing the Public Domain' just over a quarter of a century ago.[1] And yet Lange's piece is a curious place to start indeed in that he sparks a debate about the public domain without making any attempt to articulate what he means by the public domain.[2] Whereas Andrews introduced us to the necessary Do-Re-Mi with which to navigate the internal workings of the diatonic scale, Lange provides us with none of the rudimentary concepts and distinctions with which to build an understanding of the public domain. One observation he does make, however, is that the public domain 'tends to appear amorphous and vague, with

---

[1]   Lange, D. (1981), 'Recognizing the Public Domain', 44 *Law & Contemporary Problems*, 147.

[2]   Lange is not alone in this regard; see, for example, Cramer, Edward M. and Block, Lauren (1991–92), 'Public Domain: Available but not Always Free', 2 *Fordham Entertainment Media & Intellectual Property Law F.* 1; Akoi, K. (1993–94), 'Authors, Inventors and Trademark Owners: Private Intellectual Property and the Public Domain, Part I', 18 *Columbia Journal of Law and the Arts*, 1; Akoi, K. (1993–94), 'Authors, Inventors and Trademark Owners: Private Intellectual Property and the Public Domain, Part II', 18 *Columbia Journal of Law and the Arts*, 191; Schiffman, S.M. (1996), 'Movies in the Public Domain: A Threatened Species', 20 *Columbia Journal of Law and the Arts* 663; Bott, Cynthia M. (1998–99), 'Protection of Information Products: Balancing Commercial Reality and the Public Domain', 67 *University of Cincinatti Law Review* 237; Griffiths, J. (2000), 'Copyright in English Literature: Denying the Public Domain', *European Intellectual Property Review*, 150.

little more of substance in it than is invested in patriotic or religious slogans on paper currency',[3] an 'impression of insubstantiality' which has been remarked upon by others since Lange, and one which is neatly captured by Pamela Samuelson's recent observation that the public domain resembles an 'uncharted terrain':

> Sometimes it seems an undifferentiated blob of unnamed size and dimensions ... a vast and diverse assortment of contents. The public domain is, moreover, different sizes at different times in different countries ... The public domain also has some murky areas. For example, some intellectual creations are, in theory, in the public domain, but for all practical purposes, do not really reside there.[4]

This is the public domain as nebula, as a space without form or clearly defined boundaries. The trope is a familiar one in much academic writing in this area and, whether consciously or not, portrays the public domain as chimerical, imprecise and lacking conceptual clarity. This slipperiness is further compounded by the fact that many who write about the public domain often use the phrase (sometimes knowingly, sometimes not) interchangeably with other equally imprecise and/or undefined terms, such as the 'public sphere' or simply the 'commons' (with variations on the theme: the 'commons of the mind', the 'intellectual commons' and the 'informational commons'). Drawing upon the work of others in this area, what follows takes as its point of departure the relationship between the public domain and one branch of intellectual property law only – copyright – with the aim of addressing two related questions: what is the nature of the public domain and how can (or should) we best define and describe it? and why bother trying to define it at all, or rather why is it significant?

2 UNDERSTANDING COPYRIGHT'S PUBLIC DOMAIN

To begin to understand copyright's public domain we need to make clear two basic distinctions concerning the related concepts of *access to* and *use of* a work. Copyright as an institutional phenomenon functions by conferring upon the owner of the copyright in a work a bundle of rights (referred to within the UK as the 'acts restricted by copyright'), which rights enable that owner to prevent others from using the work in certain ways without first asking for permission

---

[3]   Ibid., 177.
[4]   Samuelson, P. (2003), 'Mapping the Public Domain: Threats and Opportunities', 66 *Law & Contemporary Problems* 147, 148.

to do so.[5] This then provides us with our first touchstone for understanding copyright's public domain; that is, if the institution of copyright necessitates permission before use, the public domain allows for use without the need for permission.[6] This conceit of *use without permission*, however, fails to accommodate the fact that once a work has been published it has ceased to exist within the private realm of the author and instead has entered a public cultural space (let us call this the *intellectual commons*). This second consideration touches not upon the freedom to use without permission but upon a work being *publicly accessible*. An author's book may have entered the intellectual commons in the sense that we now have the opportunity to access and engage with the work (whether at a financial cost or not) but we may remain restricted in terms of how we are able to make use of that work; the work may have been made public but it will also either be copyright protected or public domain. Implicit in this, of course, is the fact that there will also exist a realm of material that may never enter the intellectual commons at all,[7] and, as with the intellectual commons, this *undisclosed domain* will be made up of works which are either copyright protected or are public domain.

This initial set of distinctions, depicted in Figure 2.1, between that which can be used without permission and that which cannot, and between that which is published and that which is not, can perhaps be said to best represent the predominant conception of the public domain – it is the 'sphere in which contents are free from intellectual property rights'.[8] In this conception, the public domain consists of two types of work: those works which fail to meet whatever threshold

---

[5] At present this involves reproducing, distributing, renting, performing, and communicating the work, or making an adaptation of the work, or doing any of the above in relation to an adaptation of the work; Copyright, Designs and Patents Act 1988, c.48 (as amended) (hereinafter CDPA), s.16(1).

[6] We should of course acknowledge at this point that there are owners of copyright materials who dedicate their work to the public; that is, they willingly waive what rights they have to control the use of the copyright work. As such, although the works are still legally within the private domain, *de facto* they fall within the public domain. Consider for example the success of the OpenSource movement, or the Creative Commons project (www.creativecommons.org). It is important to remember however that these materials only reside within the public domain as a result of a wide-ranging *a priori* permission – there is no need to ask for permission to use, as *permission has already been granted*.

[7] Consider for example someone who keeps a diary; their entries therein would almost certainly be considered to be copyright-protected, but are almost equally certain never to be made public in that they will always remain private to the individual (or lost, forgotten, destroyed and so on).

[8] Samuelson, 'Mapping the Public Domain', 149; see also Hall, J.L. (1995), 'Blues and the Public Domain – No More Dues to Pay?', *Journal of the Copyright Society of the USA*, 215; Martin, S.M. (2002), 'The Mythology of the Public Domain: Exploring the Myths Behind Attacks on the Duration of Copyright Protection', 36 *Loyola of Los*

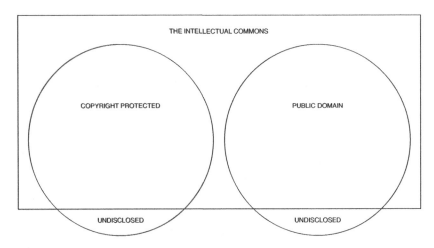

THE INTELLECTUAL COMMONS

COPYRIGHT PROTECTED

PUBLIC DOMAIN

UNDISCLOSED

UNDISCLOSED

Figure 2.1

requirements have been stipulated before protection will be attributed to them (or, more simply, those which do not qualify for protection in the first place – in the case of copyright, the non-original literary, dramatic, musical or artistic work); and second, for those intellectual properties that are time-limited, such as copyright, those works whose periods of protection have expired.[9]

As a working description of copyright's public domain, however, the distinctions set out in Figure 2.1 are too simplistic. In relation to copyright works, if the touchstone of the public domain is *use without permission*, then, as Litman and others remind us,[10] the public domain must also incorporate those aspects or features of a copyright-protected work that nevertheless do not require permission prior to such use.[11] The question now is: which aspects of a copyright-protected work is any individual free to use without having to ask the

---

Angeles Law Review, 253; Van Caenegem, W. (2002), 'The Public Domain: Scientia Nullius', *European Intellectual Property Review*, 324.

[9]   Naturally different copyright-protected works have different terms of copyright protection; in general see CDPA.

[10]   Litman, J. (1990), 'The Public Domain', 39 *Emory Law Journal* 965; see also Hawkins, C. (1998), 'Technological Measures: Saviour or Saboteur of the Public Domain?', *Journal of Law and Information Science*, 45; Uhlir, P. (2003), *Draft Policy Guidelines for the Development and Promotion of Public Domain Information*, Paris: UNESCO; Benkler, Y. (1999), 'Free as the Air to Common Use: First Amendment Constraints on Enclosure of the Public Domain', 74 *New York University Law Review* 354.

[11]   Naturally, not everyone agrees with this analysis; see for example Samuels, E. (1993), 'The Public Domain in Copyright Law', 41 *Journal of the Copyright Society of the USA* 137, 166.

copyright owner for permission? In the first place we need to make mention of the oft-cited doctrine that copyright does not subsist in ideas but only in the manner in which those ideas are expressed. This idea–expression dichotomy has never received explicit mention within the UK's legislative framework, but rather grew out of the various debates in the mid-18th century as to the very nature of property as well as the manner in which copyright was accommodated within that broader theoretical context.[12] Implicit within the very concept of copyright is the fact that the ideas expressed within any author's work are not copyright-protected and so fall within the public domain. Indeed, this brings us to one of the primary virtues of the public domain itself astutely identified by Litman:

> All works of authorship, even the most creative, include some elements adapted from raw material that the author first encountered in someone else's works … If each author's claim to own everything embodied in her work were enforceable in court, almost every work could be enjoined by the owner of the copyright in another … Because we have a public domain, we can permit authors to avoid the harsh light of a genuine search for provenance, and thus maintain the illusion that their works are indeed their own creations.[13]

That is, in ensuring that ideas, generic plots, themes and so on, as well as unoriginal materials, remain outside the private domain of copyright-protected works, the public domain enables the very process of authorial creation itself. If, as Sir Hugh Laddie pithily observes, 'the whole of human development is derivative',[14] we need to recognise that without the public domain copyright itself would not be viable.

As to the remaining types of use without permission, these can be separated into two main categories: such uses as are set out within copyright's statutory regime, and those uses which are not but which are otherwise permissible as a result of judicial intervention in that statutory regime. As to the first, within the UK, there are two types of use to bear in mind: first, use of an insubstantial part of a work;[15] and second, any use which falls within statutorily defined 'acts permitted in relation to copyright works'. The latter category is naturally the more significant of the two, allowing for use without permission in a wide range of different and varied contexts, for example, for private study, or for non-commercial research, for the purposes of criticism or review, or for reporting current events, in

---

[12]   Deazley, R. (2004), *On the Origin of the Right to Copy: Charting the Movement of Copyright Law in Eighteenth Century Britain*, Oxford: Hart Publishing.

[13]   Litman, 'The Public Domain', 1011–12.

[14]   Laddie, H. (1996), 'Copyright: Over-strength, Over-regulated, Over-rated?', *European Intellectual Property Review*, 253, 259.

[15]   CDPA s.16(3)(a).

certain educational contexts, to facilitate library and archival work, or in the interests of public administration, as well as a range of additional miscellaneous
situations.[16] Moreover, while a number of these permitted uses mandate that the
use be considered to be fair dealing,[17] some categories do allow for the use of the
work in its entirety.[18] It goes without saying of course that these statutorily defined
permitted acts can and do change over time;[19] in this regard, as the parameters of
the statutory regime shift, so too do the boundaries of the public domain.

Turning to the second general category of use without permission – those
uses which are permissible as a result of judicial intervention in that statutory
regime – we can, once again, identify two different types of use to bear in mind:
use of works which the courts refuse to protect on grounds of public policy; and
any use of copyright protected works which, while they do not fall within the
permitted acts, are nevertheless considered to be in the public interest. As to the
former, since the early 18th century, with the decision in *Burnet v Chetwood*
[1721],[20] the courts (within the UK at least) have ever assumed the ability to ad-
judicate upon the dissemination and protection of copyright material in a manner
which functions outside the bounds of the statute but falls within their *inherent
jurisdiction at common law*. In *Burnet* this took the unusual form of granting
an injunction to prevent the publication of a work that did not in fact infringe
the copyright in any other work. More typically, the courts have tended to exercise this inherent jurisdiction by refusing a claimant relief on the grounds that
the content of the claimant's work is obscene or sexually immoral, defamatory,
blasphemous or irreligious,[21] with the somewhat counter-intuitive result that
anyone is free to make use of and disseminate such works.

As to the second category, the notion that the courts can authorise use which
would otherwise be considered to be a copyright infringement so long as it is
in the public interest dates from the more recent and somewhat tentative foundations laid down in *Lion Laboratories v Evans* [1985],[22] but has recently received
a more substantive and coherent rationale with the coming into force of the
Human Rights Act 1998 [23] and the decision of the Court of Appeal in *Ashdown*

---

[16]   In general see CDPA ss.28–76.

[17]   For example, CDPA s.29.

[18]   For example, performing a literary, dramatic or musical work before an audience
of teachers and pupils at an educational establishment; CDPA s.34.

[19]   Consider for example the recent changes implemented by the Copyright and Related Rights Regulations 2003, SI 2498.

[20]   *Burnet v Chetwood* (1721) 2 Mer. 441.

[21]   See for example: *Southey v Sherwood* (1817) 2 Mer 435; *Glynn v Weston Feature
Films* [1916] 1 Ch 261; *AG v Guardian (No. 2)* [1990] 1 AC 109; *Hyde Park v Yelland*
[2001] Ch 143.

[22]   *Lion Laboratories v Evans* [1985] QB 526.

[23]   Human Rights Act 1998 c.42.

v Telegraph Group [2002].[24] In short, within the context of a discussion concerning the balance between securing the rights of the copyright owner as against the right of users of copyright-protected material to express themselves freely (albeit using the words of another), Phillips MR in *Ashdown* first accepted that copyright does indeed amount to an interference with the right to freedom of expression. He continued that while, 'in most circumstances, the principle of freedom of expression will be sufficiently protected if there is a right to publish information and ideas set out in another's literary work, without copying the very words which that person has employed to convey the information or express the ideas',[25] nevertheless:

> There will be occasions when it is in the public interest not merely that information should be published, but that the public should be told the very words used by a person, notwithstanding that the author enjoys copyright in them. On occasions, indeed, it is the form and not the content of a document which is of interest.[26]

That is, 'rare circumstances' might arise where someone's right to freely express themselves may well conflict with the copyright owner's rights notwithstanding the existence of the various permitted acts set out within the copyright legislation, and when they do the court is free to consider whether an individual's right to freedom of expression is being properly accommodated. Should such 'rare circumstances' arise, Phillips MR continued, there existed no reason as to why these might not fall under the rubric of use falling within the common law public interest defence.

To summarise then: within the context of UK law, the public domain incorporates those works which do not qualify for copyright protection, those works which do but are out of the copyright term, those works where permission to use has been granted by the copyright owner *a priori*,[27] as well as such use of those works which fall on the right side of the idea–expression line, which are allowed for within the statutory framework (use of an insubstantial part, the permitted acts), or which are permissible as a result of judicial intervention with that regime at common law (on public policy grounds, or as being in the public interest) (Figure 2.2).

---

[24] *Ashdown v Telegraph Group* [2002] Ch 149.
[25] Ibid., 165.
[26] Ibid., 166.
[27] *supra*, note 6.

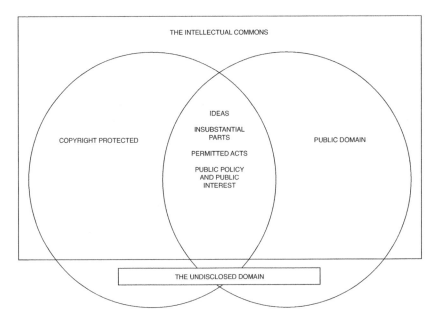

THE INTELLECTUAL COMMONS

COPYRIGHT PROTECTED

IDEAS

INSUBSTANTIAL PARTS

PERMITTED ACTS

PUBLIC POLICY AND PUBLIC INTEREST

PUBLIC DOMAIN

THE UNDISCLOSED DOMAIN

Figure 2.2

3 EXTERNALITIES AND COPYRIGHT'S PUBLIC DOMAIN

Moving from the basic relationship between copyright and the public domain, it would be foolish not to acknowledge that not only is the line between the two phenomena subject to doctrinal (or internal) development and change but it can also be profoundly affected by various external considerations. For our purposes these fall into two main categories: physical and/or technological barriers which impact upon individuals' opportunities for meaningful access to that which is public domain; and an increasing reliance upon the law of contract in requiring individuals to 'contract out' of that which they are otherwise free to do without permission (Figure 2.3). These various externalities, when overlaid upon the existing copyright regime, have considerable potential to significantly affect (that is, reduce) the shape and operation of the public domain; they have been written about by others better informed than myself, so commentary here will be brief.

Consider first the question of meaningful access. Again, there are two main aspects to this issue: regulating physical access to public domain works; and the impact of technological protection measures (TPMs) such as encryption,

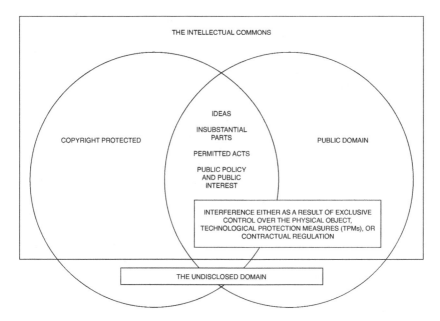

THE INTELLECTUAL COMMONS

COPYRIGHT PROTECTED

IDEAS

INSUBSTANTIAL PARTS

PERMITTED ACTS

PUBLIC POLICY AND PUBLIC INTEREST

PUBLIC DOMAIN

INTERFERENCE EITHER AS A RESULT OF EXCLUSIVE CONTROL OVER THE PHYSICAL OBJECT, TECHNOLOGICAL PROTECTION MEASURES (TPMs), OR CONTRACTUAL REGULATION

THE UNDISCLOSED DOMAIN

Figure 2.3

scrambling or copy control mechanisms. As to the first, when dealing with works which lie within the intellectual commons but which are nevertheless a scarce intellectual resource (consider for example the Dead Sea Scrolls), clearly there is significant opportunity for interplay between the ownership of the physical object, whether manuscript, book or painting, and the ability to control the subsequent use and dissemination of the text or image therein. The second and more significant issue has its origins in the implementation of the WIPO Copyright Treaty (WCT), and in particular Article 11. In Europe the WCT provided one of the catalysts which led to the Information Society Directive,[28] A.6 of which addressed the question of TPMs, and which was subsequently implemented within the UK with the passing of the Copyright and Related Rights Regulations 2003.[29] The threat posed by TPMs to the public domain is of two kinds. In the first place they could be used by content providers to technologi-

---

[28] Information Society Directive (2001/29/EC).

[29] In effect, these provisions prohibit the circumvention of any effective technological measures (such as encryption, scrambling or copy control mechanisms) designed to prevent a user unlawfully accessing any copyright work, or performing any of the acts restricted by copyright in relation to any copyright work. Moreover, any person doing anything to circumvent such measures is guilty of infringing the copyright in the work

cally lock-up works which are no longer within the copyright term. Second, in relation to works that are still within the copyright term, these TPMs can interfere with anyone's ability to engage in otherwise lawful uses without permission, whether set out in the legislation or at common law (how do you make copies from a work, whether substantial or insubstantial, fair or unfair, in the public interest or not, whenever the medium itself is copy-protected?).

The interaction between the law of copyright and the law of contract throws up some equally problematic concerns as regards the public domain in that it is increasingly the case that contractual provisions are being used by copyright owners to require end users to 'contract out' of that which they are otherwise free to do without permission. This can of course occur in a one-to-one contract negotiation, but is increasingly prevalent in relation to the delivery of copyright content online with the use of evermore generic click-wrap licensing agreements, the terms of which end users rarely ever read. For example, if you access material on Westlaw or Lexis-Nexis (or any other information database) are you legally entitled to read that material on screen only? Or does the licence also authorise you to print a hard copy of the work? Or save it on your computer's hard drive? Moreover how do these various actions relate to your ability to deal fairly with that work for the purpose of private study?[30] In this context the various principles of common law [31] and equity [32] which operate to limit the enforceability of certain types of contractual provision are likely to be of little relevance,[33] as is any of the current domestic consumer protection legislation.[34] In this light, the Broadcasting Act 1996 has specifically set out that '[a]ny provision in an agreement is void in so far as it purports to prohibit or restrict relevant dealing with a broadcast or cable programme in any circumstances where by virtue of section 30(2) of the [CDPA] ... copyright in the broadcast or cable programme is not infringed'.[35] In the absence of any similar general statutory

---

as if he had published or communicated the work to the public. For further discussion see Cahir, J., 'The Public Domain: Right or Liberty?', *infra*, Chapter 3.

[30]   CDPA s.29(1C).

[31]   The various common law mechanisms for restricting the operation of contractual provisions include duress, undue influence, restraint of trade, and public policy concerns (such as provisions promoting sexual immorality, restricting the freedom to marry, perverting the course of justice, and so on).

[32]   Equity will provide relief against bargains which it considers to be unconscionable.

[33]   See the Australian Copyright Law Review Committee (2001) *Copyright and Contract*, 148, 258: www.ag.gov.au/agd/WWW/clrhome.nsf/AllDocs/092E76FE8AF 2501CCA256C44001FFC28?OpenDocument.

[34]   Unfair Contract Terms Act 1977 c.50; Unfair Terms in Consumer Contracts Regulations 1999 SI 1999/2083.

[35]   Broadcasting Act 1996, c.55, s.137; see also CDPA ss.50A and 50B.

provision rendering null and void all contractual provisions which purport to exclude or modify the operation of what are otherwise permissible acts, then, as is the case with TPMs, the potential for contract law to impact upon the public domain remains considerable.

4 CRITIQUES OF COPYRIGHT'S PUBLIC DOMAIN

There are naturally various questions or considerations that may legitimately be raised about the appropriateness or even the value of the snapshot of copyright's public domain presented here. The first is that raised by Van Caenegem: that, as intellectual property interests have been developed and defined in accordance with Western ideologies of authorship and ownership, then similarly any concept of the public domain which operates in relation to those intellectual properties may function to justify a misappropriation, or dispossession, of traditional knowledge (whether literary, artistic, technological and so on). In his words, a Western-modelled notion of the public domain 'may inadvertently justify the denial of the otherwise legitimate claims of indigenous peoples to control intangibles'.[36] The point is well taken, and Van Caenegem is certainly right in that the public domain, described herein, is a historically, geographically, culturally and politically contingent concept, as are all intellectual properties. However this does not mean the concept, albeit contingent, is not of value. In the absence of any form of legal regulation, all works lie within the public domain (whether disclosed or not). It is the law which defines that which is removed from the original state of the public domain into the private domain of copyright protection by locating the exclusive control of certain types of use in any given individual, albeit for a certain period of time. It could equally well ascribe such controls to any given community, indigenous or not, for whatever period of time that is considered appropriate, should the political will to do so exist.

A related issue concerns not the way in which proselytising the virtues of the public domain might operate to occlude the interests of indigenous communities, but rather that it may entrench the status quo of intellectual properties wherever they currently exist, regardless of significant differences in the intellectual property interests and needs of developed, developing and least developed

---

[36] Van Caenegem, 'The Public Domain', 325; see also Coombe, Rosemary J. (2002–03), 'Fear, Hope and Longing for the Future of Authorship and a Revitalized Public Domain in Global Regimes of Intellectual Property', 52 *DePaul Law Review* 1171. In this volume see Gibson, J., 'Audiences in Tradition: Traditional Knowledge and the Public Domain', *infra*, Chapter 12, and Taubman, A., 'The Public Domain and International Intellectual Property Law Treaties', *infra*, Chapter 4.

countries. Again this is a valid comment, but not one which touches upon the public domain *per se*. Rather, it raises the issue as to what is considered to be in the *public interest* as regards those developing and least developed countries, and as a consequence whether the public domain should mean the same thing for everyone in equal measure. In point of fact, different public domains already exist for different interest groups. Within the UK, that which librarians can do with copyright-protected works is different from that which teachers can do, or that which those working in public administration can do, and so on.[37] There is no reason why the boundary between that which is copyright-protected and that which is public domain should not vary for other such interested parties, whether they are represented by the Royal National Institute for the Blind[38] or by the government of a less developed country. For example, additional cost-neutral permissions might be negotiated in an attempt to redress existing imbalances and inequities as to the manner in which the international intellectual property regime impacts differentially upon various nation states.[39] In reality, these would amount to no more than another set of 'permitted acts', and again they are simply matters of political will and institutional fact.

That the nature of the public domain may differ according to which interested party wishes to make use of any given work also throws into sharp relief the fact that, should we try to detail the nature and extent of the public domain in any given national jurisdiction (never mind in a regional or international context), the exercise is bound to fail. That is, not only do the permitted acts vary across different interest groups, as well as across jurisdictions, but as there cannot exist any bright-line test for determining that which is mere idea rather than the expression of an idea (or that which is insubstantial, fair, non-commercial, immoral, or in the public interest, and so on) it will always remain impossible to determine with accuracy, at any given time, that which is public domain and that which is not. That it is impossible to accurately articulate the public domain in this way does not mean, however, that there is no value in accurately *conceiving* the public domain. It is to be remembered that the private domain (of copyright) and copyright's public domain necessarily share the same boundary – that which is not copyright-protected is public domain and vice versa – and that the actual limits and extent of that which is copyright-protected is no more readily identifiable and subject to coherent and complete articulation than that which is public domain. The boundary between the two is and always will be

[37]   In general see CDPA ss.28–76. See also in this volume Bainton, T., 'The Public Domain and the Librarian', *infra*, Chapter 8.
[38]   Copyright (Visually Impaired Persons) Act 2002, c.33.
[39]   See for example the recommendations in Commission on Intellectual Property Rights (2002), *Integrating Intellectual Property Rights and Development Policy*, London: CIPR.

inherently unstable and unknowable, but that it is unstable and unknowable does not operate to conceptually discredit either phenomenon.

What is perhaps more important is that acknowledging that the public domain can never be accurately captured serves to remind us that copyright is an extraordinary type of property in the sense that its boundaries are equally imprecise. If indeed in this regard the public domain is 'an undifferentiated blob of unnamed size and dimensions', 'a vast and diverse assortment of contents', if it is murky and unknowable, then so too is the private domain that is copyright. Many academics have of late commented upon an unsettling and unwarranted 'reification' of copyright – the tendency to think of copyright as equivalent to any other ordinary (tangible) property. In 1999 Benkler neatly captured this sentiment in remarking upon the way in which copyrights, patents, et al. have within the last 50 years become subsumed under the umbrella term of 'intellectual property', which 'semantic umbrella has infused these laws with the conceptual attitudes we have toward property in physical things'.[40] To accept that copyright as a phenomenon is, in all practical terms, as nebulous as the public domain is to remind ourselves that copyright is not akin to other forms of property, or rather that there is property *and there is property*. This perhaps represents one of the greatest benefits of contemplating the nature and dimensions of the public domain – not what it tells us about the public domain itself, but what it reminds us about as regards copyright. That is, in better understanding the public domain we perhaps begin to better understand the nature of copyright, including both its limits and limitations.

5   CONCLUSION

The parameters of this short comment have been modest indeed; its conclusions equally so. I have not attempted to set out some economically predetermined perfect balance between the copyright-protected and the public domain (I leave that for the legal economists), or even to comment upon the recent shifts in legal policy and legislative fact that have altered what balance exists between the two phenomena (I leave that for another time). Rather, in a very simplistic, Andrewsesque fashion (would that I had the voice), I have sought to do little more than provide some useful, if basic, conceptual distinctions for articulating the relationship between copyright and the public domain. In so doing, I hope to have

---

[40]   Benkler, 'Free as the Air', 355. In a similar vein, see also Lemley, Mark A. (1997), 'Romantic Authorship and the Rhetoric of Property', 75 *Intellectual Property* 307; and Vaver, D. (2000), 'Intellectual Property: The State of the Art', 116 *Law Quarterly Review* 621.

introduced the reader to the Do-Re-Mi of copyright's public domain, while at the same time drawing attention to two significant forces external to the copyright regime which exhibit considerable potential to impact detrimentally upon that public domain. Also, exploring the concept of the public domain through the prism of copyright has provided an opportunity to highlight the role which the public domain plays in facilitating the operation of the copyright regime itself, as well as the role it can play in reminding us about the fundamental nature of copyright as a constantly evolving, artificial and institutional construct.

3. The public domain: right or liberty?

John Cahir

1 INTRODUCTION

The 'public domain' has become a totemic object for those who oppose the application of property rights to informational objects, particularly in the Internet environment. Persons who object to the expansion of copyright law maintain that there exists a public domain of information and ideas that both *is* not and *should* not be within the realm of private property. Recalling the political fault lines of the 19th and 20th centuries, exponents of this viewpoint identify (and exalt) general rights and interests of the public in the hope that in so doing they will ultimately achieve a diminution in the private rights conferred on individuals by copyright law.

Although the current controversy has many facets, one issue in need of clarification is whether it is, legally speaking, correct to claim that persons have 'rights' to the public domain. The language of rights is so central to modern political and judicial discourse that to be recognised as a true 'right' is an important victory in itself. Moreover, if the public at large can be said to have vested rights in the public domain, arguments in favour of limiting the application of digital rights management (DRM) technology and/or circumscribing the exercise of private contracting powers that have the effect of limiting the public domain are considerably strengthened.

The aim of this chapter therefore is to ascertain whether, under the common law system of copyright, there exist 'rights' to the public domain. All manner of interests and claims can be loosely classified as 'rights'. Such casual application of language, however, only serves to obfuscate the true legal status of these interests. Under analytical jurisprudence the term 'right' connotes a particular legal state of affairs, one that needs to be distinguished from the closely related concept of 'liberty' or 'privilege'.

It is accepted that the enquiry as to whether there are *ought to be* rights to the public domain is an entirely separate matter. Nevertheless, the race to recognise the public domain has resulted in many claims being made that are based on the supposition that there already exist rights to the public domain. Below, the merits of these claims in relation to imposing limits on the application of DRM technology and the exercise of private contracting powers will be evaluated, in the light of the analysis of whether rights to the public domain at present exist.

2   LEGAL RIGHTS AND PRIVILEGES

Elsewhere in this volume,[1] the meaning of the 'public domain' in copyright law has been examined in great detail. For present purposes, the concept shall be taken to mean those instances where individual rights are *not* conferred on owners of copyright works (or anyone else). Accordingly, the concept applies where the term of copyright has expired, where a work fails to qualify for protection (for example, owing to lack of originality) and in those situations where particular uses of still protected copyright works are exempted from the application of individual property rights. Into this last category fall both uses of copyright works that are not within the remit of the copyright owner's exclusive rights[2] (for example, reading a literary work) and uses that are expressly stated not to infringe the rights conferred by copyright law (for example, fair dealing under sections 29 and 30 of the Copyright, Designs and Patents Act 1988). With this generous understanding of the 'public domain' in mind, we can begin to question whether there are properly speaking 'rights' to the public domain.

What is meant by the term 'right' is a topic that has been investigated extensively in contemporary jurisprudence.[3] For present purposes there are three analytical perspectives on legal rights that need to be taken account of:

2.1   Logical Structure of Rights and Duties

Generally speaking, rights and duties are analysed conjointly. When a person is recognised as holding a right, it is necessarily implied that one or more persons (or entity such as the state) owe the beneficiary of the right a correlative duty.[4] Thus the logical structure of legal rights is usually in the following form:

---

[1]   Deazley, R., 'Copyright's Public Domain', Chapter 2.

[2]   The sum total of the rights conferred under UK copyright law are set out in sections 16–21 of the Copyright, Designs and Patents Act 1988 (CDPA).

[3]   E.g. Harel, A. (2004), 'Theories of Rights' in Golding, M. and Edmundson, W. (eds.), *Blackwell Guide to the Philosophy of Law and Legal Theory*, Oxford: Blackwell; Kamm, F., 'Rights', in Coleman. J. and Shapiro, S. (2002), *The Oxford Handbook of Jurisprudence and Philosophy of Law*, New York: Oxford University Press; and Waldron, J. (ed.) (1984), *Theories of Rights*, Oxford: Oxford University Press.

[4]   It should be noted that some authors have expressed doubts about whether rights and duties are always logically equivalent – e.g. MacCormick, N. (1982), 'Rights in Legislation', in Hacker, P. and Raz, J., *Law, Morality and Society: Essays in Honour of H.L.A. Hart*, Oxford: Clarendon Press.

X has a right to A against Y. The classical explanation of rights as duty-imposing norms was by the early 20th-century American jurist, Wesley Hohfeld.[5] Hohfeld offered a typology (Table 3.1) to distinguish rights from similar, but distinct,

Table 3.1

Rights (claim) v duties	X has a right to A entails that Y is under a duty to X with respect to A. For example, under a contract, X has a right to £50 entails that Y is under a duty to pay A £50.
Privileges (liberties) v no right	Privileges, or 'naked liberties' as they are sometimes called, are different from rights because they do not impose any correlative duty. For example, the proposition 'X has a privilege to travel to Spain' entails that no one has a right to interfere with X's actions; it does not imply that anyone is under a duty to facilitate X's travel. In common discourse rights and privileges are often confused.
Powers v liabilities	A person has a legal power when, by some act, he can alter his, or someone else's, legal position. For instance, in many legal systems individuals have the power to create contractual obligations. When I enter a loan agreement with a bank, I exercise that power and hence give rise to new legal rights (i.e. a right to receive a sum of money) and duties (i.e. a duty to repay the sum with interest). Hohfeld's correlative of a power – a liability – does not imply a disadvantage in the sense that it does when one speaks of criminal liability. Rather, it implies that persons are susceptible to having their legal position altered.
Immunity v disability	An immunity is a lack of susceptibility to having one's legal position altered. Its correlative is an absence of a power, that is, a disability, on the part of another person to alter one's legal position. Constitutional protections that limit government exercises of power are an example of where immunities and disabilities arise. A constitutionally protected right of free expression will normally entail that individuals have an immunity from government passing laws that interfere with their exercise of free expression.

---

[5] Hohfeld, W. (1978), *Fundamental Legal Conceptions as Applied in Judicial Reasoning*, ed. by W.W. Cook, Westport, CT: Greenwood Press [first published as two articles – Hohfeld, W. (1913), 'Some Fundamental Legal Conceptions as Applied in

jural relations. For present purposes, the relevant distinction is between *rights v duties* and *privileges v no rights*. The key feature about a right is that it imposes a duty on some other person; whereas with a privilege other persons simply have no right to interfere with the benefit – they are not positively obliged to see it honoured.

2.2   Substance of Rights

Understanding the logical structure of rights is extremely important, but does not reveal the substance of rights, that is, the question of what *concerns* are protected by rights. Legal theorists have developed two approaches for answering this question – the 'choice theory' and the 'interest theory' of rights. The choice theory of rights holds that rights protect the exercise of choice by an individual.[6] Rights under this approach are about carving out an autonomous zone in which individuals have space to make choices without fear of interference by others. One drawback of this theory is that it fails to explain how persons without full agency, such as infants and the mentally unsound, can hold rights (which in fact they do in most developed legal systems).[7]

The 'interest theory' of rights holds that a person is the bearer of a right when a duty is imposed *in order* to serve or protect his/her interests.[8] This theory stresses the status of right-holders as passive beneficiaries of supportive duties owed by others, and thus allows for a more expansive conception of rights. An interest is some basic value that concerns the nature of an individual's well-being. In other words, underlying all rights is some individual interest. In a normative analysis one can legitimately question whether the purported interest of the individual is in fact served by the right so conferred; that is, is there a causal relationship between the two? The interest theory of rights tends to be favoured over the choice theory because it embraces a wider category of legal rights.[9] In truth, both theories serve valid explanatory purposes.

Judicial Reasoning', 23 *Yale Law Journal* 16 and Hohfeld, W. (1916), 'Fundamental Legal Conceptions as Applied in Judicial Reasoning', 26 *Yale Law Journal* 710].

  [6]   Hart, H.L.A. (1982), *Essays on Bentham*, Oxford: Clarendon Press, pp. 174–93.
  [7]   Kramer, M. (2001), 'Do Animals and Dead People Have Legal Rights?', 14 *Canadian Journal of Law and Jurisprudence* 29.
  [8]   See Raz, J. (1984), 'Legal Rights', 4 *Oxford Journal of Legal Studies* 1.
  [9]   Penner, J. (1997), 'The Analysis of Rights', 10 *Ratio Juris* 300.

2.3 General v Special Rights

Following Hart, one can divide rights into two distinct categories. First there are general rights, that is, rights that everyone under a legal system possesses by virtue of their status as human beings, such as the right to life. Secondly, there are special rights, that is, rights that arise because of particular events that occur in an individual's life, such as a right to receive £50 that arises under a contract.[10] The former are of general application whereas the latter are contingent on an individual's particular circumstances.

Waldron has drawn attention to the importance of this distinction in the context of assessing the justifiability of property rights.[11] A *special-right based argument* is an argument in favour of private property rights based on an interest that has an importance because of the occurrence of some contingent event, such as mixing labour with an unowned resource. A *general-right based argument* is an argument in favour of private property rights based on an interest that has a qualitative importance in itself, such as having one's personality extend to the external world.

2.4 Is There a Right to the Public Domain?

Following the analysis above, if one asserts that individuals have some *right* to the public domain, the logical corollary is that some other individual or entity is under a positive duty to do some act or refrain from doing some act with respect to the interest that is protected by that right. In this author's view there is no valid basis for making such claim in relation to the public domain as understood vis-à-vis contemporary copyright law. Under Hohfeld's analysis, the correct view is that individuals have a privilege to use or dispose of objects in the public domain, which as we shall see significantly undercuts arguments for restricting the deployment of DRM technology and clickwrap licences.

First, consider works whose term of protection has expired or which do not qualify for protection in the first place. These works are held 'in common', that is, they are absented from the application of proprietary norms.[12] Like the air we breathe or the outer reaches of space, they are in a legal limbo, where no individual or entity has any rights to them at all. Likewise, no one is under a duty to others with respect to their disposition or use of these resources. Rather, we

---

[10]   Hart, H.L.A. (1984), 'Are There Any Natural Rights?', in Waldron, J. (ed.), *Theories of Rights*, Oxford: Oxford University Press.

[11]   Waldron, J. (1988), *The Right to Private Property*. Oxford: Clarendon Press, pp. 106–24.

[12]   Cahir, J. (2004), 'The Withering Away of Property: The Rise of the Internet Information Commons', 24 (4) *Oxford Journal of Legal Studies* 619–41.

all have the *privilege* or *liberty* to do what we like with these works (for example, stage a Shakespeare play); the only corollary is that other persons have *no right* to prevent us from so doing (for example, the direct descendant of William Shakespeare has no right to prevent me staging Macbeth). This state of affairs is the jural reverse of copyright ownership. A copyright owner has, for example, the exclusive *right* to reproduce a literary work and all others are under a duty to refrain from making reproductions. It seems reasonably clear therefore that, under the conventional language of rights theory, there is no right to works wholly in the public domain.

At first glance, the statutory exceptions to the exclusive rights of copyright owners have more a 'feel' of rights about them: they are, after all, specifically mentioned in statute. It is submitted that, under a close analysis, there is no *right* to avail oneself of copyright exceptions either; they too are examples of privileges recognised under the law.

Taking one obvious example, nowhere under the law can it be said that a user of a copyright work has a *right* to reproduce copyright works in the course of a criticism;[13] instead, all that is conferred on him/her by the copyright statute is the *privilege* to use copyright works for that purpose.[14] What this means is that a copyright owner has *no right* to succeed in copyright infringement proceedings with respect to such uses of protected works. The copyright owner is not, however, under a legal duty to make such uses available to any particular individual; he is merely disabled from taking infringement proceedings in the event that a permitted act takes place. A literary critic, for instance, has no cause of action under the 1988 Act against an author to obtain access to his/her unpublished manuscript for the purpose of criticism or review.

Recent changes to copyright law brought about as a result of the implementation of the Information Society Directive might imply that, when technological protection measures are applied to copyright works, the position has changed. Section 296ZE of the 1988 Act establishes a procedure whereby persons who are prevented from availing of a permitted act by a technological protection measure can issue a notice of complaint to the Secretary of State.[15] The Secre-

---

[13]   Section 30 of CDPA states: 'Fair dealing with a work for the purpose of criticism or review, of that or another work or performance, does not infringe copyright in the work provided that it is accompanied by a sufficient acknowledgement.'

[14]   A 'rights' conception of copyright exceptions was recently advanced by the Canadian Supreme Court in *CCH Canadian v Law Society of Upper Canada* [2004] 1 SCR 339, where it described the Canadian fair dealing for the purpose of research or private study as a 'user's right'. This may be simply a matter of terminological confusion, as the court did not point to any duty to which the right correlates.

[15]   Only the permitted acts listed in CDPA Schedule 5A fall within the complaint's procedure.

tary of State will grant a direction to the copyright owner requiring that he make available to the complainant the means necessary to carry out the permitted act. A failure to comply with such a direction is a breach of statutory duty.[16] The reason why this author maintains that this provision does not confer a general right to avail oneself of the permitted acts is that it is extremely limited in its application. First, one must be a 'lawful user' of copyright works in order to fall within the terms of section 296ZE, that is, have authorised access to a copyright work. Secondly, the Secretary of State will only issue a direction where satisfied that no voluntary measure or agreement is in place with the effect of enabling a person to carry out a permitted act. Thirdly, and most importantly, the complaints procedure is not available where copyright works are made available to the public 'on agreed contractual terms in such a way that members of the public may access them from a place and at a time individually chosen by them', that is, any situation where a copyright work is made available via the Internet and accompanied by a set of contractual terms.[17] The combined effect of these three limitations is to render the complaints procedure inapplicable to most commercial offerings of information made available via the Internet. It is reasonable to conclude therefore that there is no general right under UK law to avail oneself of copyright exceptions when prevented from so doing by DRM technology or a contractual provision.

In sum, the true position is that there are no rights to the public domain for the simple reason that under UK copyright law no person is recognised as being under a duty to honour the interests allegedly advanced by the public domain.

3   PRIVATE ORDERING AND THE PUBLIC DOMAIN

The emergence of the Internet and digital technology more generally at first appeared to pose a serious challenge to the continued viability of copyright law. The decentralised communicative architecture of the Internet and the ease by which perfect digital copies could be rendered raised doubts as to whether copyright laws could in practice be enforced in cyberspace.

At this stage of the Internet's development, we can surmise with reasonable confidence that predictions of copyright's demise have proven misplaced. Instead two novel exclusionary practices, in particular, have emerged which offer right-holders the prospect of securing even greater effective control over their works than was possible under traditional means of dissemination – DRM technology and clickwrap licences.

---

[16]   Section 296ZE(5).
[17]   Section 296ZE(9).

The prospect that self-help protection measures such as DRM technologies and clickwrap licences will become the principal exclusionary practices for ordering access to and use of informational resources in the Internet environment has met with a generally negative reaction. [18] Fears have been expressed that such practices will result in information being 'locked-up' and that privileges enjoyed by consumers in the pre-Internet environment will be lost. However credible these fears may be (and they are difficult to estimate at this stage), this author is of the view that the use of DRM technology and clickwrap licences to regulate access to and use of informational works is *prima facie* justified as being a legitimate exercise of individual rights and powers. Furthermore, the author will argue that the use of these exclusionary practices does not infringe any rights that the public purportedly has to the public domain.

This part will therefore examine whether (1) the use of DRM technology is conducive to a liberal conception of rights; (2) the application of clickwrap licences is a valid exercise of contractual powers; (3) the deployment of DRM technology and clickwrap licences has the potential to violate 'consumer rights' to the public domain; and (4) legislative measures against anti-circumvention of technological protections are justified.

3.1 Digital Rights Management Technology

When an individual applies a DRM technology to an informational work that he makes available via the Internet, he exercises a natural liberty[19] with respect to how he may use and dispose of his legitimately acquired tangible property (computer hardware) and accompanying software tools. Under liberal rights theory we assume that a person has a liberty to use and dispose of his legitimately acquired property provided that he does not violate the rights of other

---

[18]   E.g. Esler, B. (2003), 'Protecting the Protection: A Trans-Atlantic Analysis of the Emerging Right to Technological Self-Help', 43 *Idea* 553 at 606, expresses the fear that 'with strong TPM publicly granted monopolies such as copyright could also become irrelevant as right-holders replace legal sanctions with technological remedies. This, of course, is the publisher's dream, but if allowed to proceed unchecked it could be the consumers' nightmare.' For similar sentiments with respect to the equivalent American provisions, see Cohen, J. (2000), 'Copyright and the Perfect Curve', 53 *Vanderbilt Law Review* 1799.

[19]   Use of the terms 'natural power' and 'natural right' should not be confused with rights that are justified under natural law. The subject of natural rights attempts to discern how human social interaction should be structured so as to facilitate human happiness; natural law addresses the problem of how we ought to live our lives if we want to live a good life: see Barnett, R. (2003), 'The Imperative of Natural Rights in Today's World', *Boston University Public Law and Legal Theory Working Paper* (available at https://ssrn.com/abstract_id=437400) at 2–3, for a fuller explanation.

persons.[20] This author's initial intuition is that if we concede that a homeowner is entitled to place a padlock on his front door, we should also concede that the use of electronic locks and tolls is justified as being an exercise of one's legitimate property rights and the powers appurtenant thereto. It is important to recognise that, from a rights perspective, the use of technological protection measures as an exclusionary measure differs fundamentally from the method of engineering exclusion through copyright laws. With the former, exclusion is achieved by the individual exercising his own rights; with the latter, exclusion is achieved by the government imposing restrictions on how other persons may exercise their rights with respect to the use and disposition of their tangible property (such as printing presses and photocopiers).[21]

The rights conferred by copyright law are the outcome of a political decision-making process, and therefore reflect the bargaining positions of the various negotiating parties. In contrast, the use of self-help protection measures is a natural incident of owning computer hardware and DRM software tools and does not require any direct government intervention to take effect: one engineers exclusion without having to call on the assistance of a state enforcement or regulatory agency. The role for government in regulating exclusionary practices is likely to be considerably reduced in the light of the new-found power to self-protect information goods. From a liberal rights perspective we would only justify constraints on the use of self-help protection measures if it could be shown that their use conflicts with the rights or liberties of other persons, a matter that is addressed in section 3.3 below.

Simply *not liking* the self-serving way in which commercial operators may potentially use DRM technology to advance their economic interests is not, it is submitted, a sufficient basis for imposing mandatory use restrictions. The whole point of liberalism is to carve out zones of liberty in which individuals can peaceably pursue their own objectives. For some information producers that may mean maximising their personal wealth through regulated pay-per-use services; for others it may mean donating their product to the information commons.

---

[20] This is simply a restatement of the Millsian 'no harm' principle. For contemporary expositions on liberal rights theory, see Barnett, R. (1998), *The Structure of Liberty: Justice and the Rule of Law*, Oxford: Clarendon Press.

[21] Bell, T. (2003), 'Authors' Welfare: Copyright as a Statutory Mechanism for Redistributing Rights', 69 *Brooklyn Law Review* 229; and Palmer, T. (1990), 'Are Patents and Copyrights Morally Justified? The Philosophy of Property Rights and Ideal Objects', 13 *Harvard Journal of Law and Public Policy* 817.

3.2 Clickwrap Licences

Turning to clickwrap licences, the basic issue is whether we accept the legitimacy of so-called 'contracts of adhesion' or whether we view them as a lesser
form of contractual obligation. Putting aside the question of their legal validity,
this author takes the view that enforcing contractual obligations which arise
under a properly constituted clickwrap licence is justified under liberal rights
theory. The issue at hand is not whether we regard contractual obligations *per
se* as justified: every major branch of moral philosophy upholds the principle
of legally recognising contractual rights and duties.[22] Rather the question is
whether we think that contractual obligations can only come into being following negotiation between the parties of equal bargaining power to the point where
they are fully informed as to the detail of every obligation that they undertake
(promissory theory) or whether mere *consent*, that is, clicking 'I agree', to assume contractual obligations suffices for their instantiation (consent theory).[23]

It is conceded that 'contracts of adhesion' are sometimes viewed with scepti-
cism.[24] In the literature we can find three reasons for their negative reception,
none of which stands up to scrutiny. First, clickwrap licences are thought to lack
moral force because individuals who accede to them often do so without inform-
ing themselves of their terms: the lack of actual knowledge or informed consent
is regarded as a de-legitimising factor. It is undoubtedly true that consumers
often take a calculated risk and consent to standard term contracts without ap-
praising themselves of their details: that is their choice, but it is not one that
they are obliged to make. A cautious consumer can take the time to read the
terms and conditions, and if he is not pleased he can decline to proceed with
the purchase. The fact that most consumers do not carry out such scrupulous
investigations is for very sound reasons. Standard terms generally define default
rules on the allocation of risk for foreseeable, but statistically rare, outcomes.
If a contractual document does not set these default rules, the courts ultimately
will. Most consumers have the good sense to know that the effort required to
familiarise themselves with all foreseeable risk allocations is not worth the investment of their time and resources. The most important contractual term for
consumers is *price*, and few consumers have difficulty in ascertaining that information. With information goods consumers will also want to know the
permissions that they are granted, such as whether back-up or private copies
can be made. Again the effort required to become familiar with such essential

---

   [22]   Atiyah, P. (1983), *Promises, Morals and Law*, Oxford: Oxford University Press.
   [23]   Barnett, R. (1986), 'A Consent Theory of Contract', 86 *Columbia Law Review*
289.
   [24]   E.g. Kessler, F. (1943), 'Contracts of Adhesion – Some Thoughts About Freedom
of Contract', 43 *Columbia Law Review* 629.

information is minimal, and in most cases it will be provided along with the marketing information used to induce consumers. The 'lack of knowledge' objection to clickwrap licences is therefore without substance.

The second common objection to standard term contracts is that there is often an inequality in bargaining strength between drafters of these contracts (suppliers) and individual consumers. No one disputes that a supplier is likely to be better resourced, more knowledgeable about market conditions and in receipt of superior legal advice in comparison with the average consumer. In competitive markets, however, the greatest pressure on suppliers to provide a high-quality product or service comes not from the demands of a single consumer but from the competitive challenges posed by other suppliers.[25] A licence term is simply another attribute of a good or service, and suppliers are just as likely to compete on licence terms as they are on price or quality.[26] A high street clothes store is under no legal obligation to refund a customer who has second thoughts about a rash purchase, but most nowadays do so without asking any questions. Such a consumer-friendly approach is brought about by the operation of market forces and not because of mandatory consumer protection legislation. It is wrong therefore to posit the bargaining power of a supplier against that of a single consumer. The better view is that, in a competitive market, a supplier is responsive to the aggregated power of consumer choice.

The third common objection to clickwrap licences is that they threaten to upset the delicate 'balance of interests' allegedly struck by the legislature in drafting copyright statutes. Some authors argue that copyright legislation should limit the exercise of private contracting powers because it is an ideal (or preferable) expression of how producers and consumers ought to order their relationship.[27] If the copyright statutes can be said to pre-empt private contract-

---

[25]   One possible objection to this argument is that markets in information goods are inherently anti-competitive because of the 'monopoly' effects of copyright law. The 'monopoly' conferred by copyright law and a real economic monopoly are very different creatures and should not be confused: Kitch, E. (2000), 'Elementary and Persistent Errors in the Economic Analysis of Intellectual Property', 53 *Vanderbilt Law Review* 1277. Economists generally treat markets for information goods as examples of 'monopolistic competition', i.e. where there are many producers and consumers in a given market of substitutable, but not identical, goods – Varian, H. and Shapiro, C. (1998), *Information Rules: A Strategic Guide to the Network Economy*, Cambridge, MA: Harvard Business School Press.

[26]   Friedman, D. (1998), 'In Defense of Private Orderings: Comments on Julie Cohen's "Copyright and the Jurisprudence of Self-Help"', 13 *Berkeley Technology Law Journal* 1151; and Nimmer, R. (2002), 'Licensing in the Contemporary Information Economy', *Washington University Journal of Law and Policy* 99 (both arguing against the imposition of mandatory licence terms).

[27]   Lemley, M. (1998), 'Beyond Pre-emption: The Law and Policy of Intellectual Property Licensing', 87 *California Law Review* 111.

ing powers so that suppliers cannot contractually limit the privileges conferred on consumers by statute, it must also mean, however, that suppliers are incapacitated from licensing consumers to carry out acts that would otherwise be infringing acts, such as downloading a work to one's hard drive. The idea that the copyright statutes are an iron cage is untenable and finds no support in either authority or reason.[28] The copyright acts stipulate various default rules, which parties are free to vary by contract. In any case, there is no reason to believe that strict government regulation of licence terms would serve the interests of producers or consumers.

It is submitted therefore that the use of DRM technology and clickwrap licences to achieve exclusion and hence order information markets is *prima facie* consistent with liberal rights theory.

3.3   Consumer 'Rights'

Under liberal legal systems, we countenance restrictions on the exercise of individual rights where it can be shown that other persons' rights are threatened. For instance, an individual's right to travel freely is limited by the duty not to trespass on private land (except where a public right of way exists). Likewise the right to use a knife that one owns is limited by the duty not to harm other individuals. With respect to the application of DRM technology to informational works – an exercise of one's property rights – we must ask ourselves whether it entails the violation of other persons' rights. If it can be shown that DRM technology has such potential, we can justify government/judicial regulation.

There are, it is submitted, two potential grounds for challenging the right of an individual to apply DRM technology to an informational work: (a) because the use of DRM technology conflicts with a general public right to have *access* to information; and (b) because the application of DRM technology to a work prevents individuals from availing themselves of the privileges conferred by copyright law. Both these grounds will be rejected and it will be concluded that the use of DRM technology does not entail the violation of other persons' rights and hence that there is no justification under liberal rights theory for government-imposed restrictions on the use of DRM technology.

3.3.1   A public right of access to information?
There is no sound ethical basis for holding that the public has a free-standing general *right* to gain access to information that is protected by DRM technology. To uphold such a principle would mean that all individuals in possession of in-

---

[28]   One exception is the mandatory exceptions relating to computer programs and databases – CDPA ss. 296A and 296B.

formation would be under a *duty* to make that information available to other persons on demand. If this were true, the temperamental poet who destroyed the only copy of his masterful epic would be said to have infringed the 'rights' of others to have access to the said poem; similarly the diarist who locked his journal in a safe would be held to infringe public rights of access thereto. One might even go so far as to say that the public would be justified in breaking into the recalcitrant bibliophile's home in order to gain access to his extensive collection of books. The absurdity of these propositions indicates the heavy burden that lies on those who argue for a general public right of access to information capable of overriding the right of individuals to engage in self-help exclusionary practices.

The first question that we must ask ourselves is this: are there interests at stake that warrant the imposition of a duty on individuals in possession of information with respect to how they make use of DRM technology? We can certainly support the claim that there is a *general public interest* in gaining access to educational and cultural information:[29] information that educational and cultural providers may potentially ring-fence with DRM technology. In an ideal world all educational and cultural materials would be free for general public access and use. There is, however, a long distance to travel from the point where one identifies a non-individuated socio-economic interest to justifying the imposition of duties on specific individuals or organisations that limit the exercise of their settled rights.

Amongst the topics that most animate contemporary political theory is the extent to which the state is expected to give effect to individual rights that are grounded in non-individuated socio-economic interests. All sides of the political spectrum agree that rights are important, and that the state is bound to protect certain rights. The political fault line is between those who hold that the state is required to protect only *negative rights* of non-interference,[30] such as the right to life and property, and those who believe that the state should also actively advance *positive rights* – rights that require some positive or redistributive act on the part of state authorities in order for them to come into being, for example, social welfare rights. [31] Opinion is clearly divided on this issue. It is nevertheless

---

[29]   See Suthersanen, U. (2003), 'Copyright and Educational Policies: A Stakeholder Analysis', 23 (4) *Oxford Journal of Legal Studies* 585, for an analysis of how educational policies are advanced through copyright law.

[30]   In 20th-century political philosophy the *locus classicus* of the minimalist position is Nozick, R. (1974), *Anarchy, State and Utopia*, New York: Basic Books. See also Palmer, T. (2001), 'Saving Rights Theory from Its Friends', in Machan, T. (ed.), *Individual Rights Reconsidered*, Stanford: Hoover Institution Press.

[31]   The leading exponents of 'positive' rights include: Dworkin, R. (1978), *Taking Rights Seriously*, Cambridge, MA: Harvard University Press; and Raz, J. (1986), *The*

generally agreed that if non-individuated socio-economic interests are to be recognised as grounding individual rights they can, at most, impose duties on the state; they do not legitimate, under either negative or positive rights theory, the imposition of duties directly on private actors. A number of examples serve to illustrate this point. Many countries recognise that a child has a right to receive a basic education.[32] The recognition of such a right does not mean that a teacher owes a legal duty to his next door neighbour's child to provide him/her with an education. Equally, the recognition of a general right to receive medical treatment does not imply that a given doctor owes a legal duty to all and sundry to provide them with medical treatment. These rights impose duties on state authorities, not on private individuals.

The reason why socio-economic interests of this nature, when deemed worthy of advancement, impose duties on the state rather than on private individuals is that only a centralised authority with the power to redistribute economic resources through taxation is capable of discharging such obligations in an effective and consistent fashion. The mere fact of identifying a public interest in gaining access to information should not therefore lead one to impose a duty on individual owners of DRM technology to refrain from deploying their technology as they wish. If the state wants to recognise and honour non-individuated socio-economic interests it can do so directly itself; alternatively it can procure educational and cultural material from private suppliers on agreed economic terms.

3.3.2   A right to avail oneself of copyright infringement exemptions?

Above we concluded that, as a matter of positive law, there is no right to avail oneself of the exceptions to copyright infringement recognised under law. Should we nonetheless recognise such a right? One could argue that the logic that motivated the legislature to recognise user privileges with respect to copyright infringement applies *mutatis mutandis* to information protected by self-help technological measures. Foged states that position in the following terms:[33]

Morality of Freedom, Oxford: Oxford University Press. A particularly strong expression of the positive rights thesis is Holmes, S. & Sunstein, C. (1999), *The Cost of Rights: Why Liberty Depends on Taxes*, New York: Norton, which argues that because both negative and positive rights are contingent on political decision-making, there is a strong case for an expanded government role in advancing 'welfare' rights.

[32]   Article 26(1) of the Universal Declaration of Human Rights, 1948, states: 'Everyone has the right to education. Education shall be free, at least in the elementary and fundamental stages. Elementary education shall be compulsory. Technical and professional education shall be made generally available and higher education shall be equally accessible to all on the basis of merit.'

[33]   Foged, T. (2002), 'US v EU Anti Circumvention Legislation: Preserving the Public's Privileges in the Digital Age', 24 *European Intellectual Property Review* 525

The problem with encryption is that it threatens the public's privileges by permitting copyright owners (and others) to overprotect their works. Technological measures prevent access not only for potential infringers, but may additionally prevent access for those who have a legitimate right to access, for example because of fair use. Furthermore, technological measures effectively prevent access, not only to copyright material, but also to other information and ideas that may not be subject to copyright but may be protected by the same technological measure.

There are numerous flaws to this type of reasoning.[34] Most of all it wrongly assumes that copyright law is the only legitimate source of legal norms for determining how information markets may be ordered. Such a view turns liberal rights theory on its head. Common law contractual powers and tangible property rights predate copyright law, and have a far more distinguished pedigree.[35] This author can see no reason why the spoils of previous political bargains should override the new-found ability to self-protect by legitimate private means.

3.4 Anti-circumvention Measures

Article 6(1) and (2) of the Information Society Directive oblige Member States to provide 'adequate legal protection' against the circumvention of effective technological protection measures and against trafficking in anti-circumvention devices or services. The Copyright and Related Rights Regulations 2003[36] have implemented these provisions into UK law by creating three categories of liability for anti-circumvention related activities: (a) section 296ZA makes persons *civilly* liable for engaging in acts that circumvent effective technological measures applied to a copyright work; (b) section 296ZB makes persons *criminally* liable for trafficking (for example, manufacturing, selling, possessing in the course of business) in anti-circumvention devices or services; and (c) section 296ZD makes persons *civilly* liable for trafficking in anti-circumvention devices or services. In this section we will broach the question of whether the creation of civil and criminal liability for anti-circumvention related activities is justified under liberal rights theory.

At the outset we need to recognise that the practice of self-protecting information via DRM systems has only come about as a result of relatively recent

at 526. See also Heide, T. (2001), 'Copyright in the EU and the United States: What "Access Right"?', 23 *European Intellectual Property Review* 469.

[34] E.g. (a) in the space of two sentences the author has conflated public 'privileges' with a 'legitimate right to access'; and (b) use of the phrase 'to overprotect their works' implies wrongly that there is an objective measure of optimal protection standards.

[35] For a strong defence of common law contract and property rights over copyright law, see Palmer, T., *supra* note 30.

[36] S.I. 2003/2498.

technological developments. The issues that we are confronting may therefore have no direct connection to issues that arose with previous exclusionary practices. We need to be prepared to approach the question of the justifiability of imposing civil and criminal liability for anti-circumvention related activities from first principles.

We have already concluded that the right of individuals to protect information via DRM and similar systems is justified under liberal rights theory, as being a legitimate incident of property ownership. It should be remembered that the right we are concerned with is the right to protect information via DRM systems, and *not* a right to information itself. From the aforementioned conclusion, it follows logically that other persons should be under a duty to refrain from interfering with the operation of DRM systems. Where an Internet information supplier, such as Westlaw, applies DRM technology to information that is made available via its server, it is wholly reasonable to expect that persons accessing its website refrain from circumventing a technological protection measure (such as a restriction on downloading information). When a legal system recognises a legal right, the rule of law demands that the courts and enforcement authorities vindicate that right through appropriate legal sanction. We can justify therefore, without any hesitation, section 296ZA civil liability for engaging in acts of anti-circumvention.[37]

The creation of civil and criminal liability for manufacturing and trafficking in anti-circumvention devices and services is more problematic. It is one thing to hold that persons should be under a legal duty to refrain from circumventing a technological protection measure; it is a step further to hold that persons should be prevented from using their own skills and tools to develop and market a product that can cause no physical harm to another person. The locksmith who makes replica keys is entitled to carry on his business even though he may sometimes inadvertently assist in the crimes of a burglar.

The reason for being somewhat equivocal about indirect acts that facilitate circumvention is that there is not always a necessary connection between the manufacture and supply of anti-circumvention technology and an illegal act of circumvention. It is plausible that a manufacturer could produce a device or offer a service that facilitates both legitimate and illegitimate activities. If blanket civil and/or criminal liability is imposed, the legitimate as well as the illegitimate uses will be precluded.[38] In such circumstances it is reasonable for the manu-

---

[37] Furthermore the exemption contained in CDPA s. 296ZA(2) from liability for cryptography research (an exemption not explicitly required by the Directive) seems a reasonable safeguard for the cryptography industry.

[38] A very similar conflict arises where indirect or contributory copyright infringement is concerned. This matter has not been broached in any great detail by the UK courts; however the US courts have some quite advanced jurisprudence. In the leading case *Sony*

facturer/distributor to argue that he/she should not be held responsible for the illegal activities of others, when there are alternative legitimate uses available. Furthermore, one can argue that prohibiting the manufacturer of devices/provision of services that do have legitimate purposes perpetrates an injustice against *bona fide* consumers of those devices/services.

A fair compromise to the conflict between the right to protect information via DRM systems and the right to manufacture devices and supply services to consumers that have legitimate purposes is to have a sliding scale of liability. Where it can be shown that the sole or primary function of a device/service is to facilitate the circumvention of a technological measure, it is fair that liability be imposed on manufacturers and traffickers. The manufacture and proliferation of such devices can seriously undermine a person's ability to exercise the right to protect information via DRM systems, and is not saved by reason of its serving alternative legitimate functions. On the other hand, where it can be shown that a significant legitimate purpose is achieved through the use of the device/service, no liability should be imposed on manufacturers/traffickers. Significantly, sections 296ZB and 296ZD do contain a compromise on the lines just described. For either civil or criminal liability to arise, the offending device, product or component must be 'primarily designed, produced, or adapted' for the purpose of enabling or facilitating the circumvention of effective technological measures.[39] It would seem therefore that devices which have alternative legitimate purposes are exempted from liability.

On balance therefore we can justify the imposition of liability for manufacturing and trafficking in anti-circumvention devices and services. These measures support the right to self-protect information with technological measures, and strike a reasonable balance between that right and the right of honest manufacturers and traders to pursue their legitimate ends. The question of whether criminal liability is a *proportionate* response to the threat posed is a separate matter: one that is impossible to assess at this early stage of DRM-ordered information markets.

4 CONCLUSIONS

The 'discovery' in recent years of the public domain has resulted in much tendentious writing about the ills of copyright law, the emergence of information

---

v Universal City Studios 464 US 417 (1984), the sale of VCRs, which purchasers could use for infringing purposes, was held not to constitute contributory infringement because VCRs were held to have 'substantial non-infringing' use (i.e. they could be used for time-shifting programmes – a fair use).

[39]   CDPA ss. 296ZB(1) and 296ZD(1)(b)(iii).

'feudalism', and the supposed swallowing up of cultural and scientific information into some plutocrat's vault. Yet virtually no empirical or even hearsay evidence has been produced by dissenters to support claims that citizens are being starved of information or having their freedom of expression rights violated as a consequence of copyright law and the new exclusionary practices analysed above. On the contrary, the Internet and digital technology more generally have unleashed a flood of high- (and low-) quality information, which seems relatively impervious to the supposed threats of copyright law allied with self-help exclusionary measures.

Conscious of the charge of peering at the issue through a Panglossian lens, this author does not dispute that there are fair arguments to be made in favour of improving the existing legislative framework. Nevertheless, these arguments can only be advanced in a coherent fashion by avoiding imprecise uses and rhetorical abuses of 'rights' language. The debate as to the proper place of the public domain in copyright law should obviously continue, but it is this author's hope that it can do so without mention of the 'R' word.

4.   The public domain and international intellectual property law treaties

Antony Taubman*

When 'Omer smote 'is bloomin' lyre, He'd 'eard men sing by land an' sea;
An' what he thought 'e might require, 'E went an' took – the same as me! (Rudyard Kipling, *Barrack-Room Ballads*)

Every text is from the outset under the jurisdiction of other discourses which impose a universe on it. (Julia Kristeva, *Desire in Language: A Semiotic Approach to Literature and Art*, 1980)

1   INTRODUCTION: THE INTERNATIONAL FACE OF PUBLIC DOMAINS

This chapter, too, has many faces. The agonistic yet symbiotic *pas-de-deux* between public domains and international intellectual property (IP) treaties[1] can offer unexpectedly diverse aspects for reflection, from several vantage points:

- international public goods as a link between the public domain and the IP system;
- the conception or construction of an international public domain;
- the public domain status of treaties as texts in themselves;

---

*   This chapter expresses personal views of the author and explores ideas that have no connection with any official appointment; the views expressed should not be attributed to WIPO, its Member States or its Secretariat. Based on research undertaken at the Australian Center for Intellectual Property in Agriculture (ACIPA), College of Law, Australian National University.

[1]   The following treaties are discussed in particular: the Stockholm Act of the Paris Convention for the Protection of Industrial Property (1967), henceforth 'Paris'; the Paris Act of the Berne Convention for the Protection of Literary and Artistic Works (1971), henceforth 'Berne'; the Patent Cooperation Treaty (1970), henceforth 'PCT'; the Agreement on Trade-Related Aspects of Intellectual Property Rights (1994), concluded as an annex to the Agreement Establishing the World Trade Organization (WTO), henceforth 'TRIPS'; and the WIPO Copyright Convention (1996), henceforth 'WCT'.

- the influence of treaties on national public domains;
- a public domain perspective in international norm-setting.

International IP treaties illustrate the multiplicity and polyvalence of public domains. They express in concrete form key questions that are begged by applying a single, presumptuous definite article to 'the' public domain, when actual publics and their domains are numerous and diverse. Mapping the formal legal structure of international treaties across to 'the' or 'a' public domain can, perhaps incongruously, illuminate the multi-faceted character of public domains as social constructs.[2] Diversity in the nature of publics as collective entities and diversity in the kind of domains they maintain finds an attenuated echo in the formal recognition of distinct states under the treaty system, in the consequent territoriality of IP rights, and in the scope for diversity of values and identities acknowledged in international treaties.

The independence of IP rights[3] is itself a building block of public domains under national laws, underpinning differences in the form, reach and content of public domains. As an objective measure of this diversity, Wikimedia Commons, a public domain depositary of media files that 'must be free of use in any jurisdiction,'[4] recently replaced a single 'public domain' tag for media content with over 100 different public domain tags that denote different jurisdictions, different legal status and different modes of entry into the public domain.[5]

The territoriality of public domains mirrors the territoriality and independence of IP rights granted under a patchwork of national laws.[6] Even proposals 'to

---

[2] Thus Esma Moukhtar: '[w]hat we today call the "public domain" consists of a multiplicity of places and virtual spaces, in which people do gather, but not primarily to find differences, but to find agreement. Agreement with that which at that particular moment constitutes your chosen identity. Thus the differences search for their own place and direction. Each their own public domain as an extension of what is private', Frequently Asked Questions about the Public Domain, dedigitalbalie, 2004, at www.debalie.nl/artikel.jsp?articleid=12829.

[3] Paris, art. 4*bis*(1).

[4] 'Commons: Criteria for inclusion', at commons.wikimedia.org/wiki/Commons:Criteria_for_inclusion, last visited 20 December 2005.

[5] In addition to the many 'public domain' tags, there are other categories of 'free' and 'unfree' tags at commons.wikimedia.org/wiki/Commons:Copyright_tags, last visited 5 January 2006.

[6] A direct practical problem, for instance, for web publishing of 'public domain' works. The principal Project Gutenberg site (www.gutenberg.org) notifies the copyright status of most works (including antiquities such as Burton's *Anatomy of Melancholy*) as follows: 'Not copyrighted in the United States. If you live elsewhere check the laws of your country before downloading this ebook.' The Australian site advises that one 'cannot legally download or read books posted at Project Gutenberg of Australia if one is in a country where copyright protections extend more than 50 years past an author's

allow national buttressing of the public domain … [or] to redraw the international map more radically, to use it to constrain member states from invading the borders of public space'[7] would ultimately work through the multiplicity of national legal domains that operate within the treaty system. And the different forms of IP recognised within the treaty system correspond to distinct modes of public domain: there are public domains of freely reproducible forms of expression, of freely applicable technologies, of signs and symbols freely used to denote or connote in the marketplace, of functional and aesthetic designs free to apply to products, of ideas[8] and ephemeral news,[9] and of 'accessible knowledge.'[10]

The Patent Cooperation Treaty (PCT) may not, for instance, be conventionally construed as a mechanism for augmenting any public domains: it is essentially seen as facilitating the acquisition of national and regional patents. Yet its legal operation and practical administration together yield a steadily growing body of technological knowledge which enters an international public domain of information that is freely *knowable* and accessible (if not necessarily free for any use), in international languages, soon after its inception. (This is in contrast to knowledge which is inaccessible owing to legal constraints such as confidentiality, or which is inaccessible through simple failure publicly to disclose it, through lack of resources or of interest, so that information does not enter the domain of the freely knowable and accessible. It also stands in contrast to national patent information systems which are in the public domain but still difficult in practice to access or use in many countries. This aspect of practical accessibility as a factor in a healthy public domain is explored below.)

PCT publications form a public resource of state of the art information, international in character.[11] While it is readily accessible as knowledge, its true public domain status as freely usable technology – its impact on freedom to operate – will only be determined under national law, and by an applicant's choice to pursue protection in some jurisdictions and to forego it elsewhere. In practice, this knowledge does fully enter the public domain in most jurisdictions worldwide, given that few international patent applications mature into in-force

---

death. The author's estate and publishers still retain their legal and moral rights to oversee the work in those countries.' See also onlinebooks.library.upenn.edu/okbooks.html#whatpd.

   [7]   Dinwoodie, G.B. and Dreyfuss, R.C. (2005), 'Patenting Science: Protecting the Domain of Accessible Knowledge', in Guibault, L. and Hugenholtz, B. (eds), *The Future of the Public Domain in Intellectual Property*, available at http://ssrn.com/abstract= 698321.

   [8]   TRIPS art. 9.2; WCT art. 2.

   [9]   Berne art. 2.8.

   [10]   Dinwoodie and Dreyfuss, note 7 *supra*. Knowledge may also be 'accessed' to be known, to be disseminated or, to be used.

   [11]   www.wipo.int/patentscope/en/.

national patents in more than a minority of countries worldwide. The PCT also produces extensive metadata of freely usable public domain information about technology – such as information about patterns of technological activity and ownership, about directions in technological development, about the activities of individual inventors and firms, about other documents relevant to the novelty and inventiveness of claimed inventions, and about preliminary assessments of the validity of claims. This metadata is, in turn, a valuable resource in safeguarding the effectiveness of the public domain, inasmuch as it can help dispel uncertainty and clarify the jurisdictional boundaries of applicable claims.

The PCT therefore illustrates several faces of the public domain: its territoriality (technology patented in one country will be in the public domain in a widely variable, but generally high, number of other countries), and the link between the content of a public domain and the uses reserved for the public (freely accessible knowledge *qua* knowledge, freely usable technology to be applied, or freely reproducible form of expression of the disclosure). It shows how a public domain is defined not merely by content or subject matter, but also by forms of use – the entitlement to use public domain material is construed in terms of the absence of rights to exclude certain forms of use. PCT documents are widely distributed internationally as a freely available information resource, even as a consequence of individual choices to pursue patent protection in multiple jurisdictions. Such patent specifications will normally be in the public domain in the sense of being freely reproducible or freely accessible, but not necessarily in the sense of being free for all to use as technology until the status of patent applications is resolved. Yet, in some jurisdictions, at least, copyright constraints may apply to some material in a lapsed patent application, even though the disclosed technology enters the public domain when the application lapses,[12] and even though some aspects of copyright must be waived.[13] Again, this relatively straightforward case of exemplary public domain material points to the multi-faceted, jurisdictionally-bound quality of public domains, and the systemic interplay between IP protection and public domains.

---

[12]   United States, Consolidated Patent Rules, 70 FR 56119 (Sept. 26, 2005), § 1.71 (d) and (e); § 1.84(s).

[13]   'A copyright or mask work notice may be placed in a design or utility patent application adjacent to copyright and mask work material contained therein. … Inclusion of a copyright or mask work notice will be permitted only if the authorisation language set forth in paragraph (e) of this section is included at the beginning (preferably as the first paragraph) of the specification', § 1.71(d), Consolidated Patent Rules, Title 37 – Code of Federal Regulations: Patents, Trademarks, and Copyrights.

2 IP, PUBLIC DOMAINS AND INTERNATIONAL PUBLIC GOODS

Public domains and IP systems are closely, even integrally, linked. From different policy perspectives, the relationship between a public domain and an IP system may be characterised variously as harmonious synergy; pragmatic, uneven accommodation; or inherent tension. Policy discourse or ideological leanings may favour one side of this coin over the other. But even critiques of the embedded values in the IP system yoke IP law and the public domain together: 'indigenous peoples have rarely placed anything in the so-called "public domain", a term without meaning to us ... the public domain is a construct of the IP system and does not take into account domains established by customary indigenous laws.'[14] Even so, it is a natural analytical and polemical tendency to associate interests with one side or another of such a fundamental distinction as that between proprietary knowledge resources and 'the' public domain.[15] This can lead to an assumption that international IP treaties are antithetical in spirit to the maintenance of a healthy public domain, and that development of international IP law is a steady, even inexorable, incursion on the public domain. But the treaty system can facilitate a more diverse conception of the many public domains that abut, overlap and otherwise interact within and between national jurisdictions. There are too many public domains, and clarity about their metes and bounds too essential for their effective operation, for a zero-sum calculation of interests to be an adequate guide for practical policy-making. The complex relationship between international treaties and the multifarious public domains they shape or influence underscores the need for analysis that transcends a presumption of polarised interests.

Yet polarisation seems implicit and inevitable, even when working at the level of basic definitions. IP[16] and public domain are generally defined in binary

---

[14] Document WIPO/GRTKF/IC/5/3. See also Gibson, J., 'Audiences in Tradition: Traditional Knowledge and the Public Domain', Chapter 12 in this volume.

[15] Taubman, A. (forthcoming 2006), 'TRIPS Jurisprudence in the Balance: Between the Realist Defence of Policy Space and a Shared Utilitarian Ethic', in Lenk, C., Hoppe, N. and Andorno, R. (eds) (2007), *Ethics and Law of Intellectual Property. Current Problems in Politics, Science and Technology*, Aldershot: Ashgate Publishing.

[16] This chapter distinguishes intellectual property (IP) from the legal rights stemming from ownership of IP, and thus only uses the term 'IP right' in the latter context; thus a patent for an invention or a trade mark, as forms of IP, will be distinguished from the specific exclusive rights conferred by title in the patent or trade mark. Critics of current IP systems have suggested terms such as 'commercial privilege' in place of 'intellectual property', although current practice is for most forms of IP to be dealt with as other forms of intangible property such as a chose in action; but, even if this approach is taken, it would be helpful to distinguish between a 'privilege' and the rights it confers (to exclude certain

opposition: the two concepts intrinsically yoked together, but pulling in opposite directions. The public domain may be defined in terms of the absence of exclusive rights; but the proper scope of IP subject matter can also be determined by reference to a prior conception of the necessary public domain. Taking the first approach, Wikipedia defines the public domain as 'the body of knowledge and innovation ... in relation to which no person or other legal entity can establish or maintain proprietary interests.'[17] For instance, one clear category of public domain material is that for which IP titles have lapsed or expired:[18] the subject matter of the lapsed IP enters the public domain.[19] This means that the general public gains rights to use this material precisely in the ways that the exclusive IP rights had until then precluded. So the cessation of IP protection augments the public domain by adding a general entitlement to *certain uses* of the protected material (the public had always been entitled to use the protected material in accordance with fair use and other permitted exceptions). Thus the nature of IP can shape both the content and the forms of use of a certain public domain.

Public domains can only be intelligibly described with reference both to content and forms of use considered integrally. Not all uses of 'public domain' material are permitted – a genericised trademark enters the public domain of descriptive language, but a trader must still use it accurately to denote or

---

defined acts by third parties). The oral argument in the US Supreme Court case *JEM Supply v Pioneer Hi-Bred International* illustrated the potential confusion, as the counsel for the appellant conducted a confused exchange with the bench, directly contradicting the Chief Justice when he (the counsel) conflated the idea of subject matter protected by a plant or utility patent with the scope of the rights conferred on the right-holder.

[17]   en.wikipedia.org/wiki/Public_domain.

[18]   The public domain appears explicitly in Berne in this sense only, concerning the transitional arrangements for the protection of existing works, providing in particular (art. 18) that the Convention 'shall apply to all works which, at the moment of its coming into force, have not yet fallen into the public domain in the country of origin through the expiry of the term of protection. If, however, through the expiry of the term of protection which was previously granted, a work has fallen into the public domain of the country where protection is claimed, that work shall not be protected anew.'

[19]   But only in the national jurisdiction concerned; policy, legal and factual differences between jurisdictions must be assessed before assuming, as the Wikipedia definition does, that such 'information and creativity is considered to be part of the common cultural and intellectual heritage of humanity, which in general anyone may use or exploit' (ibid.). However, the 'rule of the shorter term' – when optionally applied under a national law – relevantly links entry into the public domain of material in the country of origin to copyright protection in third countries: 'the term shall be governed by the legislation of the country where protection is claimed; however, unless the legislation of that country otherwise provides, the term shall not exceed the term fixed in the country of origin of the work' (Berne, art. 7(8)). See in general the discussion in Deazley, R., 'Copyright's Public Domain, Chapter 2, and Cahir, J., 'The Public Domain: Right or Liberty?', Chapter 3 in this volume.

describe goods or services. An ethical and legal argument might be made to limit certain usages of traditional knowledge and genetic resources that are strictly in the public domain as determined by national laws. Yet it is too restrictive to consider only that material to be unequivocally in the public domain when applicable IP rights have definitively lapsed (the public domain as a 'kind of city of the dead, a necropolis'[20]) – even if, in some contexts, it is a necessary safeguard against careless misappropriation.[21] In general, it is not enough to point to the absence of rights alone to define the public domain; there is a strong legal and policy basis for inherent public domain status for some material. Much material begins life in the public domain and is inherently not susceptible to IP coverage at all by virtue of how it is categorised[22] or its particular characteristics, including how it is *read*,[23] or is required to be in the public domain by the explicit operation of IP law.[24] Public domain status for some material is advocated for policy reasons whatever its actual legal status may be.[25] Generally, is the public domain a simple residue, just all that is left after IP right-holders have

---

[20]   Baron, R.A., 'Making the Public Domain Public', at www.studiolo.org/IP/VRA-TM-SF-PublicDomain.htm.

[21]   For instance, as clarified by the Nigerian Delegation to the fifth session of the WIPO Intergovernmental Committee on Intellectual Property and Genetic Resources and Folklore (IGC): 'Caution should be used when referring to folklore as being in the "public domain" in the copyright context. The Delegation explained that the expression "public domain" tended to indicate something which had once been protected when this protection had lapsed. While protected under customary legal systems, expressions of folklore had never been protected under IP laws, yet this should not suggest that because a work was accessible it was already in the public domain and available freely', WIPO/GRTKF/IC/5/15 (4 August 2003), at paragraph 35.

[22]   WCT art. 2 precludes copyright protection for *'ideas, procedures, methods of operation or mathematical concepts as such'*.

[23]   Such as descriptive terms in the common language, although the public domain status of a term will differ between jurisdictions and potentially between language communities within a jurisdiction, just as the connotation and/or denotation of a term, and their legal recognition, vary.

[24]   Such as a 'work of the United States Government': U.S. Copyright Act 1976, §§101, 105; again, cross-jurisdictionally, raising the question of whether this provision amounts to a waiver of copyright and effective public domain status in other jurisdictions where this law is not directly applicable.

[25]   For instance, there have been calls for the human genome to be recognised as 'part of the common heritage of humanity' (Statement on the Principled Conduct of Genetics Research, HUGO Ethical, Legal, and Social Issues Committee Report to HUGO Council, 1996, at www.gene.ucl.ac.uk/hugo/conduct.htm), and that 'DNA molecules and their sequences, be they full-length, genomic or cDNA, ESTs, SNPs or even whole genomes of pathogenic organisms, if of unknown function or utility, as a matter of policy, in principle, should be viewed as part of pre-competitive information' so that efforts to 'map all SNPs and put them into public domain, are welcomed' (HUGO Statement on Patenting of DNA sequences, 2000, at www.gene.ucl.ac.uk/hugo/patent2000.html).

marked out the boundaries of their rights? Or is there a positive sense of public dominion over public domain material?

In fact, IP law and policy frequently define IP rights by invoking a positive, prior conception of a public domain: the bounds of IP set as allowable exceptions to public domain material that are justifiable on explicit policy grounds. This is how the Statute of Monopolies[26] was drafted, defining patents of invention as exceptions to the rule that otherwise rendered commercial monopolies 'utterly void and of none effect'. So frequently cited as a seminal patent law statute, this legislation principally aimed at the 'great grievance and inconvenience' caused to the public by illegitimate incursions on the public domain (in this instance, the content aspect of the public domain being commercially useful technology and trades, and the use aspect being the freedom to carry out such legitimate trades). Similarly, the Canadian Supreme Court invoked 'society's interest in maintaining a robust public domain that could help foster future creative innovation' to set a standard of originality in copyright law that goes beyond 'a mere copy or [simply showing] industriousness' and the need for 'room for the public domain to flourish as others are able to produce new works by building on the ideas and information contained in the works of others.'[27] The Court thus defined this key test for subsistence of copyright in terms of the policy rationale for the flourishing of a 'robust' public domain. In this way, IP is defined by a logically prior conception of the public domain. Identifying the necessary scope of the *inherent* public domain was also the starting point for the US Supreme Court in charting the bounds of fit subject matter for copyright:

> Facts, whether alone or as part of a compilation, are not original and therefore may not be copyrighted. … [Finding copyright in facts would distort] basic copyright principles in that it creates a monopoly in public domain materials without the necessary justification of protecting and encouraging the creation of 'writings' by 'authors.'[28]

Further, some perspectives on the public domain might entail a stronger conception of true public ownership, a form of domain defined not merely by the absence of exclusive private rights but by a positive sense of public ownership or collective sovereignty. This is domain as *dominion*: the sense of 'domain'

---

[26]   Statute of Monopolies of 1623, 21 Jac. 1, c. 3.
[27]   See also Litman, J. (1990), 'The Public Domain', 39 *Emory Law Journal* 965, at 969; and Craig, C.J. (2002), 'Locke, Labour and Limiting the Author's Right: A Warning against a Lockean Approach to Copyright Law', 28 *Queen's Law Journal* 1, cited by the court in this judgement.
[28]   *Feist Publications v Rural Tel. Serv. Co.*, 499 US 340, 350, 354 (1991); the same court invokes the 'public domain' in charting the bounds of patentable subject matter in *Graham v John Deere Co.*, 383 U.S. 1 (1966).

recalled in the concept of 'eminent domain',[29] the sovereign's residual entitlement to assume use of private property for public use, based on a superior form of sovereign dominion over property. In copyright law, this might be expressed as Crown prerogative (discussed below). The public domain may span the two notions in Roman property law of *res communes* (non-excludable, and incapable of appropriation and hence ownership altogether) and *res publicae* (owned by the public as such). The contested notion of *res communis humanitatis*, or common heritage of humanity, entails a conception of international collective ownership that might be construed as a form of international public dominion, distinct from strict *res nullius*. In addition, what have been termed 'user rights' may also be construed as a form of public domain defined by a limited positive entitlement of the public to use IP-protected material.

Whatever side of the coin is given conceptual priority in defining public domain and in marking out the bounds of IP rights, there is a loss of policy context in setting these concepts in bare opposition to one another.[30] Zero-sum interest-based solipsism that can impede effective public policy-making: tragedies of the commons[31] or of the anti-commons[32] may be compelling analyses within specific contexts, but lack sufficient inductive basis to guide policy-making overall. A broader perspective[33] would equally assist in assessing the role of international IP treaties in the context of the public domain.[34]

Two forms of justification are generally offered for the constraints on the public domain that are created by the recognition of IP: a natural law argument for an inherent entitlement to exclusive rights rooted in intrinsic justice or

---

[29] 'Dominium eminens est, quod Civitas habet in Cives, et res Civium ad usum publicum', *In Hugonis Grotii Jus Belli Et Pacis Commentatio.* – Grotius (De Jure Belli, Book I, iii.§6) defines 'dominium eminens' as 'quod civitas habet in cives et res civium, ad usum publicum', translated as a 'superior right' for the public good. See also the discussion in Macmillan, F., 'Altering the Contours of the Public Domain', Chapter 6 in this volume.

[30] 'The two halves of the creative pie – public domain and copyright, which we tend to think of as polar and contradictory in nature – in the United States Constitutional system are, in fact, fundamentally interdependent; they reinforce and sustain each other through a Constitutionally mandated scheme in which competing self-interests are balanced against each other', Robert Baron, 'Reconstructing the Public Domain', VRA-ARLIS NINCH Copyright Town Meeting, 'The Changing Research and Collections Environment: The Information Commons', *Today,* 23 March 2002.

[31] Hardin, G. (1968), 'The Tragedy of the Commons', *SCI.*, 13 Dec. 1243.

[32] See Heller, M.A. and Eisenberg, R.S. (1998), 'Can Patents Deter Innovation? The Anticommons', in *Biomedical Research, Science Mag.*, 1 May.

[33] See Van Caenegem, W. (2002), 'The Public Domain: Scientia Nullius', *European Intellectual Property Review*, **24** (6), 324–30.

[34] See in general Dinwoodie and Dreyfuss, note 7 *supra*, on the role of TRIPS Articles 7 and 8 in relation to an international public domain of accessible knowledge.

equity; and the utilitarian deployment of IP to yield specific public welfare gains. International treaties have typically been neutral as to the public policy basis for IP rights, and may allow more cultural elbow room than is often assumed. Even within the Berne system 'the very concept of copyright from a philosophical, theoretical and pragmatic point of view differs country by country.'[35] TRIPS does introduce an explicit utilitarian ethic as the basis of IP protection, in the form of the objective set out in Article 7; its critics characterise TRIPS as a vehicle for privileging IP rights over the public interest,[36] but it has acted as a vector for introducing public international law and a formalised construction of the public policy basis of IP protection into the international jurisprudence of IP.

The choice of analytical approach may influence whether public domain status or recognition acquires conceptual priority. If IP rights are justified by invoking intrinsic natural law, a process of discovery would reveal the contours of those rights, leaving the residuum of subject matter, lying beyond legitimate property claims, in the public domain. The Lockean rationale for property, often applied in IP debate, formulates an entitlement to appropriate material from the public domain in terms of the addition of labour.[37] By this model, the public domain is construed as source material for appropriation, rather than as a final destination for expired IP. Potential tendentiousness arises from the presumption that material such as genetic resources and traditional knowledge (TK) are raw material in a public domain of *scientia nullius*,[38] for others to appropriate through their exertions, as this undervalues other forms of 'labour', such as indigenous science and traditional forms of conservation of biodiversity. Under an utilitarian conception of IP law as a positivist construction, as a strict 'creature of statute'[39] shorn of common law roots or claims of natural law, IP statutes would ideally be structured according to a determination of what privately held exclusions from the public domain of otherwise non-excludable knowledge resources are required to harness sufficient private interest to provide for the production of certain public goods that would not otherwise come into existence. These forms of justification are not mutually exclusive. When establishing the basis for IP laws in practical policy and actual lawmaking processes, it is

---

[35] Masouye, C. (1978), *Guide to the Berne Convention*, Geneva: WIPO.
[36] See in general Taubman, note 15 *supra*.
[37] 'Whatsoever [someone] removes out of the State that Nature hath provided, and left it in, he hath mixed his Labour with, and joyned to it something that is his own, and thereby makes it his Property', Locke, J. (1690), *Second Treatise of Government*, 3rd edn, Oxford: Blackwell, 1966, s.27.
[38] Van Caenegem, note 33 *supra*.
[39] *CCH Canadian Ltd v Law Society of Upper Canada*, [2004] 1 S.C.R. 339, 2004 SCC 13 (CanLII), at 9 (McLachlin C.J.).

common to draw on a hybrid set of rationales, mixing general claims to justice and equity with public policy objectives. Thus the *CCH Canada* court cites the fundamental balance as between a (utilitarian) 'public interest in the encouragement and dissemination of works' and the idea of 'a just reward for the creator'.[40]

An idealised view of the creation of IP laws would situate the objective law-maker behind a Rawlsian veil of ignorance, to preclude favour for sectoral interests, and from there to determine what exclusions from the public domain would be just, or legitimate, or effective in an utilitarian sense. Setting the appropriate form and level of exclusion is the act of 'balancing' between private right and public interest that is central to most conceptions of IP policy-making: 'balance between promoting the public interest in the encouragement and dissemination of works of the arts and intellect and obtaining a just reward for the creator ... The proper balance among these and other public policy objectives lies not only in recognising the creator's rights but in giving due weight to their limited nature.'[41]

From a policy perspective, the public domain and the IP system are often viewed as standing in binary tension, the policy-makers' 'balance' as a strict trade-off between public and private domains. The formation of new IP law at the municipal or international level is accordingly assumed to be an inherent incursion on the public domain or an enclosure of the commons. Yet, to capture the full character of the lawmaking process, a richer, more nuanced policy palette is required: to set the process at least one level of abstraction above a simple, linear trade-off between public and private domains. From an international perspective, the conception of global public goods[42] provides one framework for assessing policy choices, reconciling justice and utilitarian arguments, and illuminating the policy rationale for international standards that influence the extent of exclusive rights under national law.

Public good analysis is strictly a methodology for determining how optimally to provide ('a pure theory of government expenditure') for public goods ('collective consumption goods'[43]). It concerns a technocratic assessment of the

---

[40]   Note 39 *supra*.

[41]   *Théberge v Galerie d'Art du Petit Champlain inc.*, 2002 SCC 34 (CanLII), [2002] 2 S.C.R. 336, 2002 SCC 34, at paras. 30–31 (Binnie J.), cited in *CCH Canadian Ltd* (*supra*, note 39). For a discussion on the inclusion of the public in setting the priorities in the policy-making process see Bruce, A., 'The Public Domain: Ideology vs Interest', Chapter 14 in this volume.

[42]   Kaul, Inge et al. (eds) (1999), *Global Public Goods: International Cooperation in the 21st Century*, New York: Oxford University Press Inc.

[43]   Samuelson, P.A. (1954), 'The Pure Theory of Public Expenditure', 36 *Review of Economics and Statistics* 387, 388.

optimal deployment of public resources to furnish society with necessary facilities. Yet choices of what public goods are to be provided can betray an ethical intentionality, cultural bias, and a privileging of certain policy objectives. Even to label certain public goods as such effectively sets them apart as being of intrinsic worth to society, a judgement with utilitarian and normative aspects:[44] a public good 'becomes public by the social decision to treat it that way.'[45] Debate about global public goods therefore focuses on the optimal ordering of collective priorities and the choice of international policy objectives, not on how best to provide such public goods. '[I]nternational debates on global public goods often address only the question of which goods to produce,' not 'how much of each to produce and at what net benefit to whom.'[46]

The concepts of 'public domain' and 'public good' both have strong positive connotations and inherent appeal, quite apart from their formal legal character and their role in the analysis of public economics respectively. The public domain of knowledge is, in principle, non-rivalrous and non-excludable: by definition, a public good. Yet the, or a, public domain cannot be conflated with the, or a, public good; it can be tendentious or reductionist, or even a category error, to assume that public domains are inherent public goods. This conflation assumes a certain ordering of public goods and overlooks the differing policy bases of public domain and public good status. It may confuse analysis of how optimally to provide public goods through the judicious establishment of legal exclusions. Rather than implicitly ordering policy objectives in the choice of certain public goods, public policy may need to consider two sets of distinctions among public goods: (i) basic material goods (roads or water as collective consumption goods) as against higher-order public goods, with a more abstract or ethical dimension (equity, good governance and efficiency in the provision of roads and water); and (ii) innate or natural public goods (clean air) as against those that are a construct of public policy (public libraries).

The IP system probes the distinction between the public domain and the provision of public goods, as it constrains public domains (domains of language, say, or of knowledge) consciously to construct or induce higher-order public goods as an artefact of public policy, such as the availability of useful new technologies, the fostering of cultural activity, or the accurate and fair operation of commercial signifiers (as distinct from knowledge, cultural works, or terms in themselves). By creating excludability and allowing the right-holder to

[44]   See, e.g., Drahos, P. (2004), 'The Regulation of Public Goods', 7 *Journal of International Economic Law* 321.

[45]   Malkin and Wildavsky, cited in Sagasti, F. and Bezanson, K. (2001), *Financing and Providing Global Public Goods*, Stockholm: Ministry of Foreign Affairs, p. 5.

[46]   Kaul, I. et al. (2002), 'How to Improve the Provision of Public Goods', in *Providing Global Public Goods*, Oxford: Oxford University Press, p. 43.

appropriate returns from protected material,[47] the IP system is intended to generate incentives for certain public goods to be provided (notably technological innovation and the disclosure of enabling knowledge about inventions) when these would not otherwise come about. The law of trade marks, geographical indications and the suppression of unfair competition aim at the production of other higher-order public goods, such as consumer knowledge, merchant responsibility, and equitable protection of reputation in the marketplace. The challenge for IP policy-makers is therefore to make the judgement as to what form of exclusion of legally protectable material from the public domain is likely best to provide for such public goods. But this simply begs the question of what public goods are to be privileged over others.

One way of analysing the role of international treaties would be to consider how they shape diverse conceptions of the public domain at the national and possibly the international level; what forms of exclusion from the public domain they facilitate; and what forms of public good they promote. The current focus of policy debate is on the public domain of knowledge; but IP laws help to shape and set bounds to other forms of public domain, such as the public domains of language[48] and symbols,[49] commercial discourse,[50] forms of expression of knowledge,[51] functional designs,[52] useable technology (as distinct from ideas[53] or knowledge *per se*), or specific forms of regulatory data.[54] In each case, the framing of the public domain as against legitimate exclusions from it requires a distinct conception of the public and private domains, and how the interplay between them should be ordered to optimise the creation of public goods.

Knowledge *per se* is 'a global or international public good,'[55] being inherently non-rivalrous and non-excludable (and of evident social utility). But policy interests (including, in some constructions, natural rights and equity considerations, not merely utilitarian objectives) may require exclusions, driving a wedge between public good and public domain. IP mechanisms intervene

---

[47]   Stiglitz, J.E., 'Knowledge as a Global Public Good', available at www.worldbank. org/knowledge/chiefecon/articles/undpk2/.

[48]   TRIPS, art. 24.

[49]   Paris, art. 6 *ter*.

[50]   Paris, art. 10 *bis*; see also the law of personality rights, and the debate over freedom of expression between the majority and the dissent in *White v Samsung Elecs. Am., Inc.* 989 F.2d 1512, 1516 (9th Cir. 1993).

[51]   Berne, art. 2.1.

[52]   TRIPS provides for an exclusion of designs dictated essentially by technical or functional considerations (art. 25).

[53]   TRIPS provides that 'Copyright protection shall [not] extend to ... ideas, procedures, methods of operation or mathematical concepts as such' (art. 9(2)).

[54]   TRIPS, art. 39.3.

[55]   Stiglitz, note 47 *supra*.

to yield higher-order public goods, precisely by ensuring that material is not left in the relevant public domain.

The debate over international legal measures to protect traditional knowledge (TK) exposes the limitations of a strictly utilitarian approach to the ordering of international public goods, showing how a simple conception of knowledge as a public good risks commodifying knowledge and stripping it of its public interest characteristics in the way that overzealous IP protection is claimed to do. This debate is therefore a critique both of the values embedded in the existing treaty system and of the legal presumptions structuring the public domain as it is conventionally ordered. The conflation of public domain and public good may set utilitarian public interest in tension with the values and interests of a specific community. This is because misuse of TK can

> cause severe physical or spiritual harm to the individual caretakers of the knowledge or their entire tribe from their failure to ensure that the Creator's gifts were properly used, even if misuse was used by others outside of the tribe, or by tribal members who were outside of the control of customary authority. For this reason ... misappropriation and misuse [is] not simply a violation of 'moral rights' leading to a collective offense, but a matter of cultural survival for many indigenous peoples.[56]

This perspective can subvert the conventional conception of knowledge as a global public good, the contribution of TK to global well-being. '[T]he skills, knowledge and institutions evolved by people on the margins, who have already been coping with [environmental] stresses for the last several millennia, will become a major source of survival. Is this the reason why global institutions are suddenly finding so much merit in local knowledge?'[57]

A widely voiced critique of the international IP treaty system concerns its lack of explicit recognition for the distinct knowledge systems and collective values of indigenous and other cultural communities. Some forms of collective ownership and collective creativity and innovation may be recognised within this framework, but greater recognition has been called for. The same critical perspective, though, also creates a basis for restricting the public domain of knowledge. Rather than perceiving TK as a non-excludable public good, this entails withholding TK from the public domain to pursue a higher-order public good – such as equity in the dispensation of knowledge resources, the cultural integrity of indigenous communities, and preservation of diverse spiritual values and world-views. Whether this result can be justified, in contrast to the utilitarian

---

[56]   Representative of the Tulalip Tribes of Washington; see IGC, note 21 *supra*, at 56. See also comments by Gibson, Chapter 12, *infra*.

[57]   Gupta, A.K. (Sep. 2002), 'Centres on the Periphery: Coping with Climatic and Institutional Change', 13 *Honey Bee* 1.

value of a more plentiful public domain including TK, depends on the hierarchy of competing public goods within the public policy process. The international treaty system is one important site for this ordering of public goods, and a strong influence on the boundaries drawn between private and community domains and 'the' public domain, including conceptions of a global public domain, or more correctly a public domain structured directly by international law, rather than national public domains as artefacts of national laws influenced, in turn, by international standards.

3   THE INTERNATIONAL PUBLIC DOMAIN

This section considers the international character of the public domain. Calls for strengthened protection of TK probe the conventional contours of the relationship between public domain and private right, by forcing us to question the legitimacy of the established conception of the public domain, and by making us recast the public – or *a* public, at least (that is, the traditional community) – as the right-holder and as the collective beneficiary of a direct, rather than indirect, interest in TK protection. Its inter-generational character and the continuing obligations under customary law also challenge the assumption that any sufficiently old material 'falls' naturally into the public domain worldwide. In short, it can form a point of resistance against the presumption of a single international public domain, that would set aside the more conventional invocation of national sovereignty and territoriality of rights and public domains.

International relations theory has long explored evolving notions of sovereignty[58] and the limitations of an excessive focus on the sovereign nation state as international actor. And international law is an incomplete picture of the actual constraints and influences on actors in the international sphere. International law has developed notions of collective international dominion, such as common heritage of humanity,[59] which may prefigure a true international public domain. Even so, the international IP system retains the formal Westphalian structure in which sovereign states define and transact their rights and obligations towards one another through treaties. International IP treaties do not protect IP directly; they oblige (but do not compel) signatory states to define and protect it in certain ways, and harmonise, support and predetermine how it is administered within national jurisdictions. Even the European patent, a product of an exceptionally

---

[58]   Linklater, A. (1996), 'Citizenship and Sovereignty in the Post-Westphalian State', *European Journal of International Relations*, **2** (1), 77–103.

[59]   FAO International Undertaking on Plant Genetic Resources, 1983 (genetic resources as the common heritage of mankind).

high degree of regional harmonisation of IP law, has its legal effect as a bundle of national patent rights. Hence, if the public domain is to be defined in counterpoint to IP, there is no single international IP right whose lapse or absence would directly confer international public domain status. While one might argue that the treaty system defines a private and a public domain, it is in practice the national legislator or judicial authority who determines its effective scope and who is responsible for policing the boundary between public and private domains. Perhaps the international public domain could be construed as a congeries of national public domains. Ultimately, the passage of time might yield a *de facto* global public domain, as national IP rights lapse. But some forms of conventional IP protection do not lapse with the mere passage of time. Effective management of geographical indications and trade marks would envisage their perennial effect; standards against unfair competition are not time-bound. Perpetual protection is extended under national laws to some copyright works[60] and more widely to national folklore and TK.[61] As observed, the presumption that material 'falls' naturally into the public domain lies at the centre of the critique of the IP system in the TK debate. The lapse, early cancellation or restriction of scope[62] of a patent should in principle lead to the unequivocal entry – or return[63] – into the public domain of the claimed knowledge, but even this presumption may be questioned for certain TK-related inventions, where the cancellation of questionable patents may be conceived more of a repatriation of the knowledge. Signs and symbols may enter and leave the public domain, as aspects of them acquire or lose signification: the bare word 'Orange' is plainly in the public domain, but its use may be circumscribed in strikingly different ways in different jurisdictions.[64]

Acknowledgement of common heritage of humanity status to IP subject matter such as knowledge or cultural works is a possible option, but again cannot be assumed automatically. Genetic resources, once possibly categorised as common heritage, have more recently been subject to reassertion of national sovereignty. An international public domain may, perhaps, be conceived under several aspects:

---

[60]   United Kingdom, Copyright Designs and Patents Act 1988 (c. 48), s.301, Schedule 6.

[61]   Agreement Revising the Bangui Agreement on the Creation of an African Intellectual Property Organisation (Bangui, 24 February 1999).

[62]   E.g. US Patent 5,663,484 (assigned to RiceTec, Inc., issued 2 September 1997 and re-examined, narrowing scope of claims, originally entitled 'Basmati Rice Lines and Grains').

[63]   E.g. US Patent 5,401,504 ('Use of turmeric in wound healing').

[64]   Taubman, A.S. (forthcoming (2007), manuscript on file with author), 'Geographical indications, international trade and linguistic communities: thinking locally, acting globally'.

1. knowledge, works or expressions, and signs, symbols or text, of universal public-domain status, unequivocally free of exclusive use rights under any national law,[65] such as Archimedes' principle, the *Odyssey*,[66] Thomson's *The Seasons*,[67] the chemical composition of quinine[68] and almost all copyright- and patent-protected material after the expiry of the longest term under any national law (apart from TK and folklore protected or recognised as such);

2. an international public domain of readily accessible knowledge that is free to *know* (combining a legal entitlement to gain access with the worldwide practical possibility of access), regardless of any use constraints under national laws: the information function of the PCT, described above, arguably creates such an international knowledge domain, fuelled by the applicants' obligation to disclose and the role of public institutions in facilitating practical access;

3. conceptions of an international public domain characterised more by a positive sense of custodianship or collective obligation to safeguard against loss, such as intangible cultural heritage[69] and biological diversity[70] (without prejudice to claims of sovereignty, or collective or individual ownership that may constrain particular forms of access or use), or a domain characterised in terms of a collective entitlement to use and to derive benefit, such as common heritage of mankind;[71] although (to the extent that it is accepted at all) this concept has largely covered natural resources rather than the intangible subject matter associated with IP systems.[72] This third conception

---

[65] Not altogether 'free': many other legal constraints on use may yet apply to this 'public domain', ranging from laws on blasphemy to regulation of GMOs.

[66] *Christoffer v Poseidon Film Distributors Ltd* [2000] ECDR 487.

[67] *Millar v Taylor*, 4 Burr. 2303, 98 Eng. Rep. 201 (K.B. 1769); *Donaldson v Beckett*, 2 Brown's Parl. Cases 129, 1 Eng. Rep. 837; *Hinton v Donaldson* (1773) Mor 8307 (Ct of Sess).

[68] *Merrell Dow Pharmaceuticals Inc. v H.N. Norton & Co. Ltd* [1996] RPC 76, at 88.

[69] For example, the Andean Cosmovision of the Kallawaya and the Darangen Epic of the Maranao People, Bark cloth making of the Baganda people, proclaimed as Masterpieces of the Oral and Intangible Heritage of Humanity, and therefore to be incorporated in the Representative List of the Intangible Cultural Heritage of Humanity to be established under the Convention on the Safeguarding of the Intangible Cultural Heritage upon its entry into force.

[70] Convention on Biological Diversity, 1992.

[71] See United Nations Convention on the Law of the Sea 1982 (art 136, 'Common heritage of mankind'); Agreement Governing the Activities of States on the Moon and Other Celestial Bodies (1979) (art 11).

[72] Genetic resources are 'manifestations of … nature, free to all men and reserved exclusively to none', *Funk Bros. Seed Co. v Kalo Inoculant Co.*, 333 US 127, 130 (1948).

is closer to international public goods, and exemplifies the distinction between maintenance of resources as a public good and the entry into the
public domain of material as legally free to use.

Inasmuch as the conception of public domain is tied to the IP legal system,
strictly speaking an international public domain can only, ultimately, be a congeries of national public domains, which in turn comprise the sum of those
elements that can be characterised as having public domain status under national
law. This is a consequence of:

- the territorial scope and formal independence of IP rights, and the application of the principle of comity in international law;
- the differing scope of protection under the IP law of national jurisdictions,
  both in practice (the simple choice to patent an invention in certain countries is, in effect, a choice to deliver it unequivocally to the public domain
  elsewhere) and in principle (in the absence of international rules to the
  contrary, folklore may, as a policy choice, be protected perpetually in one
  country and in the public domain in another);
- the need to recognise the effect of national sovereignty and policy prefer-
  ences, and to avoid conflating more general international standards with
  the actual contours and boundaries of the public domain within any national jurisdiction;
- the diverse contexts of use and the implications of the social environment
  for the application of the law, mostly clearly so in surveying the different
  connotation and denotation of linguistic terms and symbols within different communities, but also the diverse social values reflected in different
  formulations and applications of exceptions to IP protection on such
  grounds as morality, public order, social utility and cultural status.

Even so, the *de facto* convergences brought about by technological, social and
economic trends do limit the actual independence of national jurisdictions.
There is a degree of effective internationalisation of IP rights in established
national laws, evident in extraterritorial effects felt beyond national jurisdictions, as courts wrestle with the extra-territorial implications of IP rights and
related areas of law, and the broader choice of law questions raised by trans-
jurisdictional patterns of commerce and technology;[73] as the law of contract

---

[73]   Contrast *NTP v Research-In-Motion* (Fed. Cir. 2005) (finding that infringement
may possibly be found even where a component is physically located outside the jurisdiction) with *F. Hoffmann-La Roche Ltd v Empagran S.A. (F. Hoffman-La Roche v
Empagran*, 542 U.S. 155 (1994)) (applying the principle of comity – ambiguous statutes
are construed 'to avoid unreasonable interference with the sovereign authority of other

and the operation of private international law stitch together distinct jurisdictions; as enforcement of judgements[74] between jurisdictions is enhanced; and as some IP rights may be recognised in a limited sense in quasi-international legal domains.[75]

4 PUBLIC DOMAIN STATUS OF INTERNATIONAL IP TREATIES

It is therefore uncertain whether a truly international public domain can be construed as a legal construct set in counterpoint to the international IP treaty system, even if other conceptions of an international public domain can be usefully developed – including the international domain of accessible knowledge generated by the international patent system. But what is the public domain status of the international treaties as texts – or works, or publications – in themselves? The international treaties, as much as any other texts, are a case study in inter-textuality. Following Kristeva's formulation, these texts are 'constructed as a mosaic of quotations; any text is the absorption and transformation of another.'[76] Much hinges, too, on the context in which these texts are read, the authority of the reader potentially being greater than that of the 'original' authors, and the way texts are read determines key policy choices, including choices with direct impact on the scope and contours of public domains.

---

nations' – in determining that anti-trust violation in the United States cannot be based on injuries exclusively incurred abroad, provided damages were truly independent of effects on the US market); see also *Dow Jones & Company Inc. v Gutnick* [2002] HCA 56 (10 December 2002).

[74] E.g. Convention on Choice of Court Agreements adopted by The Hague Conference on Private International Law on 30 June 2005; but, relevantly for the *de facto* establishment of an international public domain, this Convention specifically excludes judgments on the validity or infringement of IP rights other than copyright and related rights, except where infringement proceedings are relevant to breach of contract; its application is limited to international business-to-business agreements that designate a single court or the courts of a single country for resolution of disputes ('exclusive choice of court agreements') and, again relevantly for the conception of an international public domain, it explicitly excludes agreements that include a consumer as a party, such as many click-through agreements.

[75] For instance, the settlement of disputes over domain name registrations in accordance with the Uniform Domain Name Dispute Resolution Policy, adopted on 26 August 1999, available at www.icann.org/udrp/udrp-policy-24oct99.htm.

[76] Kristeva, J. (1986), 'Word, Dialogue, and the Novel', in T. Moi (ed.), *The Kristeva Reader* at 37, Oxford: Basil Blackwell.

Criticised by some as embodying a narrow conception of individual author-ship[77] and innovation,[78] the treaties themselves seem closer to the very forms of non-conventional authorship and collective ownership of intangible property highlighted by their critics. They are collaborative works[79] of collective,[80] possibly or partially anonymous[81] authorship; and they are cumulative expres-sions, moulded by collective experience, passed down to new generations to interpret and rework,[82] in the light of evolving social values and technological change.[83] The texts are typically a mosaic of inter-textual quotations and re-workings. The language of TRIPS is to some extent a critical reading of the 'original' texts that contributed to it, and the WCT in turn takes up the TRIPS text and re-reads it in a distinct legal context. If these texts are 'owned' as liter-ary property, it is ownership closer in character to the collective custodianship of some traditional works, a responsibility more than an economic or moral right in the text. The texts have legal custodians[84] who are empowered to

---

[77]   'There is a politics to "authorship": as presently understood, it is a gate through which one must pass in order to be given property rights, a gate that shuts out a dispro-portionate number of non-Western, traditional, collaborative, or folkloric modes of production', Boyle, J. (1996), *Shamans, Software, and Spleens: Law and the Construc-tion of the Information Society*, Cambridge, MA, 195.

[78]   'The TRIPS Agreement itself does not provide any protection for the traditional knowledge and innovations of indigenous and local people ... [and o]n the whole, con-ventional intellectual property law does not cover inventions and innovations of indigenous and local peoples', John Mugabe (1988), 'Intellectual Property Protection and Traditional Knowledge', Panel discussion on Intellectual Property and Human Rights, WIPO, Geneva, 9 November, at www.wipo.int/tk/en/hr/paneldiscussion/papers/pdf/mugabe.pdf.

[79]   See for example the description of the extensive drafting process of the PCT in History of the Patent Cooperation Treaty (PCT/PCD/1, WIPO/BIRPI, 16 October 1970). The treaty has since been amended, on 28 September 1979, and modified on 3 February 1984, and 3 October 2001.

[80]   See, for example, the reports of drafting committees of numerous diplomatic conferences.

[81]   Berne, Article 7 (3).

[82]   The current (Paris) Act of Berne is fully characterised as 'of September 9, 1886, completed at PARIS on May 4, 1896, revised at BERLIN on November 13, 1908, com-pleted at BERNE on March 20, 1914, revised at ROME on June 2, 1928, at BRUSSELS on June 26, 1948, at STOCKHOLM on July 14, 1967, and at PARIS on July 24, 1971, and amended on September 28, 1979'; early drafts drew on draft text prepared by an NGO, the International Literary and Artistic Association (ALAI).

[83]   See the discussion of the effect of social and technological trends on the evolution of performers' rights in Taubman, A. (2005), 'Nobility of interpretation: equity, retro-spectivity, and collectivity in implementing new norms for performers' rights', 12 *Journal of Intellectual Property Law* 351–425.

[84]   For instance, the text of the latest (Stockholm) Act of Paris is deposited with the

establish[85] or certify[86] the authenticity of the text, a faint echo of the question of 'authenticity' of indigenous cultural works.[87] Actual authorship of international legal texts is diffuse, and variable: among international IP treaties, first or 'original' drafts have been prepared by NGOs,[88] by national government officials within national systems or collectively, and by international civil servants at the direction of governments. Modifications during negotiations may yield texts sufficiently distinct to be viewed as derivative works of distinct authorship. Original authorship of international legal texts may therefore need to be construed so diffusely as to defy conventional copyright analysis: a US court goes so far as to reason that 'the citizens are the authors of the law, and therefore its owners, regardless of who actually drafts the provisions, because the law derives its authority from the consent of the public, expressed through the democratic process.'[89] Could the same reasoning apply at the international plane, substituting 'sovereign governments' for 'the citizens' and 'the public'?

If legal authorship is difficult to ascribe, interpretative authority is still more diffuse and potentially contested. The treaties, as texts, are detached from their original authors and enter a kind of public interpretative domain, to be read according to 'the ordinary meaning to be given to the terms of the treaty in their context and in the light of its object and purpose.'[90] The interpreter shows some residual deference to the express intentions of negotiators (or the 'authorial intentionality' in literary theory) during the drafting process[91] – it would overstate matters to report the 'the death of the author', but the reader increasingly assumes ownership in a manner still recalling Barthes:

Government of Sweden (Paris, art. 29(1)(a)); the PCT text is deposited with the WIPO Director General (PCT, art. 68).

[85]   Official texts of the Stockholm Act of Paris were 'established by the Director General, after consultation with the interested Governments' (Paris, art. 29(1)(b)).

[86]   The Government of Sweden certified the official copies of the Stockholm Act (Paris, art. 29(3)).

[87]   See 'Indigenous Arts Certification Mark', in Janke, T., *Minding Culture: Case-Studies on Intellectual Property and Traditional Cultural Expression*s (WIPO/GRTKF/STUDY/2, 2003), and more recently the Cultural Indications (CI) Index concerning certain indigenous cultural works, at www.ididj.com.au/authenticity/label.html.

[88]   E.g. Association littéraire et artistique internationale (ALAI), 'Projet de convention pour constituer une Union générale pour la protection des droits des auteurs sur leurs oeuvres littéraires et artistiques' (1883), distributed by the Swiss Government as a basis for work on the draft Berne Convention.

[89]   *Building Officials and Code Adm. v Code Technology, Inc.,* 628 F.2d 730 (1st Cir. 1980), at 734.

[90]   Vienna Convention on the Law of Treaties (1969), art. 31.1.

[91]   Supplementary means of interpretation, when needed to avoid ambiguity, obscurity or absurd or unreasonable readings, include preparatory work and the circumstances of a treaty's conclusion (Vienna, art. 32).

> Thus is revealed the total existence of writing: a text is made of multiple writings, drawn from many cultures and entering into mutual relations of dialogue, parody, contestation, but there is the reader, not, as was hitherto said, the author. The reader is the space on which all the quotations that make up a writing are inscribed without any of them being lost; a text's unity lies not in its origin, but in its destination![92]

The interpretative 'literalism'[93] of the WTO Appellate Body is, in this sense, an assertion of the primacy of the reader as interpreter in the choice of interpretative domain, an assertion of ownership of the text that is more far consequential than copyright ownership. The introduction of IP into international trade law and the incorporation of IP treaties into the trade law framework, both through the vector of TRIPS, create an interpretative quandary that can be construed as a 'contestation' of authorial cultures and different readerships. 'Multiple writings' such as the Paris and Berne Conventions are embedded within the text of TRIPS, the unity of the treaty's text indeed lying in its destination. The paramount interpretative question is whether there is a specific trade-law reading of these embedded international IP treaties which diverges from the reading that would be obtained by a reader imbued in the separate institutional traditions of Paris and Berne.[94] How this question is resolved in turn directly influences the boundaries of public domains defined under national law.[95]

Considered on the plane of copyright works, international treaties are widely reproduced and generally assumed to be in the public domain. But this appears to be a matter of practice rather than a consequence of their precise legal status as works or as publications. There is a strong policy rationale for widespread dissemination, reflected in the General Assembly resolution on the UN Decade of International Law,[96] which aimed *inter alia* to encourage the dissemination of international law, building on the custodial responsibilities of the UN Secretariat.[97] This policy rationale led legal information institutes to declare that

---

[92]   Barthes, R. (1977), 'The Death of the Author', in S. Heath (ed.), *Image, Music, Text*, Glasgow: Fontana-Collins, p. 147.

[93]   Bacchus, J., 'Appellators: The Quest for the Meaning of And/Or', Advisory Centre on WTO Law, at www.acwl.ch.

[94]   Netanel, N.W. (1997), 'Comment: The Next Round: The Impact of the WIPO Copyright Treaty on TRIPS Dispute Settlement', 37 *Virginia Journal of International Law* 441; and Dinwoodie, G. (2001), 'The Development and Incorporation of International Norms in the Formation of Copyright Law', 62 *Ohio State Law Journal* 733.

[95]   The scope of certain aspects of the public domain being directly at issue in WTO disputes DS 114: Canada – Patent Protection of Pharmaceutical Products, DS 160: s110 US Copyright Act, and DS 170: Canada – Term of patent protection.

[96]   UNGA Resolution 44/23 of 17 November 1989.

[97]   The United Nations Charter (art. 102) requires registration with and publication by the Secretariat of 'every treaty and every international agreement' that any UN Member enters.

public legal information from all countries and international institutions is part of the common heritage of humanity; maximising access to this information promotes justice and the rule of law; public legal information is digital common property and should be accessible to all on a non-profit basis and free of charge; independent non-profit organisations have the right to publish public legal information and the government bodies that create or control that information should provide access to it so that it can be published.[98]

Recalling the distinction between public good and public domain, a strong policy rationale for dissemination of international law texts does not *necessarily* entail the exclusion or waiver of exclusive rights over the text. One public-interest legal information service clarifies that it is 'proudly a "free to air" service,' but that its mark-up 'is absolutely not in the public domain as far as any sort of commercial reproduction is concerned'; it further clarifies that many public authorities retain 'copyright on their decisions, legislation and other materials … to reproduce these materials, you should seek permission from the relevant copyright holder(s)'.[99]

Indeed, there is no settled practice on the public domain status of national legislation,[100] and there are diverse possibilities for the subsistence of copyright. One commentator points out that legislation may fail the test of originality when it draws extensively on international treaty language.[101] National legislation may be in the public domain;[102] subject to government ('Crown') copyright that may be exercised, waived altogether or conditionally waived;[103] held by parliament in

---

[98]   Defining public legal information as that 'produced by public bodies that have a duty to produce law and make it public'. This impliedly comprises international law and the role of international organisations.

[99]   www.austlii.edu.au/austlii/faq/#q5.3.

[100]   Berne (art. 2(4)) expressly cedes to the national level of policy-making the question of whether copyright should subsist in 'official texts of a legislative, administrative and legal nature'.

[101]   Perry, M. (1998), 'Acts of Parliament: Privatisation, Promulgation and Crown Copyright – Is There a Need for a Royal Royalty?', *New Zealand Law Review*, 493–529.

[102]   Through legislation, explicitly (New Zealand Copyright Act 1994, s.27(i)) or implicitly (legislation as a government work under US law); or through judicial decision (in the *United States, Banks v Manchester*, 128 U.S. 244, 9 S.Ct. 36 (1888): 'the law, which, binding every citizen, is free for publication to all'), citing *Nash v Lathrop*, 142 Mass. 29, 6 N.E. 559 (1886) (the legislature cannot deny access to statutes).

[103]   E.g. United Kingdom Copyright Designs and Patents Act 1988 (c. 48). For further discussion see Susskind, R., 'The Public Domain and Public Sector Information', Chapter 11 in this volume; NSW, 'Copyright in Legislation and other Material', published in *Gazette* No 110 of 27 September 1996 and varied in *Gazette* No 20 of 19 January 2001.

its own right;[104] or subject to a change of status on enactment.[105] From these diverse forms of exclusivity and *de facto* or *de jure* public domain status, one can abstract a broader custodial responsibility for legal texts, construed and applied through widely different mechanisms.[106] Conditional waiver of copyright, for example, aims at promoting wide dissemination of laws while preserving the integrity, even the dignity, of legislation.[107] Conventional copyright over legislative materials may be subsumed within the far broader reach of Crown prerogative,[108] which has been construed as a form of custodial responsibility for legal texts.[109] Choosing how to do this exemplifies the defining paradox of IP law and policy: how can a legal exclusion from the public domain best function to promote the widest dissemination of an authentic text, consistent with public policy and legitimate private interest? How is the answer to this question modified by changing social and technological factors, as cost and modes of reproduction and access evolve?

This diversity at the national level carries over to the status of international legal texts, but with an additional layer of complexity. The public domain being a construct, ultimately, of national law, the status of treaties, considered as copyright works, may in principle differ between national jurisdictions. A

---

[104]   See Ireland's Copyright and Related Rights Act, [No. 28.] 2000, s.192, vesting copyright in bills and enactments in the Houses of the Oireachtas.

[105]   In the UK, draft legislation is subject to parliamentary copyright, but once enacted enters the public domain.

[106]   The rationales for two contrasting approaches are critically reviewed in Vaver, D. (1996), 'Copyright and the State in Canada and the United States', 10 *Intellectual Property Journal* 187.

[107]   E.g. Office of Public Sector Information, 'Guidance – Reproduction of United Kingdom, England, Wales and Northern Ireland Primary and Secondary Legislation', 27 October 1999, revised 9 May 2005, at www.opsi.gov.uk/advice/crown-copyright/ copyright-guidance/reproduction-of-legislation.htm; see also the Hon. J.W. Shaw QC, MLC, Attorney-General, 'Notice: Copyright in Legislation and other Material', *NSW Government Gazette* No. 110 (27 September 1996) p. 6611: 'Any publisher is by this instrument authorised to publish and otherwise deal with any legislative material, subject to the following conditions: [*inter alia*] any publication of material pursuant to the authorisation is required to be accurately reproduced in proper context and to be of appropriate standard. ... The State will not enforce copyright in legislative material to the extent that it is published or otherwise dealt with in accordance with the authorisation. For this purpose, the authorisation has effect as a licence binding on the State.' See generally Susskind, Chapter 11.

[108]   Confirmed in *The Attorney-General for New South Wales v Butterworth & Co.* 110 (1937) 38 SR(NSW) 195.

[109]   '[T]he real reason and origin of the prerogative in regard to statutes [is], namely, the duty resting upon the King, as first executive magistrate, to superintend the publication of acts of the legislature and acts of state of that description, carrying with it a corresponding prerogative', ibid., at 229.

country outside the treaty system may elect to have no copyright law at all. And the custodians of international legal texts may also make different choices to assert or to waive copyright in different circumstances, even if the goal of the widest dissemination of 'their' texts is a common objective. Different players will deploy or eschew exclusivities in different ways, but with a common goal of optimising the undoubted international public good of wide accessibility of accurate texts of international legal instruments.

Even when vesting the Crown with copyright over legal statutes, Long Innes CJ recognised the difficulty of ascribing true authorship to the government.[110] The still more diffuse origins of international legal texts implies, *a fortiori*, that authorship would provide an uncertain base for copyright over these texts. But there are several other avenues for situating international legal texts in a national copyright environment and thus determining their public domain status.

One point of entry would be to apply the same principles to international legal texts as to national statutes. From a hard monist position, 'international law is simply part of the law of the land',[111] so that the public policy considerations that impel the entry of 'the law' into the public domain would apply to the international treaties that constitute applicable law. Literally more prosaically, international treaties often contribute to the wording of national laws, either through direct reproduction of text or through annexure, so that any considerations that would deliver national law to the public domain would carry with them text elements of international provenance. One need not enter the monist/dualist debate to observe that international treaties are frequently drawn on as a source of text, if not strictly of 'law' (to apply hard dualism), suggesting that a claim of originality (in the copyright sense) on the part of parliamentary drafters would be difficult to sustain.[112]

How this might affect public domain status of treaties is suggested in *Veeck v SBCCII*,[113] which considered 'the extent to which a private organisation may assert copyright protection for its model codes, after the models have been adopted by a legislative body and become 'the law'. The court found that, inasmuch as a text has become 'the law,' it has entered the public domain. The text in question was indisputably subject to copyright, and was obtained from the

---

[110] *Attorney-General v Butterworth*, note 108 *supra*, 258–9.
[111] Kirby, M. (1988), 'The Growing Rapprochment between International Law and National Law', in Sturgess and Anghie (eds), *Visions of the Legal Order in the 21st Century*, at www.hcourt.gov.au/speeches/kirbyj/kirbyj_weeram.htm, See also *Chow Hung Ching v R.* (1948) 77 CLR 449 at 477, noting Blackstone's view to this effect but rejecting it as 'without foundation'.
[112] A point also made by Perry, note 101 *supra*, 15.
[113] *Veeck v Southern Building Code Congress Int'l Inc*, No. 99-40632 (5th Cir. 2002).

copyright owner as a model law; but it was *read as* the municipal building codes of the towns of Anna and Savoy, and its copyright status determined accordingly. *Read that way*, the text was in the public domain – here, the destination, or reader, not the source, or author, governed how it was read as a text and then how its legal status was construed under copyright law. The same analysis may apply to international treaties, when their text is in some sense *read as* the 'law of the land'. The assertion of Crown, or government, or parliamentary, copyright over international elements of laws would then have more of the character of a reversion to Crown prerogative, with the underlying public policy basis of custody over the texts constituting the law of the land, and responsibility for their dissemination. Picciotto[114] suggests that, if the concern is to protect against inaccurate versions of texts which damage the integrity or authenticity of the source material, the prerogative might be better construed as an extended form of moral right.

As already noted, Berne provides flexibility under national law to determine the copyright status of official texts, and this may perhaps be interpreted to apply to international treaties along with national laws. On the other hand, many national copyright laws give distinct recognition to texts prepared under the authority of or first published by international organisations.[115] The UCC articulates this rule,[116] which arguably verges on customary international IP law and is a consequence of recognition of the legal personality of intergovernmental organisation (IGOs). This formulation would encompass international treaties, the first, authoritative publication of which is typically a formal treaty responsibility of an international organisation. Crucially, this allows copyright to vest in the organisation even without resolving the question of authorship. In any event, IGOs do, in practice, routinely exercise copyright in publications including treaty texts.[117] A general trend seems to be to allow free non-commercial

---

[114]   Picciotto, S. (1996), 'Towards Open Access to British Official Documents', 2 *The Journal of Information, Law and Technology* (JILT), elj.warwick.ac.uk/elj/jilt/leginfo/2picciot/.

[115]   For example, UK Copyright Act, s.168; New Zealand Copyright Act, s.28; Australian Copyright Act, s.187.

[116]   The Second Protocol to the Universal Copyright Convention (1971) applies copyright protection to 'works published for the first time by the United Nations [and] by the Specialized Agencies in relationship therewith'.

[117]   The site in question in *Veeck* (note 113 *supra*) also included the Chicago Convention, and an email exchange in which the International Civil Aviation Organization (ICAO) asserted copyright in its conventions 'in order to preserve the authenticity and integrity of ICAO publications and to protect their successful commercial distribution'. The ICAO currently posts a copyright notice on its website, prohibiting various use or reproduction of material from the site 'unless such activity is solely for educational or other non-commercial purposes, and also provided the source is fully acknowledged'.

and educational use subject to acknowledgement or other conditions,[118] but to reserve commercial uses, so the material is not considered to be in the public domain.[119] The WTO site reserves the right for commercial use for publications in general, but interestingly makes a distinction for official documents and legal texts, including treaties, which 'are free for public use.'[120] Given its role in developing and propagating standards, the International Telecommunications Union (ITU) has a tailored policy, referring in particular to use 'to further the work of the ITU or any standards body developing related standards, to provide guidance for product or service development and implementation and to serve as support documentation associated with a product or service'.

The principal custodian of international legal texts is the UN Secretariat itself, in the light of its depositary responsibilities under the UN Charter.[121] Its management of the United Nations treaty collection (comprising over 158 000 treaties and related actions) illuminates the complexity of the public domain status of international legal texts, and is itself a case study of how the conscious exclusion from the public domain may advance global public goods, in this case the public good of effective practical access to legal texts, and higher-order public goods such as acceptance of, and respect for, the principles of international law and its progressive development.[122] To this effect, a series of General Assembly resolutions[123] approved a fee-based structure for on-line provision of the treaty collection, which would generate sufficient revenue to recover costs, compensating for lost revenues from past sales of hard copies.[124] Accordingly, the on-line UN Treaty Collection offers a fee scale that in practice deploys legal and technological constraints on access to the treaty collection to cross-subsidise preferential public sector, educational and developing country access. Legally, the usage conditions advise that the treaty collection 'contains copyrighted material and/or other proprietary information' and that materials 'may be

---

[118]   See, for example, copyright notices of the FAO, UNESCO and WHO.

[119]   Regional law-making institutions follow a similar practice, such as the Council of Europe Treaty Office: 'Reproduction is authorised, provided the source is acknowledged, save where otherwise stated. For any use for commercial purposes, a prior permission by the Council of Europe must be obtained.'

[120]   www.wto.org.

[121]   Note 97 *supra*.

[122]   UN General Assembly Declaration on the Decade of International Law.

[123]   A/RES/51/158, A/RES/52/153 and A/RES/53/100 ('the United Nations Treaty Series involve high costs and additional costs which result from the need to maintain, update and improve the service; the revenues generated from hard copy sales are inadequate to cover these costs and will increase as a result of their on-line availability; accordingly, it will be appropriate to charge a fee from users of the on-line version to generate revenues to fund at least the maintenance and improvement of the service').

[124]   Note of the Secretary-General, A/52/363 of 26 September 1997.

copyrighted by the United Nations and, thus, are protected by copyright laws and regulations worldwide', and provide that, unless 'expressly permitted by applicable law', a wide range of copying, redistribution, publication and commercial exploitation requires the prior written permission of the United Nations.[125]

Even if public goods analysis is effectively an ordering of policy priorities, overwhelming policy reasons would surely situate access to the text of international treaties as a public good. This was central to the prevailing spirit at the birth of multilateralism in the aftermath of the First World War – the very first of Wilson's Fourteen Points called for 'open covenants of peace, openly arrived at, after which there shall be no private international understandings of any kind but diplomacy shall proceed always frankly and in the public view.'[126] Yet visibility and even accessibility are not necessarily dependent on public domain status, or the absence of copyright altogether. There are modes of subsistence and exercise of copyright akin to a custodial responsibility, including an obligation to promote practical access to the texts. The uncertain and diffuse provenance of treaties as text perhaps renders difficult, and possibly undesirable on a policy basis, the attribution of copyright over treaty text on the basis of its authorship.[127] And the incorporation of treaties both as law and as texts in the 'law of the land' shifts the frame so that public domain status may be asserted as a consequence of domestic policy settings. Yet treaties, as international texts, may be viewed as copyright works by virtue of the specific legal personality of international organisations and their express entitlement to copyright in works prepared and published under their authority. This may be construed as a custodial responsibility, akin to the Crown prerogative. In practice, this can entail free public domain status for the texts through the formal or *de facto* waiver of copyright, although promoting equitable access to the texts may also entail imposing certain exclusions, limiting full public domain status to promote such higher-order public goods as Wilson's first 'Point'. Considered as texts, the international treaties on IP do not fall into any distinct legal category. It is notable, however, in the light of the diverse practices of international agencies, that access policies in this part of international law appear to be more open than in several other areas.

---

[125] untreaty.un.org/English/usage.asp.

[126] Woodrow Wilson, speech to Congress, 18 January 1918, text available at en. wikipedia.org/wiki/Fourteen_Points.

[127] Long Innes CJ observed that 'it is probably true in the legal sense that legislation has no author, even though the text is undoubtedly drafted by identifiable individuals' (*Attorney-General v Butterworth*, note 108 *supra*, at 259).

5   THE PUBLIC DOMAIN SHAPED BY INTERNATIONAL IP TREATIES

The final point of inquiry is to consider public domains as a legal construct and the various ways in which international IP treaties help to define a public domain. Certainly, the entry point for much analysis of the public domain and the operation of the international IP treaty system is to consider the treaty system as inherently, even constitutionally, set against the public domain, with the suggestion that this process has accelerated in recent years. International IP treaties are viewed with concern and apprehension by many who defend the public domain. It is assumed that – whether by direct legal effect or by promoting a value system that favours exclusion and property rights – the treaty system is a major driver in privatising knowledge and foreclosing the public domain. Current proposals for a treaty to safeguard access to knowledge[128] have been developed at least in part as a response to the perceived negative impact of international treaty-making on the public domain, and to pre-empt or counterbalance proposals for further international IP treaties – essentially out of concern that further treaty-making will lead to new constraints, which will in turn exclude further material from the public domain.

In practice, given the many faces of public domains, treaties exert influence in many different aspects, limiting public domain in some aspects and preserving it in others. Focusing on public domains under national law, forms of constraint introduced by international treaties include:

- the simple greater geographical reach of treaties, as the majority of countries adhere to most key international texts, in many cases doubly so as commitments under treaties such as Paris and Berne are accepted as direct obligations and as a consequence of WTO membership: very few countries now lie outside the treaty system altogether;
- principles of non-discriminatory access to protection under national IP laws,[129] so that foreign works and works published by international organisations cannot be simply deemed to be public domain material;
- substantive constraints both on exceptions to protectable subject matter and on the availability of limitations and exceptions to rights granted, and the imposition of minimum durations for term of protection;

---

[128]   E.g. the Treaty on Access to Knowledge (draft 9 May 2005), at www.cptech.org/a2k/consolidatedtext-may9.pdf, which aims to 'protect, preserve and enhance the public domain, which is essential for creativity and sustainable innovation' and affirms the right to circumvent digital rights measure and technological protection measures for 'works consisting predominantly of public-domain material'.

[129]   In particular, the principle of national treatment under Paris, Berne and TRIPS.

- increased practical activity, for instance a greater number of registration-based industrial property titles, which may be facilitated by elements of the treaty system.

To some extent, a national public domain is a reading of a treaty, both as law and as text. Yet it is difficult to gauge the full effect of the treaty system on national public domains. Public domains are multi-faceted, from the aspect of subject matter and use entitlements. Differences in law, policy, practice and custom mean that national public domains differ widely between countries bound by the same treaties. And to address this question objectively entails resolving a counterfactual: what options would each country have chosen in the complete absence of international treaties? How to isolate that precise layer or elements of IP law that can be directly attributed to the treaty system and not to domestic choices? What elements are attributable to the legal effect of the treaty? and What elements result from its non-legal influence as a text? Sometimes, the influence is plain: certain categories of patentable subject matter are protected as a direct consequence of international substantive standards. On other issues where the proper scope of the public domain is contested, such as copyright term, the recent drivers have been domestic law-making and litigation[130] and bilateral and regional treaty-making. The last fundamental shift on copyright term in the multilateral treaty system was virtually a century ago, when the Berlin conference set copyright term at life of the author plus 50 years.[131]

In other respects, international treaties may provide positive recognition of and enhanced access to public domains, for instance:

- in setting standards for inherently unprotectable subject matter, such as the TRIPS and WCT requirement that copyright be limited to expressions only, and not be extended to 'ideas, procedures, methods of operation or mathematical concepts as such,'[132] reflecting the policy basis for defining copyright scope in terms of the public domain as discussed above;
- in defending notions of collective public property, not susceptible of appropriation by individuals, either through use ('possession') or through assertion of an exclusive right ('property'): for example, the protection against appropriation of various signs and symbols with either public or international status under Paris 6 *ter*;
- in providing a legal framework to assert and defend choices to exclude certain subject matter from protection, to maintain a public policy choice

---

[130]   *Eldred v Ashcroft* 123 S. Ct. 769 (2003) 153.
[131]   Revised Berne Convention for the Protection of Literary and Artistic Works (Berlin, 13 November 1908), art. 7.
[132]   TRIPS, art. 9.2; WCT, art. 2.

to preclude exclusive rights on such material as diagnostic, therapeutic and surgical methods,[133] or to preserve the public domain of descriptive terms 'customary in common language';[134]

- in constructing an international public domain of accessible knowledge as discussed above, including the early publication of technological information through the PCT system ensuring its worldwide public domain status, the creation of a corpus of socially beneficial metadata, and practical tools established by international treaties[135] for enhanced, systematic access to public domain information;
- at the regional level, constructing alternative forms of public domain – material free for use, but subject to liability rules, for collectively held tradition-based materials, in particular the creation of the *domaine public payant*.[136]

Ultimately, the forms of influence on the public domain exerted by international treaties are as diverse as the conceptions of public domain. While international IP treaties, by their nature, facilitate and even precipitate the formulation of policy-driven exclusions from the public domain – and indeed may exceed themselves and generate exclusions with questionable policy basis – they do also provide a platform, a basis, for appropriate definition and defence of the public domain under national law. This is, indeed, one of the very reasons why the international law expressed by the treaties is a pre-eminent international public good.[137]

6 A PUBLIC DOMAIN VIEW OF INTERNATIONAL NORM-SETTING

The IP policy-maker is not confronted with making a simple choice along a linear scale that ranges along a single dimension between absolute private

[133] TRIPS, art 27.3 (a).
[134] TRIPS, art 24.6.
[135] Strasbourg Agreement concerning the International Patent Classification (IPC), Nice Agreement concerning the International Classification of Goods and Services for the Purposes of the Registration of Marks, Locarno Agreement establishing the International Classification for Industrial Designs, and Vienna Agreement establishing the International Classification of the Figurative Elements of Marks.
[136] Bangui Agreement, note 61 *supra*, art. 59 (Paying Public Domain and Exploitation of Expressions of Folklore).
[137] For discussion on how such a defence would be constructed, see for example Dinwoodie, note 7 *supra*; see also ICTSD-UNESCO, 'Resource Book on TRIPS and Development' (2005).

monopoly and a wholly unbounded public domain; and IP legislation is not
simply a matter of selecting a point on such a scale according to a zero-sum
balance between one cluster of interests ('users') and another ('producers'). The
inter-textuality that treaties exemplify highlights that every producer of text is
a user of text, that access to text helps to create text. The policy-maker's task is
rather to craft the optimal dynamic interplay between public domains and forms
of legal exclusion, so as to optimise the production of those public goods which
the policy process sets as priorities. These public goods can be abstract in nature,
higher-order public goods that would transcend commodifying knowledge as a
simple public good akin to a public utility, so that the 'health' of the public domain is not measured solely by its girth. Literal public domain status is of scant
utility if knowledge is practically inaccessible: various modes of accessibility
may be promoted by exclusions from the public domain. Forms of management
of international treaties illustrate at least some of the options.

The international IP treaty system, ideally conceived, is a concretion of a
complex set of judgments about what form of interplay between private interest
and public access is most effective in ensuring the cooperative delivery of international public goods. As law, too, it should provide a more or less stable
platform for establishing and defending the domestic policy choices that determine the shape and the health of national public domains. The 'policy space'
in which legal flexibilities are explored is itself a form of public domain, defining legislators' freedom to operate.

Practically constructing this domestic policy space within the constraints
of treaty system is an active form of reading and interpreting treaty texts: the
kind of reading that imposes authority, subordinating text to the reader's context. In this way, a national law is a textual critique of the international text,
as a reading of a party's rights and obligations expressed by that text. Sometimes this reading is overly uncritical, and the legislator as interpreter may
needlessly cede authority to the 'original' author.[138] Recursively, the readings
of treaty text in national laws are then drawn on to interpret the import of the
treaty text. This interpretation is also coloured by the complex inter-textuality
of treaties; texts authored in one forum are re-authored as they feed into a
mosaic of text negotiated in other forums. The incorporation of treaty text into
national law is a further form of re-authoring. When the treaty text enters national law, it is read in a new aspect, both as law and as a text: this can affect
its public domain status, since public policy considerations may overrule
ownership of the treaties as literary properties precisely because they have
entered national law.

---

[138]   See discussion of the legislator as treaty interpreter in Taubman, A., 'Nobility of
Interpretation', note 83 *supra*.

The public domain status of international IP treaties as texts depends, recursively, on those very texts and on how national laws read them. In the absence of a true international public domain, even the treaties that set international standards are subject to the national IP laws that they themselves help to determine. But the consideration of the public domain status of treaties also highlights broader forms of custodianship and of authority, sovereign prerogative or public dominion over IP subject matter, recalling that public domain may be construed as a form of positive ownership, and as a concretion of use rights rather than through the absence of rights.

Treaties are works of collaborative, collective, incremental and at times anonymous literary handiwork. Their very existence as law and their practical accessibility as texts are two forms of higher-order global public goods, which are promoted in part by conscious constructions in which exclusion buttresses accessibility. Considering the public domain status of treaty texts offers an intriguing study in public policy, authority and custody over texts, and promotion of public goods through the interplay between exclusivity and access. The interplay between exclusive right or prerogative and public domain status is not a static zero-sum game. Ideally, it is a dynamic process of crafting policy settings allowing for a positive feedback loop between private exclusivities and public domains, with the effect of producing fundamental public goods that transcend the legal infrastructure, defined by particular texts and the specific rights and entitlements that they provide for.

5. The public interest in the public domain

Gillian Davies

Copyright is a 'tax upon the public' ... [it should] not last a day longer than is necessary for the purpose of securing the good. (T. Macaulay)[1]

1 INTRODUCTION

The public domain in copyright parlance means all literary and artistic works and other subject matter which are no longer protected by copyright or related rights because the term of protection applicable to them has expired. When the term of protection comes to an end, the works fall into the public domain, meaning that they may be freely used in any form or manner by anybody, either for private use or for public purposes, whether for commercial gain or otherwise. There is no requirement to ask for authorisation from the authors of the works or to pay any remuneration for the use. The protection of the international conventions also falls away, as recognised by the Universal Copyright Convention (UCC), which provides:

> This Convention shall not apply to works or rights in works which, at the effective date of this Convention in a Contracting State where protection is claimed, are permanently in the public domain in the said Contracting State.[2]

Works also fall into the public domain if they are not eligible for copyright protection for any reason, such as lack of originality, and, in countries where compliance with formalities is still required, if these are not complied with. It is possible that a work as such is not in the public domain but a particular right

---

[1] *Hansard*, House of Commons, Vol. 56, 5 February 1841, at 348.
[2] UCC, Art. VII. Art. 18, Paris Act of the Berne Convention for the Protection of Literary and Artistic Works, 1971, also refers to the public domain in the context that the Convention shall apply to all works which have not yet fallen into the public domain.

in the work is; for example, where the term of protection for different rights varies.

In some countries, the copyright law specifies that certain subject matter and works fall into the public domain. For example, the Copyright Law of the United States of America[3] provides that copyright does not subsist in ideas, systems or works of the federal government, such as laws, government reports, and so on. By contrast, in the United Kingdom, government publications are not public domain works. Other subject matter commonly agreed to fall outside the ambit of copyright protection includes methods, facts, utilitarian objects, titles, themes, plots, words, short phrases and idioms, literary characters and style.

The public domain represents a vast body of information, literature and other creative works with great cultural and historical significance. There is a public domain for all subject matter of intellectual property, for example, in the fields of patents and trade marks. This discussion is limited to the public domain in works protected by copyright and related rights.

The scope of the public domain shifts from time to time according to new legislation and the outcome of litigation. The public domain is, moreover, different sizes at different times and in different countries. Sometimes the public domain grows, as when patents or copyrights expire, or as in the aftermath of decisions such as *Feist Publications, Inc. v Rural Telephone Service*, which held that uncreative compilations of facts cannot be protected by US copyright law. Sometimes it shrinks, as when the European Union promulgated a directive requiring EU member states to protect the contents of databases or when US courts decided that business methods could be patented.[4]

The public domain during the 20th century came to be severely curtailed as a result of the fact that copyright laws worldwide extended the scope of copyright by granting more expansive rights to intellectual property right-owners and by protecting an array of new subject matter. The importance to the public interest of a vibrant and extensive public domain took second place to the expansion of rights. In the public interest, however, it should be accepted that 'recognition of new intellectual property interests should be offset today by equally deliberate recognition of individual rights in the public domain'.[5]

---

[3]   17 USC 1976, as amended, §105 (2002).

[4]   Samuelson, P. (2003), 'Mapping the Public Domain: Threats and Opportunities', 66 *Law & Contemporary Problems* 147.

[5]   Lange, D. (1981), 'Recognising the Public Domain', 44 *Law & Contemporary Problems* 147.

2   THE DURATION OF COPYRIGHT VERSUS THE PUBLIC DOMAIN

The Statute of Anne 1709[6] and the copyright clause of the US Constitution 1787[7] both embodied the concept that providing protection for the author against un-authorised reproduction for a limited period would encourage and promote learning and progress, and preserve the public domain, thus acting for the public good. From the inception of the common law copyright system, therefore, it has always been recognised that protection should be limited in time, in order to protect the rights of the public to have access to works.

> Copyright is a monopoly ... It is good that authors should be remunerated; and the least exceptionable way of remunerating them is by a monopoly. Yet monopoly is an evil. For the sake of the good we must submit to the evil; but the evil ought not to last a day longer than is necessary for the purpose of securing the good.[8]

The public domain was born of the limitation of the duration of copyright. It provides a free resource of culture, knowledge and information, which is avail-able to society as a whole. It is a cultural patrimony which is crucial to the spread of knowledge and culture, benefiting education, business, government, archives and libraries, as well as the cultural industries and the general public.

The question of how long copyright should last has been a controversial matter from the outset. In the United Kingdom, the debate focused on maintaining the balance between the public interest in stimulating creativity by means of protect-ing right-owners and the public interest in dissemination of and access to works protected by copyright. Although, at the international level, the principle that copyright should be limited in time has prevailed in the wider interests of the public, proponents of the theory that, since copyright is a property right, it should be perpetual remained vocal for many years and their arguments were met in part by a gradual extension of the term of protection. Thus, for example, in the United Kingdom, the term of protection in the Statute of Anne was 14 years, extendable if the author was still living for a further 14 years; in addition, works already published by 1710 were given a single term of 21 additional years.

---

[6]   The Statute of Queen Anne, 1709, Ch. XIX: 'an Act for the encouragement of learning, by vesting the copies of printed books in the authors or purchasers of such copies, during the times therein mentioned'.

[7]   Constitution of the United States of America, Art. I, 8, cl.8. Clause 8 vests Con-gress with the power 'to promote the progress of science and useful arts, by securing for limited times to authors and inventors the exclusive right to their respective writings and discoveries'.

[8]   Macaulay, T. in *Hansard*, House of Commons, Vol. 56, 5 February 1841, at 347–8.

Gradually the term of protection increased but until the end of the 20th century the norm was to protect authors for their lifetimes and 50 years thereafter and to protect other right-owners for 50 years from publication. Today, in order to comply with EU legislation[9] on the subject adopted in 1993, the UK has extended the term of protection for literary, dramatic, musical and artistic works, as well as films, to 70 years after the death of the author (*post mortem auctoris* (p.m.a)).[10] The trend in the EU's trading partners worldwide in recent years has also been to increase the term of protection beyond the standard of 50 years p.m.a. originally set by the Berne Convention in 1908,[11] although 50 years p.m.a. does remain the standard of the Berne Convention and of the TRIPs Agreement[12] at present. The United States of America enacted legislation soon after the EU to extend the term of copyright protection by 20 years.[13] As a result of this trend, many works which were about to fall into the public domain now remain protected. Moreover, because the new legislation was applied retroactively, certain works which had fallen into the public domain received renewed protection.

Clearly, the trend towards longer periods of protection of works diminishes the public domain for the benefit of the right-owners and to the detriment of society and acts as a disincentive to creation. The opportunity to build upon works within the public domain is a fundamental need of the creative community. 'All authorship is fertilised by the work of prior authors and the echoes of old work in new work extend beyond ideas and concepts to a wealth of expressive details.'[14] As Ricketson has pointed out:

> there comes a point at which these works should cease to be subject to private rights and pass into the public domain ... With the passing of time ... they become 'common property', a part of the general resources of a nation and the world at large. At this stage, it can be argued that they should be free for anyone to use in whatever way he or she may choose. Education and general cultural life will be enhanced as a result, and a useful basis is provided for further derivative creative endeavours.[15]

This is not a theoretical argument. The interest of present-day society in the public domain is vividly demonstrated by looking up 'public domain' on the

---

[9] Directive 93/98/EEC on the Duration of Copyright and Related Rights.

[10] Duration of Copyright and Rights in Performances Regulations 1995 (SI1995/3297).

[11] Art. 7, Berlin Act of the Berne Convention, 1908.

[12] Arts. 9 and 12, Agreement on Trade-Related Aspects of Intellectual Property Rights, Marrakesh, 1994.

[13] The Sonny Bono Copyright Term Extension Act, Pub. L. No. 105-298, 112 Stat. 2827 (1988).

[14] Litman, J. (1990), 'The Public Domain', 39 *Emory Law Journal* 965 at 968.

[15] Ricketson, S. (1987), *The Berne Convention for the Protection of Literary and Artistic Works: 1886–1986,* Kluwer, para. 7.3.

Internet. Countless websites advertise public domain information and offer assistance to potential users with identifying works of all kinds which are in the public domain, from music and lyrics to books, images and films and a huge variety of government, institutional, academic and commercial literature freely made available to the public.

3   PUBLIC POLICY ATTITUDES TO THE PUBLIC DOMAIN

3.1   The Shifting Balance

The traditional bargain between copyright protection for limited times for the right-owners, followed by works falling into the public domain in the interests of the general public having the widest possible access to works, has been compromised in the last twenty years or so by the steady increase in the terms of protection in Europe and the United States of America.

The debate leading to the adoption of the 70 year p.m.a. term by the EU (in spite of the fact that only three of the then 12 Member States previously protected certain works for longer than 50 years p.m.a.[16]) was dominated by the representatives of the right-owners representing powerful commercial interests, from collecting societies to the publishing, film and record industries and the computer software industry. The principal concern of the EC Commission as expressed in the Recitals to the Term Directive was to harmonise periods of protection throughout the Community in view of the completion of the Single Market.[17] Harmonisation upwards at a high level was thought necessary 'since these rights are fundamental to intellectual creation and ... their protection ensures the maintenance and development of creativity in the interests of authors, cultural industries, consumers and society as a whole'.[18] Upward harmonisation was also considered simpler to achieve in view of the difficulties inherent in cutting back acquired rights.[19] Other arguments deployed in favour of the extension included longer life expectancy of authors and the desire to protect the interests of their direct descendants for two successive generations.[20] The Recitals make no reference to the public domain, which together with the public interest appears not to have played any role in the debate. That the

---

[16]   France (70 years for musical works only), Germany (70 years for literary, artistic and musical works) and Spain (60 years for literary, artistic and musical works).

[17]   Term Directive, Recital 2.

[18]   Ibid., Recital 10.

[19]   Ibid., Recital 9.

[20]   Ibid., Recital 5.

United States of America subsequently extended the term of protection by 20 years was described by one commentator as 'Keeping up with the Joneses in the European Union'. In her view, because the public domain is a crucial counterpart to the copyright system, 'Congress should not have revised the 1976 Copyright Act's balance between protected and expired works without compelling reasons for term extension. It is not clear that such reasons have been demonstrated.'[21]

The granting of intellectual property rights in general, not only copyrights but patents, trade marks and other rights too, is predicated on the assumption that at some point, in the public interest, the monopoly rights fall into the public domain for the benefit of all. The continual erosion of the public domain by the extension of copyright terms represents a real tax on the public, on knowledge and information. With Macaulay, the present author believes that long terms of protection 'inflict grievous injury on the public, without conferring any compensating advantage on men of letters'.[22] Copyright protection is only acceptable, and then only for limited times, in order to resolve the conflict of public interest between a fair return to the creator and the desirability of the public having an unrestricted right of use.

The public domain is threatened not only by the extension of the term of copyright protection but also by other efforts to exploit or control it. Historically, a number of countries have introduced a *paying public domain*, imposing a tax on its exploitation. Other initiatives have aimed at *safeguarding the public domain* by various means of control. The subject of the protection of the public domain is currently on WIPO's development agenda.

3.2 The Paying Public Domain

The paying public domain establishes an obligation to pay for the use of works after the expiry of copyright protection.[23] During this post-copyright period (either limited in time or indefinite) royalties are collected for the general benefit of living authors or for other cultural purposes. Such payments are usually conceived as a form of tax for the use of the public exchequer or other government agency. A number of countries have introduced such schemes and continue to advocate them.

---

[21]   Ginsburg, J. (1999), 'News from US(I)',179 *R.I.D.A.* 143.

[22]   Macaulay, T. in *Hansard,* House of Commons, Vol. 56, 5 February 1841, at 349. For a more thorough discussion of these issues, see Davies, G. (2002), *Copyright and the Public Interest,* 2nd edn, London: Sweet and Maxwell.

[23]   See also the discussion on the *domaine public payante* by Gibson, J., 'Audiences in Tradition: Traditional Knowledge and the Public Domain', in Chapter 12 of this volume.

It is also argued that the right to collect and distribute funds arising from a paying public domain should be assigned to authors' collecting societies, to be used to finance welfare funds and to promote cultural and artistic activities by awarding grants and organising systems of aid to authors.

The system is sometimes portrayed as a defence for living authors against 'competition' from works in the public domain. Authors, however, do not suffer unfair competition from works in the public domain. Publishers of works publish both copyright protected works and works in the public domain. The use of the latter free of royalties compensates the risk that publishers take with contemporary authors, composers and artists.

During the 1980s a series of meetings was held by Unesco and WIPO aimed at preparing international recommendations for the protection of works in the public domain. During these meetings, the issue of the public paying domain was also addressed with a view to establishing guidelines on it. The subject turned out to be highly controversial and in December 1983 it was dropped by the Executive Committee of the Berne Convention and the Intergovernmental Copyright Committee of the UCC, which endorsed the following statement by the then Director General of WIPO:

> Revenues collected under copyright laws should go to the authors and their successors in title. Copyright laws should not provide for payment for the use of works not protected by copyright since such provisions obscure the real justification of copyright … the cultural aims financed from the revenues derived from the institution of 'domaine public payant' – in countries in which such an institution existed – were fully respectable but such aims should be financed from sources other than a kind of tax on the use of literary and artistic works, not protected by copyright.

Indeed, it is the responsibility of the state to provide welfare benefits for its authors. States should not shelve this responsibility by imposing a tax on works in the public domain at the expense of the public. Adding to the users' costs in this way discourages the use of works in the public domain, has negative results in cultural terms and results either in a reduction of profitability for those taking the risk of publishing works or in higher prices to the consumer.

3.3   Efforts to Safeguard or Control the Public Domain

For more than fifteen years, beginning in 1976 and coming to a conclusion only in 1993, Unesco was occupied with a proposed instrument for the protection or safeguarding of the public domain. The initiative was finally dropped by the General Conference of Unesco in 1993, but remains of interest, since the matter has recently resurfaced in discussions for a WIPO Development Agenda. On a proposal of the Chilean government, the following items are proposed for action by WIPO:

- Draw up proposals and models for the protection of, and access to, the contents of the public domain.
- Consider the protection of the public domain within WIPO's normative processes.[24]

The draft Recommendation which was under discussion for so many years was committed in particular to protecting the integrity of works in the public domain. It recognised that works belonging to the public domain are not only an expression of the personality of their authors but also a reflection of the cultural identity of peoples, and, because of their educational, cultural, artistic, scientific and historical value, form an integral part of a nation's cultural heritage. Owing to the ever-increasing tendency to use and adapt works in the public domain as a result of the rapid development of technology, it was suggested that the integrity of works in the public domain was vulnerable and could be distorted or mutilated, in breach of the moral rights of their original authors.

In this connection, it should be recalled that in a number of countries, including France, moral rights are granted in perpetuity. In these countries, after the author's death, the exercise of these rights is transmitted to his or her heirs and users of the author's works which have fallen into the public domain may have action taken against them for infringement of, for example, the rights of paternity and integrity.

The recommendation set out general principles on which the safeguarding of works in the public domain should be based, put forward proposals for measures that should be taken to safeguard works in the public domain and envisaged sanctions for violation of these measures.

The principles elaborated on the recognition that works in the public domain could be freely used, without permission or payment, subject to respect for the authorship and integrity of the work. Private uses envisaged included use as a source of inspiration for the creation of a new, independent work; as a source to be quoted from, with due acknowledgement; for translation, adaptation and any other transformation short of distortion or mutilation; and as the basis for parody, caricature or pastiche. Public uses included reproduction by any means, public performance, broadcasting and any other form of communication to the public either in the original form or in transformation.

The measures to be taken for safeguarding works in the public domain should apply to both national and foreign works and it was emphasised that, even in countries where moral rights were not recognised as perpetual, other means of

---

[24] Provisional Committee on Proposals Related to a WIPO Development Agenda (PCDA), 20–24 February 2006, Draft Report, Annex 1, B, points 7 and 8. See also Proposal by Chile (doc. PCDA/1/2).

legal redress should be found to protect public domain works from distortion
or mutilation.

Although, in spite of all the effort that went into the draft recommendation,
it was not adopted, the ideas behind it are still with us. The Chilean proposal
referred to above calls upon WIPO to (i) deepen the analysis of the implications
and benefits of a rich and accessible public domain, (ii) draw up proposals and
models for the protection of, and access to, the contents of the public domain,
and (iii) consider the protection of the public domain within WIPO's normative
processes (that is, consider the adoption of an international instrument on the
subject).

The concept of seeking to control the use of works in the public domain in
the way envisaged by the intergovernmental initiatives already referred to appears to the present author to be a contradiction in terms. Either the works are
in the public domain and freely available for the information and use of the
public or not. Problems likely to arise from any efforts to oversee the use of
public domain works would include those of defining the concept of works in
the public domain, of determining the nature and powers, and financing, of any
body responsible for ensuring respect for such works, and of selecting those
works which might benefit from protection. Taking into account changes in
public taste, it is essential to maintain the intellectual freedom to freely use any
and all of the works of the past. There is also the danger that the responsible
body might seek to require users to obtain advance permission to use a work in
the public domain and even to charge an administrative fee for such use.

4   RECLAIMING THE PUBLIC DOMAIN FOR THE PUBLIC

Long terms of protection 'inflict grievous injury on the public, without conferring any compensating advantage on men of letters'. [25] The publisher will not
give appreciably more for a copyright of 60 years than for one of 20. Taste and
fashion in literature and the arts change and very few books or songs have a life
of more than a few years. 'Such is the inconstancy of the public taste, that no
sensible man will venture to pronounce, with confidence, what the sale of any
book published in our days [1841] will be in the years between 1890 and
1900. [26]

The late-20th century-extensions of the term of protection of copyright to the
detriment of the public domain took place with little regard for the public

---

[25]   Macauley, T., op. cit., at 344.
[26]   Ibid.

interest. At governmental level and within the European Commission, there was 'little sustained discussion of the economic, social and cultural issues involved, and the steady trend towards longer terms has remained largely unquestioned'.[27] No effort was made to establish on a factual and economic basis what the appropriate term for copyright protection should be. Outside of academia, hardly any attention was paid to the idea that the limitation on the duration of protection is imposed in the public interest in order to provide the public with free access to copyright works as soon as possible and to promote the widest possible dissemination of such works for the benefit of the public. To extend the term of protection without first having ascertained the likely benefits and disadvantages to be derived from such extension on the basis of factual evidence and discussion of the public policy issues involved is not in the best interests of the public at large.

The trend toward longer terms of protection did, however, attract the critical attention of academics, a majority of whom were overwhelmingly opposed to term extension, as well as renewed interest in the subject of the public domain. For example, Cornish argued that

> it cannot be that an extension of the right from fifty to seventy years *post mortem auctoris* is required as an economic incentive to those who create and those who exploit works. They make their decisions by reference to much shorter time scales than these.[28]

The debate on the extension of the term of protection stimulated interest in and scholarly discussion of the public domain, its history and the threats posed thereto by recent developments in copyright protection.[29]

Historically, in Europe and the United States of America, legislators attempted to balance the arguments in favour of copyright with criticism of its monopolistic costs and dangers. Built into copyright protection from the beginning was the idea of the need for limitations on the right. 'Here there was an existent public domain, whose value we should recognise and which should have protection – perhaps even constitutional protection – against the danger that knowledge would be removed from it, or access to existing material impeded.'[30]

---

[27] Ricketson, S. (1992), 'The Copyright Term', 23 *I.I.C.* 766.

[28] Cornish, W.R. (1994), 'Intellectual Property', in 13 *Yearbook of European Law* 485.

[29] See, for example, Litman, J. (1990), 'The Public Domain', 39 *Emory L.J.* 965; Lange, D. (1981), 'Recognizing the Public Domain', 44 *Law & Contemporary Problems* 147; Samuelson, P. (2003), 'Mapping the Digital Public Domain: Threats and Opportunities', 66 *Law & Contemporary Problems* 147; Boyle, J. (2003), 66 *Law & Contemporary Problems* 33.

[30] Boyle, J., op. cit., at IX.

The public domain has been vastly extended in its usefulness and accessibility by the contribution that digital technology and the Internet has made. As Samuelson has pointed out: 'In some respects, digital information and digital networks have made the public domain more vibrant and robust, and if various digital commons initiatives attain their goals, the public domain may flourish as never before.'[31] It is a challenge for governments and the public to devise strategies for preserving and developing the public domain in the digital environment and making it available on the Internet.

5   CONCLUSION

> One of the ultimate goals of any society is the empowerment of all its citizens through access and use of information and knowledge. Every person and every nation must have equal opportunity to benefit from cultural diversity and scientific progress as a basic human right in the current information revolution and the emerging knowledge society ... A significantly under-appreciated, but essential, element of the emerging Information Society is the vast amount of information already in the public domain, or that can potentially be placed in the public domain.[32]

It is very much in the public interest that the benefits of the public domain to the public be appreciated and promoted. A recent initiative of Unesco to adopt policy guidelines for the development and promotion of governmental public domain information, taking account of both national needs and international practices, is therefore to be welcomed. The guidelines are intended as a practical guide to defining, and promoting understanding and debates on the meaning of the public domain information and to assist Member States in the development of policies and strategies in this area for the benefit of society.[33]

Access to the information available in the public domain brings undoubted benefits to the public, serving essential educational and cultural functions in every society. There are also social benefits to be derived from a more informed and educated society. There are other benefits too. For information produced by governments, placing it in the public domain brings with it transparency of government and the promotion of democracy, responding to the public's claims to freedom of information and open government. Public interest policy

---

[31]   Samuelson, P., op. cit., I.

[32]   Uhlir, P. (2003), *Draft Policy Guidelines for the Development and Promotion of Public Domain Information*, Unesco doc. CI-2003/WS/2, 1.1.

[33]   29C/Resolution 28 of the Unesco General Conference 1997; see also Uhlir, P. (2004), *Policy Guidelines for the Development and Promotion of Governmental Public Domain Information*, Unesco (CI-2004/WS/5).

objectives are also furthered by access to and disclosure of information relating to the public's welfare in matters such as health policy, environment concerns and the use of public funds. Governments therefore have a critical role to play in expanding access to and use of public domain information and must be willing to consider the benefits of making public information available.

The fostering of a vibrant public domain to serve the causes of education, information, and social and economic development should be a crucial element in any government's information and intellectual property policies.

6.   Altering the contours of the public domain

Fiona Macmillan

1   INTRODUCTION

As this volume so eloquently demonstrates, intellectual property scholarship has become deeply involved in a discourse about the relationship of intellectual property with the public domain. This has been an important debate driven by serious concerns about the imperialistic tendencies of intellectual property, as it extends its boundaries horizontally to include new types of intellectual activity and vertically to confer wider powers of control on the relevant right-holders. The frequent tendency of the debate is to create some sort of binary opposition,[1] so that we divide the whole of intellectual space between that which is proper-tised and that which is in the public domain.[2] It is not just that the public domain is other than intellectual property and vice versa, but that the two are envisaged as butting up against one another so that, if we were to conceive of this in physi-cal terms, each would fit snugly against the shape of the other. The implication of this is that, if the two also take up the whole of intellectual space, altering the contours of intellectual property will alter those of the public domain (and vice versa).

Of course, the dangers of analogies between intellectual property and physical property are considerable. It is not unknown for advocates of strong intellectual property rights to draw comparisons between the theft of physical property and that of intellectual property, nor is it uncommon to encounter the use of emotive metaphors that have somehow abandoned their metaphorical nature and acquired a life of their own within the lexicon of intellectual property.[3] The cognoscenti

---

[1]   Hemmungs Wirtén, E. (2006), 'Out of Sight and Out of Mind: On the Cultural Hegemony of Intellectual Property (Critique)', *Cultural Studies*, **20**, 165–74.

[2]   This is the underlying assumption of my own work: see, e.g., 'Public Interest and the Public Domain in an Era of Corporate Dominance', in Andersen, B. (ed.) (2005), *Intellectual Property Rights: Innovation, Governance and the Institutional Environment*, Cheltenham, UK and Northampton, MA, USA: Edward Elgar.

[3]   The classic example of this is the use of the word 'piracy' for systematic copyright

of intellectual property know only too well that the non-rivalrous and non-waste-able nature of intellectual property mean that its 'theft' is of an entirely different order from that of physical property. Like taking someone's physical property, taking someone's intellectual property may be ethically questionable but this is not because taking it deprives the owner or anyone else of its further use. How-ever, on the whole, we are much less careful about the limits of the analogy when we refer to the relationship between intellectual property and the public domain. Sometimes that carelessness can be productive. For instance, the concept of the whole of intellectual space is no more knowable than is the concept of the whole of physical space. In order to give some sort of purchase to the concept of physi-cal space, we tend to assume boundaries that are constructed by our collective limitations rather than any actual limitations of physical space.[4] We need to apply the same sort of reasoning in order to bound our concept of intellectual space, despite our understanding of the inherent malleability of its borders. However, on undertaking an analysis of the space within those borders it is necessary to be aware of the limitations of the analogy between physical and intellectual property. The following attempt at such an analysis is, accordingly, wary.

2 RELATIONSHIP BETWEEN INTELLECTUAL PROPERTY AND THE PUBLIC DOMAIN

The idea of the public domain in intellectual space is heavily dependent on Ro-man law concepts governing physical space, which recognised various dimensions of non-exclusive – but not necessarily public – property.[5] The most well-used of these so far as the intellectual property/public domain debate is concerned are *res communes* and *res publicae*. The former refers to things in-capable by their nature of being exclusively owned, while the latter refers to things open to the public by operation of law. These seem to have translated into the modern-day debate about property in intellectual space in the specific form of the concepts of the commons and the public domain. The fact that these expressions are often used interchangeably is probably not much of a surprise given that the Romans had a similar problem with *res communes* and *res publi-cae*,[6] which foreshadowed the modern-day tendency 'to mix up normative

---

infringements, despite the absence of unconstrained violence that is the hallmark of high-seas piracy.

[4] Hence the notion of the physical frontier.
[5] See Rose, C.M. (2003), 'Romans, Roads and Romantic Creators: Traditions of Public Property in the Information Age', 66 *Law & Contemporary Problems* 89.
[6] Rose, note 5 *supra*, 96, citing Borkowski, A. (1994), *Textbook on Roman Law*, London: Blackstone, p. 144.

arguments for "publicness" with naturalistic arguments about the impossibility of owning certain resources'.[7] This confusion between the commons and the public domain, *res communes* and *res publicae*, has done nothing to simplify the epistemological basis of the dichotomy between intellectual property and intellectual public space.[8] More than this, it has tended to conceal the fact that, when these concepts are traced back to their Roman law origins, neither of them seems to provide a particularly strong basis for a vibrant public or non-exclusive intellectual space in today's world.

So far as *res communes* is concerned, one might be forgiven for thinking that because of the non-rivalrous and non-wasteable nature of things in intellectual space they are all incapable by their nature of being exclusively owned or appropriated.[9] Intellectual property law has, with its useful distinction between exclusive possession/use and ownership, put paid to that idea. As is well known, there has been a tendency for law governing physical space, particularly environmental law, to foreclose or regulate the use of the physical commons. At least in some cases, this has been a benevolent response to the famous 'tragedy of the commons',[10] according to which resources held commonly are plundered, degraded and eventually exhausted.[11] The non-rivalrous and non-wasteable nature of things in intellectual space tends to suggest that this is not a reason for the foreclosure of common intellectual space, but intellectual property law has done it anyway. At least, this is what intellectual property law has tried to do. It may be that there are certain things that not even the might of intellectual property law can convert into property capable of exclusive ownership in any meaningful sense. For example, the ease of copying works available in digital form, allied with the difficulty in identifying and proceeding against unauthorised copiers, may be an indication that this part of intellectual space is incapable of the type of exclusive ownership enjoyed in relation to other types of intangible works. On the other hand, the combined effect of technology and law may render even this part of intellectual space appropriable.

Intellectual property law has not, of course, sought to foreclose all of the intellectual commons. As a body of law, it has declared that certain things are

[7]   Rose, note 5 *supra*, 96.
[8]   See also Hemmungs Wirtén, note 1 *supra*, who suggests that it is time for 'some good old epistemological soul-searching'.
[9]   Except if, and for so long as, they are kept secret: Rose, note 5 *supra*, 95.
[10] See Hardin, G. (1968), 'The Tragedy of the Commons', 162 *Science* 1243, 1244.
[11] See further, e.g., Hardin, note 10 *supra*; and Ostrom, E. (1990), *Governing the Commons: The Evolution of Institutions for Collective Action*, Cambridge and New York: Cambridge University Press, esp. Chapter 1, in which the tragedy of the commons is contrasted with other models of the commons.

incapable of being owned. Patent law, for example, rejects the concept of ownership over a range of innovations, including discoveries, scientific theories, and
methods of doing business.[12] However, its imperialising tendency means that it
is constantly pushing at the boundaries of these exclusions so that more and
more of that intellectual space concerned with inventions and technical innovations is subject to patent rights.[13] Copyright law, famously, rejects the ownership
of ideas, embracing the tenuous distinction between the unprotected idea and
the protected expression,[14] although this concept seems to be unevenly applied[15]
and subject to much erosion.[16] More generally, creative acts that do not fall
within the realm of copyright law are not appropriated.[17] However, copyright
(along with intellectual property rights related to it) has been distinguished by
a tendency to extend its reach over more and more creative or innovative acts
in intellectual space.[18] And, while intellectual property laws continue to exclude
certain parts of intellectual space from the propertised domain, it is far from
clear whether their exclusion is because they are, by their legal nature, incapable
of being owned, and therefore part of the commons, or because they should not
be brought into the private domain of intellectual property but should be kept
in the public domain. Arguably, because things in intellectual space are all incapable of ownership in the sense that things in physical space may be owned,

---

[12]   See, e.g., the UK Patents Act 1977, s 1(2).

[13]   In relation to discoveries, see e.g. *Genentech v Wellcome Foundation* [1989] RPC
147; see also Crespi, S. (1999/2000), 'Patents on Genes: Can the Issues be Clarified?',
Bioscience Law Review, 200. In relation to business methods, see e.g. *State Street Bank
& Trust Co v Signature Financial Group Inc*, 149 F 3d 1368 (Fed Cir(US)).

[14]   See, e.g., *Donoghue v Allied Newspapers* [1938] Ch 106; *Fraser v Thames Television* [1983] 2 All ER 101; *Green v Broadcasting Corporation of New Zealand* [1989]
RPC 469 and 700.

[15]   E.g., the two-dimensional/three-dimensional infringement rule in relation to artistic works in, e.g., the UK Copyright Designs and Patents Act 1988, s 17(3), arguably
breaches the idea/expression rule: see further Macmillan, F., 'Artistic Practice and the
Integrity of Copyright Law', in M. Rosenmeier and S. Teilmann (eds) (2005), *Art and
Law: The Debate over Copyright*, Copenhagen: DJØF. See also, e.g., the provisions on
the protection of preparatory design material for computer programmes in the UK Copyright Designs and Patents Act 1988, s 3(1)(c).

[16]   See, e.g., *Krisarts v Briarfine* [1977] FSR 577; *Ravenscroft v Herbert* [1980] RPC
193; *Designer Guild Ltd v Russell Williams (Textiles) Limited* [2000] UKHL 58.

[17]   See, e.g., *Merchandising v Harpbond* [1983] FSR 32; *Komesaroff v Mickle* [1988]
RPC 204; *Creation Records Ltd v News Group Newspapers Ltd* [1997] EMLR 445; *No-
rowzian v Arks Ltd (No 2)* [2000] FSR 363 (CA).

[18]   E.g., the inclusion of computer programs and preparatory design work for them
within the definition of protected 'literary works' (see, e.g., Directive 91/250/EEC on
the legal protection of computer programs and the UK Copyright Designs and Patents
Act 1988, s 3(1)) and the database right established under Directive 96/9/EC on the legal
protection of databases.

but are all – or nearly all – quite capable of being appropriated in another way by force of law, the concept of the commons or *res communes* is a difficult one to apply to intellectual space. At least, it is difficult once we concede any concept of ownership in intellectual space, unless by referring to the commons we merely mean to be descriptive and refer to those things that, as a matter of fact, have not been subsumed into the intellectual property regime.

The concept of the *res publicae*, where there is the scope for what Rose describes as 'normative arguments for "publicness"',[19] seems to offer far greater promise. In relation to *res publicae*, however, we move from the wilderness of the commons to the park,[20] that is, from the unregulated to the regulated domain. The primary reason for this, at least in relation to physical space, is that being *res publicae* implies appropriability, if not actual appropriation. Unlike the concept of *res communes*, *res publicae* in physical space does not reject the notion of private property. According to Rose, *res publicae* is always open to the possibility of ownership 'subject to the requirements of reasonable public access'.[21] One consequence of this is that it is necessary for something or someone to defend *res publicae*.

In physical space, *res publicae* is regarded as normatively justified by the need to ensure productive synergistic interactions that would otherwise be obstructed by denying public access.[22] The irony in the application of this concept to intellectual space is that precisely because things in intellectual space are non-rivalrous and non-wasteable there are not many reasons why productive synergistic interactions should not take place.[23] That is, there are not many reasons apart from intellectual property law. By regarding things in intellectual space as capable of appropriation and not therefore *res communes*, intellectual property law has created a system of obstructions to synergistic interactions. Then, in response to these obstructions, it has created its own mechanisms to defend *res publicae*. Arguably, this sounds slightly more ridiculous than it actually is. One of the reasons that productive synergistic interactions might not take place in unfettered intellectual space is because, in the absence of reward, appropriate investment and effort might not be made. Even accepting this argument and accepting that the most appropriate form of 'reward' is the creation of intellectual property rights,[24] it seems reasonably clear that to achieve productive

---

[19]   Note 7 *supra* and accompanying text.

[20]   Paraphrasing Rose, note 5 *supra*, 99.

[21]   Rose, note 5 *supra*, 99. On the attributes of *res publicae* see Rose, ibid., 96–100.

[22]   Rose, note 5 *supra*, 96–8.

[23]   See also Rose, note 5 *supra*, 102–3.

[24]   A point that is not universally accepted: see, e.g., Smiers, J., 'The Abolition of Copyrights: Better for Artists, Third World Countries and the Public Domain', in R.

synergistic interactions there needs to be a carefully calibrated balance between property rights in intellectual space and rights that preserve *res publicae*. In intellectual property law, this is generally achieved through three mechanisms: disclosure requirements, limits on duration and exceptions to the exercise of the exclusive rights. With respect to the first two mechanisms, the provisions of the law automatically defend the *res publicae*, whereas in relation to the last those seeking to use the exceptions must make a case. Despite the existence of these mechanisms, it would be straining credulity to suggest that the balance between property rights and rights that preserve *res publicae* in intellectual space is carefully calibrated. The history of intellectual property law has been marked by a progressive extension of the duration of intellectual property rights and the contraction of their respective exceptions and defences.

The law of copyright provides a particularly good example of movement along this trajectory. Its duration has expanded from the initial maximum period of 14 years[25] to the current high-water mark of 70 years after the death of the author.[26] The vitality of its fair dealing exceptions, which are essential to permitting the sort of access that allows productive synergistic interactions, has been sapped by a combination of restrictive judicial interpretation,[27] technological innovations, and new legal devices that interact with that technology.[28] Added to all this, copyright law does not require disclosure through publication. It might be argued that the existence of copyright encourages publication, which provides greater access to things in intellectual space. However, passive access and use are not quite the same things when it comes to productive synergistic interactions in intellectual space. (This is another one of those places where the

---

Towse (ed.) (2002), *Copyright and the Cultural Industries*, Cheltenham, UK and Northampton, MA, USA: Edward Elgar, 120; and van Schijndel, M. and Smiers, J., 'Imagining a World Without Copyright: The Market and Temporary Protection a Better Alternative for Artists and the Public Domain', in H. Porsdam (ed.) (2005), *Copyright and Other Fairy Tales*, Cheltenham, UK and Northampton, MA, USA: Edward Elgar.

[25] Statute of Anne 1709 (Copyright Act 1709, 8 Anne c 19).

[26] Thanks, in particular, to Directive 93/98/EEC, on harmonising the term of protection of copyright and certain related rights, and the Bono Copyright Term Extension Act 1998, the constitutional validity of which was upheld in *Eldred v Ashcroft*, 123 S Ct 769 (2003).

[27] See, e.g., *Rogers v Koons*, 751 F Supp 474 (SDNY 1990), *aff'd*, 960 F 2d 301 (2d Cir), *cert denied*, 113 S Ct 365 (1992), in which it was held that the fair use right only applied where the infringing work has used a copyright work for the purpose of criticising that work, rather than for the purpose of criticising society in general. On the significance of this case, see further Macmillan, F., 'Corporate Power and Copyright', in Towse, note 24 *supra*; and Macmillan, note 2 *supra*.

[28] The particular device in question is the anti-circumvention right. For a case that illustrates the dangers of this right, see *Universal City Studios, Inc v Corley*, 273 F 3d 429 (US Ct of Apps (2d Cir), 2001). See further Macmillan, note 2 *supra*.

analogy between physical space and intellectual space is problematic, since access to physical space implies some sort of use even if it does not embrace all sorts of uses.) Moreover, in intellectual space access to property in the name of *res publicae* is not always free or even reasonable. At the same time as the Internet has opened up an array of apparently free artefacts in intellectual space, other forms of digital technology are being used to restrict access to highly sought-after information.[29]

Patent law is hardly in a better state. Its so-called 'research' exception,[30] which is one of the few devices it has to ensure that patent rights do not obstruct scientific innovations, is very limited in scope.[31] Unlike copyright law, patent law has copious disclosure and working requirements,[32] but the caveat above concerning the difference between access to information and its use still holds. It may be true to say that under the patent regime the contraction of *res publicae* is not as dramatic as it has been in relation to copyright law. However, that is hardly much to boast about since the regime is so unbalanced in favour of right-holders. One of the things that accentuates the lack of balance in both copyright and patent regimes is the fact that the application of the exceptions is open to considerable legal disputation, which frequently means that the deep pockets of large corporate right-holders are pitted against those of more limited means. Patent law, perhaps in acknowledgement of the strength of the rights that it confers, makes some attempt to constrain bullying in the form of the action for groundless threats of infringement proceedings,[33] but this does not compensate for the gross inequalities of the legal system in which it operates.

If *res communes* and *res publicae* were the only concepts to inform our notion of the public domain as it relates to intellectual property in intellectual space, then the notion of the public domain would be somewhat impoverished. There

---

[29] A classic example of this is the dispute over access to electronic journals.

[30] See, e.g., UK Patents Act 1977, s 60(5)(b); and WTO Agreement on Trade-Related Aspects of Intellectual Property Rights, Art. 30.

[31] Because, at least in the UK version, it contains a *Rogers v Koons* type limitation to experimental uses only in relation to the subject matter of the patented invention: see *Auchinloss v Agriculture & Veterinary Supplies* [1997] RPC 397. For a more worrying case, see *Madey v Duke University*, 307 F 3d 1351 (Fed Cir 2002). See further Loughlan, P. (1996), 'Intellectual Property, Research Workers and Universities', 6 *European Intellectual Property Review* 351; and Mueller, J.M. (2001), 'No "Dilettante Affair"': Rethinking the Experimental Use Exception to Patent Infringement for Biomedical Research Tools' 76 *Washington Law Review* 1.

[32] On disclosure requirements, see e.g. UK Patents Act 1977, ss 14, 16 & 32; see further Oppenheim (1979), 'The Information Function of Patents', *European Intellectual Property Review* 344. On working requirements, see e.g. UK Patents Act 1977, ss 48–50, governing the grant of compulsory licences.

[33] See e.g. UK Patents Act 1977, s 70.

are, however, two further Roman law concepts that may be employed to flesh out the public domain in intellectual space. One of these is *res divini juris*, referring to things that cannot be owned because of their sacred or religious nature.[34] In the physical realm, ownership of things such as temples and icons was offensive to the gods. One can only speculate that offence to the gods would have been caused by general presumptuousness and by the fact that the ownership of such property would confer the type of power that might rival their own.

At first blush, the application of this category in the context of the current debate might not be obvious. These days we are not necessarily so sensitive about the feelings of divine beings; however we still recognise the cultural power of the iconic (whether of traditional religious significance or not). Like the Roman gods, if for slightly different reasons, we should be anxious about the idea that such power can be exclusively appropriated in intellectual space. To some extent, intellectual property law has eschewed exclusive rights in categories of the iconic. Rose suggests, for example, that in intellectual space this category might include 'the canon, the classics, the ancient works whose long life has contributed to their status as rare, extraordinary'.[35] Fortunately, the period of copyright duration has not yet become so long that we have to worry about the inclusion of these sorts of things in propertised intellectual space. However, Rose goes on to argue:

> [L]est we forget that all things godlike may be accompanied by lesser gods (or even false ones) and their representations, we might wish to include here too the iconography of modern commercial culture, the Mickeys and Minnies and Scarletts ... though the point is controversial, the category of *res divini juris* could well embrace this iconography and dedicate it at least in some measure to the public, as in copyright law's exception for parody.[36]

Copyright law certainly could do this, but there is little evidence currently that it would. Indeed, Mickey and Minnie have been able to rely on intellectual property law to protect them and their cultural baggage from parody.[37] The

---

[34]   Rose, note 5 *supra*, 108–10.
[35]   Rose, note 5 *supra*, 109.
[36]   Rose, note 5 *supra*, 109.
[37]   See *Walt Disney Prods v Air Pirates*, 581 F 2d 751 (US Ct of Apps (9th Cir), 1978), *cert denied*, 439 US 1132 (1979). For further discussion of this case, see Waldron, J. (1993), 'From Authors to Copiers: Individual Rights and Social Values in Intellectual Property', 69 *Chicago-Kent Law Review* 841; and Macmillan, note 2 *supra*. See also Chon, M. (1993), 'Postmodern "Progress": Reconsidering the Copyright and Patent Power', 43 *DePaul Law Review* 97; and Koenig, D.M. (1994), 'Joe Camel and the First Amendment: The Dark Side of Copyrighted and Trademark-Protected Icons', 11 *Thomas M Cooley Law Review* 803.

exception for parody is not well defined[38] and, to the extent that it must rely on the fair dealing defences, is compromised by their shrinkage. It should be added that it is far from clear that the insights about the public domain offered by *res divini juris* are confined to things in intellectual space that fall within the copyright stable. This concept appears to impose limits on what should be regarded as patentable. For instance the patenting of 'life' or of biotechnological inventions might be regarded as propertising, if not the iconic, the sacred. Anxieties about the 'morality' of such developments, and the extent to which they fall into the relevant exceptions to patenting,[39] may perhaps reflect the internalisation of a modern-day equivalent of *res divini juris*. This may also be true of attempts to stem the tide, such as the EU Directive on the protection of biotechnological inventions.[40]

The final category of non-exclusive property under Roman law that has some resonance in the context of the colonising of intellectual space by intellectual property is *res universitatis*.[41] In modern parlance, this refers to a regime that is bounded by property rights but creates a type of limited public domain (or commons) within its boundaries.[42] In physical space, this merges the advantages of productive synergistic interaction with the need to avoid the tragedy of the commons. In intellectual space, as discussed above, there is no need to avoid the tragedy of the commons, so the utility of *res universitatis*, or the bounded commons, must be to preserve productive synergies while maintaining the incentive to produce such synergies through the exercise of rights against outsiders.

As the name suggests, this type of bounded community is commonly reflected in the activities of academic and scholarly groupings.[43] It may also describe the way in which members of traditional and indigenous communities produce innovations, knowledge and other types of creative expressions. As this example serves to remind us, intellectual property law has some difficulties in recognising these types of creative or innovative communities.[44] The primary reason for this

---

[38] See, e.g., *Joy Music v Sunday Pictorial Newspapers* [1960] 2 WLR 615; *Williamson Music v Pearson Partnership* [1987] FSR 97.

[39] See Bently, L. (1992), 'Invitations to Immorality: The Oncomouse Decision', 3 *Kings College Law Journal*; Drahos, P. (1999), 'Biotechnology, Patents, Markets and Morality', *European Intellectual Property Review* 441.

[40] Directive 98/44/EC.

[41] For a description of *res universitatis*, see Rose, note 5 *supra*, 105–8.

[42] For an example of the application of this concept in physical space, see Ostrom, note 10 *supra*.

[43] See Rose, note 5 *supra*, 107–8; Merges, R.P. (1996), 'Property Rights Theory and the Commons: The Case of Scientific Research', 13 *Social Philosophy and Policy* 145.

[44] In relation to traditional and indigenous communities, see Blakeney, M. (1995), 'Protecting Expressions of Australian Aboriginal Folklore under Copyright Law', 9

is that intellectual property is always anxious to identify the owner of the relevant right, be it copyright's author or patent law's inventor. In doing this, it is likely to disregard many contributions from the relevant community and to muddle up concepts of origination, ownership and use.[45] Intellectual property does enjoy a very limited ability to recognise the concept of the bounded creative or innovative community through the devices of joint authorship and joint invention, which it transforms into joint ownership. However, these concepts are so limited in law that they can rarely do justice to the dynamic relations of a creative or innovative community.[46] In any case, the successful use of these concepts to nourish a vibrant creative or innovative community depends upon an unrealistic degree of goodwill, if not goodness, on the part of all the members of the relevant community.[47]

Creative or innovative communities bounded by intellectual property rights may also be created by cross-licensing or open-licensing devices, which are dependent on prior identification of rights and a partial or conditional waiver of them. The so-called 'creative commons movement' has, for example, come up with a way of using intellectual property law and contract law in this way to create what looks very much like the bounded community of *res universitatis*. Intellectual property rights are not eschewed, but a blanket licence is given by right-holders for the use of all or some of the exclusive rights attaching to the relevant intellectual property. The end result is a creative community that is bounded by intellectual property rights but within which there is considerable freedom to pursue productive synergistic interactions.

3 WHY DOES THE PUBLIC DOMAIN MATTER?

The importance of the various dimensions of the public domain that may be analogised to *res communes*, *res publicae*, *res divini juris* and *res universitatis* lies in the extent to which they are capable of rising to the role that the public

---

European Intellectual Property Review 442; and Blakeney, M. (2000), 'The Protection of Traditional Knowledge under Intellectual Property Law', 6 *European Intellectual Property Review* 251.

[45] See further, e.g., Chon, M. (1996), 'New Wine Bursting From Old Bottles: Collaborative Internet Art, Joint Works, and Entrepreneurship', 75 *Oregon Law Review* 257.

[46] Chon, note 45 *supra*, 270–72; Rose, C.M. (1998), 'The Several Futures of Property: Of Cyberspace and Folk Tales, Emission Trades and Ecosystems', 83 *Minnesota Law Review* 129, 158ff.

[47] See also Rose, note 5 *supra*, 107, who observes in relation to creative or innovative communities within universities: 'Here too there are opportunists, charlatans and zealots – and to some degree commercial users – who can disrupt the process.'

domain needs to play in today's world. The reason that the public domain has come to matter so much in the debate about intellectual space and its creeping propertisation is not just some intuitively appealing idea about the importance of balance between it and the propertised domain; it is rather the danger posed by the power of those few who hold so much of the really bankable property in intellectual space.[48] Intellectual space is no longer divided between a public domain and a propertised zone in which a rich diversity of author-originators and inventor-originators each wield exclusive rights over a small plot. To be sure, these people still exist as owners of intellectual property rights, but the commodifiable nature of intellectual property rights means that vast tracts of prime intellectual space have been bought up by powerful multinational corporate interests.[49] Here, the analogy with physical space similarly held is alarming – and rightly so. This power, which resides to a considerable degree in the hands of concentrated corporate sectors, means that its members are able to exert undue control over the direction of significant areas of cultural and technical development.[50] Even more seriously, the power that has been acquired by the corporate players, partly although not exclusively on the back of intellectual property rights, means that they are able to exert more and more control over the shape of intellectual property law itself.[51]

The public domain is the only place in intellectual space in which the power of the corporate giants can be challenged and resisted. One of the reasons why the power of the concentrated corporate sectors over intellectual property law is a matter of such concern is that intellectual property has a symbiotic relationship with the public domain. That is, it shapes the public domain, which might be conceived of alternatively as its progeny, rather than being in a binary opposition to it. In this lies the tragedy of the modern public domain in intellectual space. If the formation of intellectual property law is subject to the power of

---

[48] For a full exposition of this argument in relation to the copyright industries, see Macmillan, note 2 *supra*.

[49] For accounts of this process, see e.g. Bettig, R.V. (1996), *Copyrighting Culture: The Political Economy of Intellectual Property*, Boulder: Westview Press; Macmillan, note 2 *supra*; Bollier, D. (2005), *Brand-name Bullies: The Quest to Own and Control Culture*, Hoboken: John Wiley.

[50] See Macmillan, note 2 *supra*; Vaidhyanathan, S. (2001), *Copyrights and Copywrongs: The Rise of Intellectual Property and How it Threatens Creativity*, New York: New York University Press; Lessig, L. (2004), *Free Culture: How Big Media Uses Technology and the Law to Lock Down Culture and Control Creativity*, New York: Penguin Press.

[51] The classic example of this is the negotiation and conclusion of the WTO Agreement on Trade-Related Aspects of Intellectual Property Rights: see Sell, S.K. (2003), *Private Power, Public Law: The Globalization of Intellectual Property Rights*, Cambridge: Cambridge University Press.

those who dominate the propertised part of intellectual space, then it seems likely that this part will expand and the public domain will contract. As the discussion above has attempted to demonstrate, this is exactly what has happened. *Res communes* may be weakly analogised to that part of the public domain that intellectual property law deems incapable (for now) of appropriation. However, intellectual property law has shown a tendency to deem more and more of what we might have considered *res communes* as capable, after all, of appropriation. The concept of *res publicae* in intellectual space, which is justified by the importance of productive synergistic interactions, is defended (or not) by the variable and constantly changing rules on duration and a progressively weakening range of defences and exceptions. What is perhaps of equal concern to the contraction of these aspects of the public domain in intellectual space is that the public domain that has been created by intellectual property law seems to be a rather thin concept compared with the multilayered idea of the public domain in Roman law. The bounded community envisaged by *res universitatis* is poorly catered for in intellectual property, although licensing devices may be used to create something that looks rather like the bounded creative or innovative community. Such communities are capable of indirectly tilting against the power of the corporate giants by developing an alternative space for creativity and innovation, although their ability to form the basis of a direct attack on the monolith of corporate power is open to question. More capable of mounting such a direct attack is the concept of *res divini juris*, which is grounded in the idea that the potency of some symbols gives too much power to those who might seek to appropriate them. This idea does not seem to have gained much influence in intellectual property law's construction of the public domain, although it does have some atrophying tools that might be used for this purpose.

4   IS THAT ALL THERE IS?

A key aspect of the public domain in both intellectual and physical space is that in order to have vitality it needs to be defended and nurtured. It has been argued above that, in intellectual space, intellectual property law inadequately provides the means for the defence of the public domain. However, intellectual property law is not all the law there is to perform this defensive task. There is a range of other laws that regulate and order activity in intellectual space. These laws include, for instance, censorship, obscenity and blasphemy laws, defamation, laws governing national security, and laws protecting human rights, including the right to free speech. It seems that at least some of these laws have the effect of altering the boundary between the public domain and the propertised zone. For example, there is some evidence that courts will refuse to enforce intellectual property rights in material that is regarded as obscene,[52] or has been produced contrary to national security obligations.[53] In these sorts of cases it is arguable that artefacts in intellectual space are being forced out of the propertised zone and into the public domain, where they will become subject to other forms of regulation designed to ensure that the public domain remains an orderly and productive one. Of course, it might be argued that intellectual property law has attempted to internalise considerations of morality[54] and public policy,[55] with the result that it has pushed material that transgresses certain norms into the public domain, where it may be regulated by areas of law more suited to the purpose. The distinction between what is pushed out by intellectual property law and what is pulled out by other areas of law is, however, rather obscure in many cases. And it is not necessarily clear that what intellectual property law pushes out into the public domain has a significant degree of identity with that which other areas of the law might seek to pull into it.

The relationship between human rights law and intellectual property law is the clearest (if anything here is clear) example of an uncertain tussle at the borders of propertised intellectual space and the public domain. Human rights law, or at least norms driven by this area of law, seems to knock at the door of the propertised domain in intellectual space requesting the release of certain material for limited times and purposes. The classic example of this in relation to patented material has been the demands in the name of human rights for the release or waiver of some of the rights attaching to patents in order to allow the manufacture of generic anti-AIDs medications for supply to those who are unable to afford the purchase of patented medication.[56] It is tempting to argue that patent law, itself, has no mechanisms with which to recognise these types of claims. However, that would be to disregard the utility of the compulsory licence. There may be doubt about whether the contracted notion of the compulsory licence under the WTO Agreement on Trade-Related Intellectual Property Rights[57] would be sufficient to support a compulsory licence in the

---

[52] E.g. *Glyn v Weston Feature Fims* [1916] 1 Ch 261.

[53] E.g. *AG v The Guardian Newspapers (No 2)* [1988] 3 All ER 542; and see also Patfield, F. (1989), 'The House of Lords Decision in the Spycatcher Litigation', 1 *European Intellectual Property Review* 27.

[54] See, e.g., UK Patents Act 1977, s 1(3).

[55] See, e.g., UK Patents Act 1977, s 1(3); and UK Copyright Designs and Patents Act 1988, s 171(3).

[56] See UN Commission on Human Rights (2001), *The Impact of the Agreement on Trade-Related Aspects of Intellectual Property Rights on Human Rights*, Report of the High Commissioner, E/CN.4/Sub.2/2001/13, 27 June; and Weissbrodt, D. and Schoff, K. (2004), 'The Sub-Commission's Initiative on Human Rights and Intellectual Property', 22 *Netherlands Quarterly of Human Rights* 181.

[57] See WTO TRIPS Agreement, art. 31.

circumstances of the HIV-AIDs crisis facing many parts of the world. But this is not to say that a compulsory licensing scheme could never do this job. Presumably patent law could also rise to the task of mitigating other types of human rights concerns with which it has been associated. This might be true, for example, in relation to the abuse of the rights of indigenous peoples that has occurred as a result of ill-gotten gains from bioprospecting[58] or from concerns about food security that have been raised by the acquisition and exercise of rights over biotechnological inventions.[59] Both of these might be addressed by a combination of limitations on patentable subject matter, alterations to the concept of 'inventor', improvements in compulsory licensing, and/or a more extensive regime of exceptions. The question is whether or not internalising human rights concerns into patent law and allowing patent law, then, to be the sole arbiter of the line between the propertised domain and the public domain is an optimal solution.

This same question arises in relation to copyright law, although it is far from clear that copyright law actually has the tools to respond to the human rights issues that it raises. The primary human rights concern in relation to copyright law has arisen in relation to freedom of speech issues.[60] In essence, the tension is between the control that the copyright owner has over the copyright work and the argument that the work should, for certain purposes, subsist in the public domain. Despite the fact that copyright law grounds a system that might be argued to constitute extensive private control over speech, it has shown little concern with freedom of speech issues.

The key to copyright law's comparative inattention to countervailing concepts of free speech appears to be threefold. First, the role of copyright in stimulating expressive diversity is often considered to outweigh or nullify any negative effects on freedom of speech.[61] It is accepted that a certain degree of copyright protection is necessary for the maintenance of free speech, perhaps because it

[58]   See Aoki, K. (1986), 'Neocolonialism, Anticommons Property, and Biopiracy in the (Not-So-Brave) New World Order of International Intellectual Property Protection', 6 *Indiana Journal of Global Legal Studies* 11; and Blakeney, M. (1998), 'Biodiversity Rights and Traditional Resource Rights of Indigenous Peoples', 2 *Bioscience Law Review* 52.

[59]   See Blakeney, M. (2002), 'Protection of Plant Varieties and Farmers' Rights', 24 *European Intellectual Property Review* 9; and Drahos, P. (1999), 'Intellectual Property and Human Rights', 3 *Intellectual Property Quarterly* 349.

[60]   For a comprehensive overview of the relationship between copyright and free speech, see J. Griffiths and U. Suthersanen (eds) (2005), *Copyright and Free Speech: Comparative and International Analyses*, Oxford and New York: Oxford University Press.

[61]   See, e.g., Goldstein, P. (1994), *Copyright's Highway: From Gutenberg to the Celestial Jukebox*, 228ff., esp. 236. For a more nuanced approach to this proposition, see

is likely to encourage expressive autonomy and diversity, but at least because it is likely to encourage the widespread dissemination of such expressive autonomy and diversity. These are, in turn, prerequisites for the sort of vigorous public domain that is essential to maintaining a democratic political and social environment, which is the main utilitarian concern of free speech principles.[62] This does not, however, mean that we should be blind to the possibility that under certain conditions the way that copyright law restricts activities that might otherwise take place in the public domain raises serious freedom of speech concerns.[63]

The second reason why copyright has paid little attention to free speech concerns is that there is a prevailing belief that copyright has internal mechanisms that are capable of dealing with freedom of speech issues, if they arise. Particular emphasis in this respect is placed on the idea/expression dichotomy and the fair dealing defences. There is no doubt that the idea/expression dichotomy is of considerable importance here because it prevents the monopolisation of information and ideas that are capable of being expressed differently from the way in which they are expressed in the material subject to copyright protection. However, the utility of the dichotomy in relation to non-literary copyright material is dubious.[64] Where the idea/expression dichotomy cannot do the job, the fair dealing defences may provide a partial back-up. But it is only partial: despite the potential usefulness of the fair dealing defence for criticism and review, the defences are unable to take into much account the most critical factor in relation to securing free speech.

The critical factor in securing free speech in a vibrant public domain is not so much the extent to which material is subject to property rights, but rather the nature of the right-holder and, specifically, the degree of power wielded generally by that right-holder in intellectual space. This is linked, in a negative way, to the third key to copyright's inattention to free speech principles, which is that the very fact that copyright enables the exercise of private, rather than governmental, control over speech means that the risks that copyright poses to free

---

Netanel, N.W. (1996), 'Copyright and a Democratic Civil Society', 106 *Yale Law Journal* 283, esp. 347–64.

[62]   See Barendt, E. (1987), *Freedom of Speech*, Oxford: Oxford University Press, Ch. 1; Netanel, note 61 *supra*; and Macmillan, F., 'Commodification and Cultural Ownership', in Griffiths and Suthersanen, note 60 *supra*, 35.

[63]   See further Macmillan, note 62 *supra*.

[64]   See further Nimmer, M. (1984), *Freedom of Speech*, 2:05[C], 2–73, concerning photographs of the My Lai massacre; Waldron, note 37 *supra*, 858n, concerning the video film of two white Los Angeles policemen beating Rodney King, a black motorist; Macmillan Patfield, F. (1996), 'Towards a Reconciliation of Free Speech and Copyright', in E.M. Barendt et al., *The Yearbook of Media and Entertainment Law 1996*, 199, 216–19; Macmillan, note 62 *supra*, 57–8.

speech are underestimated or ignored. This is despite the fact that a vigorous public domain is as much threatened by the concentration in private hands of copyright ownership over cultural products as it would be if such ownership were concentrated in the hands of the state. In fact, an argument might even be made that concentration of such ownership in private hands is all the more dangerous because at least the state is accountable for the way it wields power both through the electoral process and through the tools of administrative law. The private sector is, of course, accountable through market mechanisms. Some questions might be raised about the effectiveness of these mechanisms in the case of the media and entertainment corporations, which have vast and valuable property rights in intellectual space and hold overwhelming power in the market for cultural products. Once these corporations have acquired the ability to shape taste and demand through selective release and other devices for cultural filtering and the ability to suppress critical speech about the process of taste-shaping,[65] then the market mechanism may work rather imperfectly.

5 REDRAWING THE BOUNDARIES

As the foregoing discussion has attempted to demonstrate, while there is a range of other laws that regulate intellectual space, only intellectual property has a symbiotic relationship with the public domain. That is, the rights attaching to intellectual property shrink and expand conversely with the alterations in the contours of the public domain. Moreover, intellectual property law is largely responsible for drawing the boundary between what is subject to property rights, when and how, and what is not. Some (shrinking) parts of intellectual space have been ignored or excluded by intellectual property law. Effectively, in Roman law terms they are for the time being something akin to *res communes*, legally incapable of appropriation. Doubtless, there are also vast swathes of intellectual space that might currently be analogised to the Roman law concept of *res nullius*, the space in which things belong to no one because no appropriation recognised by law has yet taken place. However, much of intellectual space has been colonised by intellectual property. Within that space, intellectual property law itself has declared some things to be in the public domain, either for certain limited purposes or by effluxion of time. Most of what is in the public domain for these purposes might be analogised to the concept of *res publicae*, although the current limits to this aspect of the public domain seem to be depriving it of much vitality. Other Roman law concepts of the public domain in

---

[65]   See further Macmillan, note 24 *supra*; Macmillan, F. (2002), 'The Cruel ©: Copyright and Film', *European Intellectual Property Review* 483; Macmillan, note 2 *supra*.

physical space, such as *res divini juris* and *res universitatis*, seem to have had little impact on the way in which intellectual property law creates the public domain in intellectual space.

If intellectual property law not only has a symbiotic relationship with the public domain in intellectual space but also is largely responsible for determining the boundary between it and the exercise of exclusive property rights, then an obvious way in which to give the public domain more vitality is to alter those aspects of intellectual property law that have been identified in this chapter as impacting on the shape of the public domain. Most obviously, this would involve reversing the current trend whereby more and more of intellectual space is sucked into the propertised domain. For copyright law, for example, this would involve limiting if not reversing its tendency to spread horizontally to cover new forms of activity in intellectual space, along with a renewed commitment to distinguishing between ideas and expressions and keeping the former in the intellectual *res communes*. For patent law a wider reading of the classes of innovations that are deemed not to be inventions would do much to curb horizontal spread. It might also be the case that the hurdles of novelty, inventive step and industrial applicability[66] need to be set a little higher. Owing to doubts about whether the concept of *res communes* can have any meaningful existence in intellectual space, it may be that these are really arguments about *res publicae* in intellectual space. (The line between these two concepts, if it exists in intellectual space, is not easy to apply.) What is clearer, however, is that the protection of the *res publicae* in intellectual space requires more than just a reappraisal of the horizontal scope of intellectual property laws.

In order to safeguard the vitality of the *res publicae* in intellectual space, a critical reappraisal of the duration rules is needed, particularly with respect to copyright.[67] In the early life of English copyright law, much of the justification for increases in the duration of copyright appeared to be a manifestation of the influence of romantic conceptions of the author and the author's right to control the work.[68] Given that the process of commodification divorces the author from his or her work[69] so that the author has become a somewhat marginalised figure in copyright law, extensions of the copyright interest based upon the figure of

---

[66] See, e.g., UK Patents Act 1977, ss 1(1), 2 (novelty), 3 (inventive step), and 4 (industrial applicability).

[67] On reforming the duration rules, see further Netanel, note 61 *supra*, 366–71.

[68] See Bently, L. (1994), 'Copyright and the Death of the Author in Literature and Law', 57 *Modern Law Review* 973, 979 and 979n, in which reference is made to Wordworth's support for Sergeant Talfourd's famous campaign to extend the duration of copyright. See also Vaidhyanathan, note 49 *supra*, Ch. 2.

[69] See, e.g., Gaines, J. (1991), *Contested Culture: The Image, the Voice and the Law*, Chapel Hill and London: University of North Carolina Press, p. 10.

the author seem to have little justification. A similar lack of justification affects the contraction of the defences to copyright infringement, especially the fair dealing defences, which are the other important aspect of copyright law that needs to be considered if we are to increase the protection of *res publicae*.[70] Early on in the history of copyright, as a result of the focus on the now marginalised figure of the author, there was a transition in the application of the fair dealing defences from a focus on what the defendant had added to what the defendant had taken.[71] The contraction of the right has moved forwards in leaps and bounds in recent times. Optimists may argue that subsequent decisions on both sides of the Atlantic in cases like *Campbell v Acuff-Rose Music, Inc*[72] and *Time Warner Entertainments Company LP v Channel 4 Television Corporation plc*[73] repair or mitigate some of the damage that *Rogers v Koons*[74] has done to the vitality of the fair dealing/fair use defence as a weapon for securing the intellectual commons. However, the more likely result of this mishmash of case law is to create confusion about the scope of the defence. In comparison, the one thing that might be said in favour of the various defences and exceptions that protect *res publicae* under patent law is that they are so limited that the scope for confusion is considerably less. Of course, this is not to say much. In order to preserve an intellectual space for productive synergistic interactions, serious attention needs to be given to the scope of the research exception.

So far as those parts of the public domain analogous to the concepts of *res divini juris* and *res universitatis* are concerned, as has been argued above, they hardly rate any recognition in the current organisation of intellectual space. There is potential for productive synergies in *res universitatis*, but in the prevailing climate of corporate domination too much valuable intellectual space has already been acquired by interests hostile to the type of closed creative or innovative communities that it envisages. A modern version of *res divini juris* might very well take its place alongside a reinvigorated *res publicae* in order to ensure that the power that might otherwise flow from concentrations of ownership in intellectual space does not give rise to at least some types of unacceptable abuses or limitations on the rights of others. However, even if all the different

---

[70]   On reform of the fair dealing defences, see further Netanel, note 61 *supra*, 376–82; on the need for strong fair dealing defences in the digital environment, see van Caenegem, W. (1995), 'Copyright, Communication and New Technologies', 23 *Federal Law Review* 322.

[71]   Bently, note 68 *supra*, 979n, cites *Sayre v Moore* (1785) in *Cary v Longman* (1801) 1 East 358, 359n, 102 ER 138, 139n; *West v Francis* 5 B and Ald 737, 106 ER 1361; and *Bramwell v Halcomb* (1836) 2 My and Cr 737, 40 ER 1110, as examples of this transition.

[72]   114 S Ct 1164 (1994).

[73]   [1994] EMLR 1.

[74]   Note 27 *supra*.

aspects of the public domain could be catered for using expanded versions of
the devices that intellectual property currently uses, the question of the adequacy
of these devices would remain. Other ways of drawing material out into the
public domain of intellectual space may also be needed. At present the most
obvious tools for this lie within the realms of human rights law. This area of law
does not yet seem to have adapted itself for this purpose, although its adaptation
remains a viable option. What is arguably important in any future development
of this kind is that the relevant aspects of human rights law are not subsumed
into intellectual property law. The inevitable result of such subsumption will be
the subjugation of human rights to the essentialism of the property paradigm.
Human rights will then go the way of all the other exceptions to intellectual
property law designed to maintain the public domain. Rather, to be effective in
manipulating the border of the propertised zone and the public domain in intellectual space, human rights law needs to maintain its own integrity as an area
of law in potential normative clash with intellectual property law.

The fate of the public interest defence is a classic example of subsumption
to the essentialism of the property paradigm. This has perhaps been most marked
in common law jurisdictions in relation to attempts to use it to restrict the exercise of interests attaching to copyright material. In Australia, for example, doubts
about the existence of this right as a defence to an action for copyright infringement are relatively longstanding.[75] The decision of the US Supreme Court in
Eldred v Ashcroft[76] is eloquent testament to the fact that public interest will
rarely, if ever, trump the proprietary interests of the copyright holder. In the
United Kingdom, even before the decision of the English Court of Appeal in
Hyde Park v Yelland,[77] which appeared to have killed off the right in the United
Kingdom, there was considerable evidence that the courts were unwilling to
engage with the question of the relationship between copyright and the public
interest.[78] However, the subsequent decision of the Court of Appeal in *Ashdown
v Telegraph Group*[79] shows that the public interest right may yet have a spark
of life in the United Kingdom, although it is unclear whether this decision will

[75]   See Gummow, J., in *Corrs Pavey Whiting & Byrne v Collector of Customs for the
State of Victoria* (1987), 10 *Intellectual Property Reports* 53, 70–77, and *Smith, Kline
& French Laboratories (Australia) Ltd v Secretary, Department of Community Services
& Health* (1990), 17 *Intellectual Property Reports* 545, 583.
[76]   Note 26 *supra*.
[77]   [2001] Ch. 143, CA.
[78]   See, e.g., *Secretary of State for the Home Department v Central Broadcasting*
[1993] EMLR 253 and *Beggars Banquet Records Ltd v Carlton Television* [1993] EMLR
349. See also Macmillan Patfield, note 64 *supra*, 223–5.
[79]   [2002] Ch. 149, CA.

have much, if any, application apart from preserving the right to speak freely in the overtly party political arena.

Despite this rather sorry catalogue, perhaps it is time for an attempt to reinvigorate the notion of a public interest right as an independent vehicle to defend the public domain in the circumstances where the exceptions and defences created by intellectual property law are unable to do the job. Given the flexibility of the public interest concept and the fact that its clash with intellectual property rights is not unexplored legal territory, perhaps it might be a sufficiently capacious vehicle to carry and deploy the human rights concerns that are increasingly implicated in the propertisation of intellectual space. More might even be said for it in an ideal world where it could carry part of the burden of ensuring public accountability for the exercise of private power. In any case, there is a good argument that we need to find some bulwark against the domination of intellectual space by private corporate interests that have now acquired so much power that they are able to shape intellectual property law, and its range of exceptions and defences, for their own benefit.

7. Creativity, innovation and intellectual property: a new approach for the 21st century[1]

John Howkins

1 INTRODUCTION: SETTING THE SCENE

One of the key issues facing us today is the relationship between people's crea-tivity, which is usually private, personal and local, and global governance, standards and laws on intellectual property. It is a contentious issue because it involves not only our free speech and free expression but how we choose to live in societies based increasingly on monetising ideas.

The strength of both individual ambition and corporate power can lead to conflict and bad feeling. We need a new approach. I believe the way to resolve the tension lies through a better understanding of the process of creativity and innovation. I want to explore how, at each stage of the creative process, ideas move back and forth between the private and public domains. I also want to discuss the RSA Adelphi Charter on Creativity, Innovation and Intellectual Property which arose, in part, from these concerns.

My other reference point is the creative economy. I prefer the word 'economy' to 'industry' because I want to include all parts of the process from production (supply) to consumption and use (demand). The word 'industry' puts too much emphasis on the supply-side and not enough on the demand side. I also want to include the public. One of the characteristics of the creative economy is that it is an economy based on the individual, both as creator and as user. This, by it-self, marks a dramatic difference from conventional extractive and agricultural economies, which are based on the land, and from manufacturing and service economies, which are based on the firm.

In recent years, the core creative economy has grown in size and importance. It was worth $2.2 trillion in 2001 and $2.9 trillion in 2005 and is likely to be

---

[1]   This chapter is based on discussions at the Shanghai Intellectual Property Forum, 2005.

worth around \$4.1 trillion in 2010. This core economy consists of the industries best noted for turning new ideas into new products: advertising, architecture, art, crafts, design, fashion, film, music, performing arts, publishing, R&D, software, toys and games, TV and radio, and video games. It makes up about 7.8 per cent of world trade. Growth rates average 5 per cent a year, although that figure hides wide disparities between different sectors.

This or similar groups of core industries have attracted a lot of attention recently, often skewed towards a cultural or arts theme. However, it is increasingly accepted that focusing on specific industries can be misleading. It is difficult if not impossible to set limits to the creative economy (and, given the claim of 'creativity', invidious). It is also obvious that many creative industries are also manufacturing and service industries, such as crafts and broadcasting. The importance of the creative economy is not limited to any one single group of industries. It is based on a *way of working* that is found in almost all industries. Likewise, intellectual property law is no respecter of particular industries, but is applicable to every industry and indeed to everyone in society.

The world's finance, industry, trade and even culture ministries are only just beginning to grasp this. Many policy-makers are still ignorant of and uncomfortable with the basic principles of intellectual property (IP); for example, they do not understand the balance between private rights and public access, they do not appreciate the difference between patents and copyright, they do not collect accurate data, and they are happy to leave policy-making to national patent offices and the courts. This lack of understanding is a major problem, not only because IP is now economically important but because it deals with the stuff of politics: the boundary line between what is public and what is private. What is being fought over affects how we work together, how we access knowledge and how we get rewards.

The battles around this line can be vigorous. On the one hand, there are increasing demands for more IP rights, more patentability and stricter enforcement. On the other hand, there are substantial trends in the opposite direction: towards more open access, more free collaboration and more relaxed licensing. Both groups (the defenders of private property and the defenders of the public domain) get daily more passionate and more entrenched in their views.

Although these debates use the terminology of copyright and patents, at heart they are fundamentally about the merits of free markets and the role of public regulation.

2   SOME EXAMPLES

Let me illustrate the scale of the problem with some examples. First, the Internet. The Internet is one of the most remarkable tools the world has ever known for sharing information and knowledge, and for allowing us to make contact with other people and with what they are saying, writing, making and doing. It is continually offering up new possibilities, new ideas, new friendships, new networks and new businesses.

But it presents a challenge. The Internet is a massive copying machine. It works because it allows us to upload and download, copy and share, on a massive scale. But if we apply the laws that regulate, say, copying printed books to copying Web files, then we will strangle the Web.

The nature of the Web means it is a major threat to businesses that depend on restricted access and restricted copying. The first to be hit was the music recording industry, which said on-line copying threatened its profits, if not its existence. The TV and film industries followed suit. Then the print publishers got worried. I suspect nobody knows the Internet's real impact on these industries. But it is possible to make some comments.

One, the possibility of infringement is immense. Two, it is increasingly accepted that the best solution, alongside sensible laws sensibly enforced, is better business models. Three, many if not most companies will survive. The ones that go will be replaced by others. Four, the nature of musical, audiovisual and written forms, and the way we use them, will change but not by much. My feeling is that these last two outcomes are evolutionary rather than revolutionary and I would be hard pressed to say whether they are positive or negative.

Meanwhile, companies should be moderate in their use of digital rights management (DRM). Sony's use of XCP copy protection software on CDs, which affected the user's operating system and set up links between the user and Sony without the user's permission, went too far.

From a policy-makers' perspective, it is vital at this stage to protect the Internet's essential freedoms. But we must also enable people to be rewarded for their work and investment. What is the right balance between freedom and enforcement? How do we answer that question?

Another topical Internet issue is webcasting. I believe that the draft of the WIPO Treaty on webcasting agreed at the 2005 WIPO General Assembly is not only against the interest of webcasters (I write as a former chairman of a webcasting company) but also against the interests of the public. WIPO's Standing Committee on Copyright and Related Rights (SCCR), which met in November 2005, said its new draft had won significant support. But in the words of James Love, Executive Director, CPTech, Washington DC, the proposal is 'an effort to radically change the ownership of information and knowledge goods, based upon who transmits information, rather than who creates the work'. If we extend this logic further, he asks, 'should we grant an intellectual property right to Amazon Books because it makes books available to the public?' The webcasting treaty would extend protection over distribution systems like the Internet which merely transmit other people's material – including material in the public domain. That must be wrong. Again, how do we decide?

My next example is patentability. In October 2005, the US Board of Patent Appeals decided in Ex Parte Lundgren, US Board of Patent Appeals, Appeal No. 2003-2058, 2005 (on the method of calculating a way to compensate a sales person) to allow the patenting of an idea that had no element of technology. The majority opinion said Lundgren's claim produced a 'useful, concrete, tangible result' without being a 'law of nature, physical phenomenon or abstract idea'. It is therefore patentable. Regarding the Patent Office's reference to US Patent Law, section 101, and its use of the so-called 'technological arts' test, the majority opinion said the law did not justify the test. This decision is as least as significant as the Supreme Court's decision on *State Street Bank and Trust Co v Signature Financial Group 149 F3d 1368 (Fed Cir 1998); Cert denied 525 US 1093 (1999)* in 1998, which allowed what are known as business method patents. It has profound implications for innovation and competition. Already, the US Patent Office has published patent applications for stories. I believe business method patents are absurd and should not be issued.

There is also deep concern with the patentability of the human genome. It is estimated that US companies have patented over 18 per cent of the genome. This is worrying not so much for what the patent-holders might use the genes for (and beneficial uses would be wholly welcome), but because the patent-holders will block or slow down any related research by other companies, which is wholly bad. Again, this raises the question: how do we regulate access to knowledge?

My final example focuses on the politicians who are responsible for representing the public interest in these matters. In 2005, as bird flu became widespread, the global patent system was sharply criticised because of Roche's manufacturing and marketing rights in Tamiflu. Or, to be precise, about the balance between Roche's private rights and society's need for public healthcare. The point is not to criticise Gilead, which actually invented the anti-viral, nor Roche, which acquired manufacturing and marketing rights, but to set a new balance in the light of a possible pandemic. The global community had faced this challenge before with the AIDS crisis. This time, however, the crisis affected everyone, rich and poor. Of course, TRIPS allows government patent offices to enforce compulsory licences in a public health emergency, subject to several conditions. Yet, in 2003 some 30 countries opted out of the TRIPS Section 30 exemption, which allows imports, as well as domestic production, of generic drugs in such emergencies. I believe many governments were not fully aware of what they had done. I believe they were widely out of step with public feeling. Most European countries decided to stockpile Tamiflu to treat only 27 per cent of the population. I believe that Europeans with avian flu who discovered the EU had decided not to allow imports of generics would be annoyed and justifiably so.

These examples (the Internet, the patentability of business methods and genetic sequences, and avian flu) all turn on the balance of right-holders' exclusive rights, access and enforcement. The last one also raises the question of political and public awareness.

3   A PROPOSAL

Now to my proposal. I always believe that you have to ask the right question to get the right answer. If you ask the wrong question, you never get the right answer. The obvious question is this: is the system of IP that we had in place at the end of the 20th century the right one, the most appropriate one, for the 21st century? Or, what is the right way to regulate ideas in the 21st century?

To answer this we have to ask another question: what is IP for? This question seldom gets asked. There is a phrase, 'the elephant in the room', indicating something very big and very important but also very embarrassing which everyone pretends is not there. The question, 'What is the purpose of IP?', is the elephant in the room.

What is the answer? IP laws provide a means to establish and protect one's exclusive rights. We need them to provide the incentives and rewards that are an essential part of the economic value chain. We need them to ensure business contracts are solid and robust. When I license a film on DVD, both I and the licensee need to have a common understanding which underpins what is being licensed and how the licence will be enforced.

There is a second purpose which is built into every IP law but which some policy-makers and many observers find counter-intuitive and secondary. This is that the laws enable people to have access to what has been created. For example, all patent systems require the patent to be published so that others can see what has been invented and how it works. All copyrights come with limitations and exceptions that are just as important as the rights themselves. All patents and copyrights have limited terms.

But these two objectives – linking incentives and rewards to access – are not the whole answer to the question, 'What is IP for?' There is another level, which can be described as the politics of IP. Why do we need these things – incentives, rewards, access? And, when they are in conflict, as they often are, how should we decide what to do? Which should predominate? Is there a public interest involved? Faced with formulating the right copyright policy for, say, digital media, how do we ensure the public interest is served?

This question elicits some interesting answers. The major production industries have a simple ideology. It is based on the belief that we have a basic right to our ideas, to the output of our brain, and that we have a right to charge others compensation if they want to use our ideas. In this world, incentives and rewards must always take priority, must always trump access.

This argument has a sound moral and economic base. Its morals are based on the principle that our ownership of our body, our minds and our thoughts is what defines us as independent free-thinking people. It marks out the free person from the slave. Its economics can be found in companies' revenue figures and on their balance sheets. An increasing percentage of global business depends on IP. It is understandable that these companies and their governments, who are keen to make their economies more competitive and to protect jobs, believe these intellectual assets must be protected. This attitude can be summed up in the phrase, 'the more IP the better' (that is, the stronger the rights, the stronger the economy).

But there is another approach, which puts access over and above incentives and rewards. This approach is based on three arguments. First, access to existing data, ideas and knowledge is the starting point of all *new* ideas. Second, Europe, the USA and Japan industrialised successfully in the 19th and 20th centuries, when their copyright and patent laws were weak, and many developing countries claim, as they industrialise, that they would benefit from similarly weak laws. Third, many major initiatives continue to benefit from weak laws and licences: for example, Free and Open Source Software, the World Wide Web and the majority of education and research.

The argument here is that IP certainly offers incentives and rewards but does so at the cost of slowing down and inhibiting other work. The reluctance of the USA, which is normally found in the first camp, to adopt the Rome Convention's related rights for broadcasting, or to follow the European model for protecting databases, provides provocative evidence for this argument.

These arguments are espoused by the BRICK group (Brazil, Russia, India, China and Korea) but have implications for all countries, large and small. They are also supported by a wide range of organisations under the title, 'Access to Knowledge'.

4 A NEW ANSWER

I want to suggest a new answer to the question, 'What is IP for?' It is based on what we know about the creative economy.

The phrase, creative economy, emphasises creativity's economic and financial aspects. But it is equally a cultural and social phenomenon. The social and the economic work hand in hand. How did the creative economy come about? Its origins lie in the arts and culture and, especially, in government's active promotion of their economic importance. Technology is certainly a major factor, especially TV, the computer and the Internet. Equally important are some fundamental demographic trends, such as increased population sizes, increased levels of immigration, the spread of open liberal societies, globalisation, free speech, the spread of mass education, and the growth in people's disposable income, which has created new markets for art and design.

What has emerged is a new freedom for the individual to have, share and enjoy new ideas: a freedom to make their ideas central to their lives, and to use their ideas to build up their own personality, identity and status; to build up their earning power and their own creative capital.

Of course, some people have always worked in this way, such as professional artists, writers and composers, and flourished in some places, such as cultural institutions. But the point is that creativity is no longer restricted to such people or to such places. It is now the favoured activity of millions of people and can be found almost everywhere: at home, at work, in schools, in small groups, on the street and, of course, in cyberspace. The numbers of people thinking about and using other people's ideas and creating their own ideas – ideas that may be copyrightable or patentable – can no longer be counted in thousands but run to many millions. Creativity is now part of daily life for millions of people.

We can see the emergence of three spheres of creativity. First, the business of producing and distributing commercial work (such as books, films, TV programmes), which often requires large financial investments. Then, alongside and overlapping, are two new spheres: a sphere of people, often working collaboratively, who are willing for others to use their work for non-commercial purposes; and an even larger sphere of countless people who are exploring ideas, sounds and images, and creating work with little thought of its commercial value or, to be more precise, of claiming any exclusive rights over it.

These three spheres, *taken together*, must be the basis for IP in the 21st century. We need to recognise each sphere's characteristics – and differences. Each sphere must accept the other; which means the people in each sphere must accept each other. Those in the first sphere must accept users not merely as consumers but as people with their own basic rights including the right to access knowledge and make their own work.

I am therefore proposing that we use IP law as a means of *regulating* the creative economy. We can see some immediate implications. Laws on intellectual property should not be seen as ends in themselves but as means of achieving social, cultural and economic goals. These goals should be explicitly stated and approved by parliament (in the same way as are public interest goals in other areas of society).

I suggest the goal should be to support creativity and innovation. All laws should be tested against this objective, and the tests should be open, rigorous and independent. All laws should be required to be shown to support people's basic rights and economic well-being. Intellectual property protection should not be extended over abstract ideas, facts and data.

Some of these principles are taken from the new RSA Adelphi Charter on Creativity, Innovation and Intellectual Property, which was launched in London in October 2005.[2] The Charter was prepared by an international commission of artists, scientists, lawyers, Internet experts, consumer representatives and business people (including musician Gilberto Gil, who is Brazil's Minister of Culture; Nobel laureate Sir John Sulston; and Lawrence Lessig, Chair of Creative Commons). It sets out principles for the public regulation of IP in the public interest, based firmly on creativity and innovation.

There are obvious implications for international governance, particularly within WIPO, the WTO and TRIPS as well as UNESCO. The organisations which drafted a treaty on Access to Knowledge (A2K) in 2004 had hit upon an essential wrongness about the current IP system and a novel way of putting it right. The wrongness was the system's essential bias towards private, corporate interests and the way of putting it right was to replace this bias with the principle that access to knowledge should be the starting point, not some marginal add-on.

With hindsight we can see that WIPO was going through the same convulsions as some other UN organisations had gone through in the 1980s and 1990s. The most obvious similarity is with the International Telecommunication Union (ITU), also based in Geneva, which for over 100 years has regulated telecommunications, in particular managing the electro-magnetic spectrum and setting equipment and transmission standards. In the late 1970s, government moves towards liberalisation, first in the USA and then in Europe, meant that the ITU, which till then had been the preserve of state telecom and broadcasting monopolies, was opened up to private competitive interests. With these new interests came user representatives. After a difficult few years the ITU accepted these new interests. It also recognised the particular needs of developing countries. Anyone watching the development of the ITU through the 1980s might have forecast the shocks awaiting WIPO in the 1990s.

5 CONCLUSION: ACCESS, USE AND REWARDS

As I said earlier, we know a lot about some key elements of creativity and innovation – about how to be creative and how to maximise our ability to have good ideas and make money. We have realised that these principles can be ap-

---

[2] More information on the RSA Adelphi Charter can be found at www.adelphicharter.org.

plied in almost every industry, in almost every situation. We also know how to use IP laws to support the creative economy. Governments need to apply a public interest test to ensure their IP laws protect the public domain as well as private rights, in order to support the next round of creative people.

These three factors, access, use and rewards, are the core of the creative economy. They affect how we use our creative imagination, and how each country will develop, socially and economically, in the coming years.

8. The public domain and the librarian

Toby Bainton

1 INTRODUCTION

The librarian's mission is to help people find the information they need. This goal remains valid even if the individual library users are unsure what their information needs really are. Very often librarians pursue this mission despite their comparative lack of expertise in the library user's chosen topic. Increasingly the librarian is intent on helping library users who may not have entered a building called a library but are nevertheless using materials supplied, through the intervention of librarians, to their desktop.

2 THE WORK OF THE LIBRARIAN

The concept of the public domain becomes important as soon as the requisite information has been found. Library-based information is invariably recorded information, traditionally in printed form but nowadays very often in digital formats. As such it is likely to be subject to copyright or other intellectual property rights. These rights are steadily increasing in extent, either through prolongation of term or through the establishment of new rights. In the UK the term of copyright was extended in 1995 from 50 to 70 years by the Duration of Copyright and Rights in Performances Regulations[1] and an example of a new right is the database right, introduced in 1997 by the Copyright and Rights in Databases Regulations.[2] Intellectual property rights are important for every library user since they may well restrict how the information they have discovered may be used. Only material in the public domain may safely be used by library users with complete freedom.

It follows that, to a librarian, great importance attaches to the distinction between public domain material, on the one hand, and material subject to copyright

---

[1] S.I.1995 No. 3297.
[2] S.I.1997 No. 3032.

or database right, on the other. The difference is crucial because library users very often wish to copy the material they have successfully identified as meeting their needs. They are unlikely to wish to copy it all (most students, for example, eventually learn that photocopying is an inadequate substitute for reading), but to copy selections or extracts is often convenient for future reference. Transmitting the material electronically almost invariably transgresses any rights subsisting in it. If the material in question does not lie in the public domain, librarians are unwise to abandon their users at the point when it has merely been found. Experienced library users look to their librarian for guidance about intellectual property rights, while inexperienced users, if they are not to infringe copyright or database right, may well need the guidance put before them uninvited. One outstanding challenge for the librarian is the widespread current assumption that anything that is available on the Web is, by that very fact, in the public domain and subject to no restrictions at all.

Librarians also take seriously their obligations to right-holders. They make it their professional business to accumulate stores of published works, so they have a clear duty to respect the rights pertaining to those works.[3]

In principle, the librarian's situation is disarmingly simple. If the information sought by the library user proves to be in the public domain, professional duty need be taken no further. The librarian has succeeded simply by enabling it to be found. But if the material is subject to copyright or database right, it behoves the librarian to advise how much, if any, of the material may be copied.

Of course, complexity of practice often accompanies simplicity of principle. Defining the public domain, not always straightforward even in the abstract, is notoriously difficult in the individual example presented to librarians. In the abstract one might say that the public domain embraces all recorded material in which intellectual property rights (a) cannot, in principle, subsist; or (b) have been waived; or (c) have expired. Category (a) scarcely exists with regard to material in 21st-century libraries unless one includes, for example, the publications of the United Nations and the United States federal government, whose copyrights have been officially waived en bloc. Within the European Union, even simple recorded facts, until recently clearly in the public domain, may now be subject to database right if their obtaining, verification and/or presentation has been the subject of substantial investment. Category (b) is less rare but presents the difficulty that the rights must not only be waived – they must be known without doubt to have been waived. Category (c) is where librarians, and many library users, feel more confident about the extent of the public domain.

---

[3]   Much of this assessment of the librarian's view of the public domain applies also to archivists. Archivists more frequently than librarians face the challenges of unpublished works, whose eventual entry into the public domain is problematic.

One of the relatively well-known facts about copyright in the library environment is that copyright expires 70 years after the death of the author. But when did the author die? And can the librarian be really confident in this '70 years *post mortem auctoris*' rule? British law provides about fifty different variations in copyright term alone.[4] Moreover library material may be subject to database right as well as or instead of copyright: indeed, whether or not the material looks like a 'database', the growing trend towards digital editions of published works makes this complication increasingly likely.

Academic librarians in particular have to remember the international ramifications of the public domain. This is because research is very often conducted on an international basis. Even an individual researcher may wish to consult libraries in different countries. Dr David Sutton recently compared the boundaries of the public domain, as they affect a writer's unpublished papers, in the UK on the one hand and in the USA on the other. He wrote:

> As you can imagine, in the UK we are preparing for a huge Public Domain Celebration Party on 1 January 2040 ... the most recent British copyright legislation ... virtually abolished perpetual copyright. Perpetual copyright in the UK now subsists only in the Bible, the Book of Common Prayer, and J.M. Barrie's *Peter Pan*. The perpetual protection previously afforded to unpublished works has been removed, but transitional arrangements ... gave a further period of protection for fifty years from the Act's implementation in 1989 – until midnight on 31 December 2039.[5]

Dr Sutton points out that this postponement of the public domain in the United Kingdom contrasts with the archival cut-off date in the USA of 1 January 2003: 'From 2003, for manuscripts, the 70-year post-mortem figure in the USA becomes fixed – meaning that all the manuscripts of any author who died in 1933 or earlier are now out of copyright.'[6]

To a scholar studying an author whose papers are held in libraries in different countries, the public domain becomes an immensely complicated concept, as indeed it does to any librarian attempting to give advice. Dr Sutton points out the consequences of varying terms of protection – that is, varying boundaries of the public domain – in different countries:

> This leaves us in a situation in which, for a work by D.H. Lawrence where part of the manuscript is in the University of Texas at Austin and part in the University of Nottingham Library, the Texas part of the manuscript is in the public domain from

---

[4]   Adams, J.N. and Edenborough, M. (1996), 'The Duration of Copyright in the United Kingdom after the 1995 Regulations', *European Intellectual Property Review*, **18** (11), 23–6.

[5]   Sutton, D. (2004), 'International Perspectives on Archival Copyright', in 15th International Congress on Archives, p. 4, available from www.wien2004.ica.org.

[6]   Ibid. at 6.

2003, while the Nottingham part of the manuscript remains in copyright until 2040. Any D.H. Lawrence manuscript housed in the Bibliothèque Nationale in Paris has (since he died in 1930) been out of copyright since 2001.[7]

A similar difficulty at the interface of copyright and the public domain lies in the phenomenon of the 'orphan work'. Large libraries usually contain many books that are out of print and whose authors have died. Being unobtainable commercially they are often assumed to be in the public domain. When the librarian is asked about copying them, or even asked to do the copying, the reply (explaining that copyright still subsists) disappoints the enquirer. Even more disappointing, as a rule, is the subsequent train of investigations, especially if the publisher has gone out of business, to find the current copyright holder in order to obtain any permission relating to the copyright. As the years pass it in fact becomes increasingly difficult for a law-abiding citizen to obtain reliable consent to do something restricted by copyright. The Web-based enquiry service WATCH (Writers, Artists, and their Copyright Holders[8]) reveals the challenge of tracing copyright holders for this purpose.

3   CONCLUSION

In essence the public domain is a useful concept for the librarian, and the wider the public domain, the easier it is to help library users. Unfortunately it seems highly unlikely that the boundaries of the public domain will widen – legislative proposals tend on the contrary to extend rights and reduce the area of public freedom. Cautious optimism for the future is perhaps justified on some limited fronts.

The existence of the Web – something that looks and feels like a public domain though it is no such thing – seems to be prompting public discussion. For example, the Geneva Declaration of Principles and Plan of Action from the World Summit on the Information Society, Geneva, 10–12 December 2003, contains the following at the beginning of its action line 'C3: Access to information and knowledge':

> ICTs allow people, anywhere in the world, to access information and knowledge almost instantaneously. Individuals, organizations and communities should benefit from access to knowledge and information. a) Develop policy guidelines for the development and promotion of public domain information as an important international instrument promoting public access to information.

---

[7]   Ibid.
[8]   For more information see tyler.hrc.utexas.edu.

In 2004 the European Commission held a workshop on the public domain, which concluded that:

> problematic issues in the legal framework for copyright and neighbouring rights should be addressed, in particular the exceptions to the copyright directive, to allow for greater legal certainty on issues relevant to libraries and the scientific community. User and consumer rights should be treated on a par with the prerogatives of right holders and not as mere exceptions.[9]

In 2005 the Commission's Information Society Directorate proposed a green paper on this very topic,[10] which promises to look at the pressures on the public domain and the resulting risks of 'a stifling effect on creative efforts, scientific progress and traditional user rights'.

The Creative Commons movement is a brave attempt to produce a 'near-public' domain through clear indications by right-holders setting aside some of their rights for the benefit of the public.

Early in 2005 the United States Copyright Office asked for public comments on the 'orphan works' problem and has since published a report.[11] Perhaps this might even be solved, since it afflicts big media companies as well as librarians. In order to bring large numbers of 'orphan works' into the public domain, only a small amendment to UK law would be needed, borrowing wording from section 41(2) of the Copyright, Designs and Patents Act 1988: 'An act of copying a published work does not infringe copyright if at the time the copy is made the person making it does not know, and has not by reasonable inquiry ascertained, the name and address of a person entitled to authorise the making of the copy'. Such an amendment would deprive no right-holder of any right, or even any income, unless they have allowed themselves to become unreasonably difficult to trace. At a stroke the public domain would be enlarged to embrace thousands of works that have in effect been abandoned by the current system. Librarians tend to be optimists, but no librarian expects this change to occur in the near future.

---

9 Quoted in *EBLIDA Annual Report 2004–2005*, available from www.eblida.org.
10 Work programme 2005/INFSO/010.
11 For full details of the consultation process and of the recommendations made by the US Library of Congress see www.copyright.gov/orphan.

9. The public domain and the creative author

Bill Thompson

1 INTRODUCTION

The public domain is little understood, rarely defended in the public prints and under constant attack from those who would have all works of the human imagination kept under lock and key through a combination of perpetual copyright and technological protection measures.[1] Even while it persists it is often hard to determine whether a particular piece of work is in the public domain, and since the rules differ in different jurisdictions the status of all but the most obvious – for which read 'older' – works must often be considered questionable.

The idea of the public domain is not well defined in English and Scottish law and serves only as a catch-all for the collection of works whose use is not constrained by law – the inverse of the set of 'works in copyright'. It is not even mentioned in the discussion of copyright in McNae's *Essential Law for Journalists*,[2] the standard text for UK journalism students.

Clarity over its applicability is even further diminished by its rather cavalier use in the press, where it is often called on as a longhand version of 'public',

---

[1]   One advocate of a much stronger approach to copyright is Bruce Lehman, Commissioner of Patents for President Bill Clinton. Speaking in 1995 he said: 'Creators, publishers and distributors of works will be wary of the electronic marketplace unless the law provides them the tools to protect their property against unauthorized use' and 'Creators and other owners of intellectual property rights will not be willing to put their interests at risk if appropriate systems – both in the U.S. and internationally – are not in place to permit them to set and enforce the terms and conditions under which their works are made available', Lehman, B. (1995), Statement before the Subcommittee on Courts and Intellectual Property, Committee on the Judiciary, United States House of Representatives and the Committee on the Judiciary, available at www.uspto.gov/web/offices/com/doc/ipnii/nii-hill.html. For discussion on copyright and technological protection measures see Cahir, J., 'The Public Domain: Right or Liberty?', Chapter 3 in this volume.

[2]   Welsh, T., Greenwood, G. and Banks, D. (2005), *McNae's Essential Law for Journalists*, 18th edn, Oxford: Oxford University Press.

as in *The Guardian* of 9 December 2005, where a feature on the singer George Michael describes his problems as being 'played out in the public domain'[3] when 'in public' would have been a more appropriate expression.

2   THE PUBLIC DOMAIN AND THE WRITER

Writers of non-fiction are well aware of the public domain, partly because much of their professional life seems to consist of clearing rights, finding licence-free photographs and ensuring that their use of sources is allowable. However rights are less of an issue for writers of fiction, and in consequence there is much less comprehension of the nature or importance of out-of-copyright works. While a great deal of attention is paid to the few clear cases of plagiarism, much less consideration is given to the way that writers of fiction make legitimate use of material drawn from the work of others.

Despite this lack of awareness, it is hard to overstate the practical importance of the public domain for all writers, or to exaggerate the damage caused by recent moves to restrict its scope and stop works either dropping out of copyright or being available for use when they do. Creative writers make use of the public domain in a wide range of contexts, from a literary novel like Sena Jeter Naslund's *Ahab's Wife*,[4] which appropriates characters from Melville's *Moby Dick*, to 'Tales from the Public Domain', episode 14 of *The Simpsons'* 13th season, which ruthlessly plunders *The Odyssey* and *Hamlet* for our entertainment.[5] Non-fiction writers use eyewitness testimony in books on earthquakes,[6] or reproduce documents verbatim in history books, knowing that they are out of copyright and do not need to be cleared or licensed.

However the relationship between the writer and the public domain is far from clear-cut. While many look to Newton, 'standing on the shoulders of Giants',[7] as the clearest expression of a writer's relation to the wider culture and

---

[3]   Hattenstone, S. (2005), 'There was so much death', available at www.guardian.co.uk/filmandmusic/story/0,,1662016,00.html 9 December 2005.

[4]   Naslund, S.N. (2000), *Ahab's Wife*, London: Harper Perennial.

[5]   Groening, M. (2001), *The Simpsons One Step Beyond Forever: A Complete Guide to Our Favorite Family ... Continued Yet Again*, London: Harper.

[6]   Rooney, A. (2006), *Explore It: Earthquakes and Volcanoes*, San Diego: Silver Dolphin Books.

[7]   In a letter to Robert Hooke, Newton wrote, 'what Descartes did was a good step. You have added much in several ways and especially in taking the colours of thin plates into philosophical consideration. If I have seen further it is by standing on the shoulders of Giants', Newton, I. (1676 [1959]), Letter to Hooke 5 February 1676, in *The Correspondence of Isaac Newton Vol. II 1676–1687*, ed. Turnbull, H.W., Cambridge: published for the Royal Society at the University Press, p. 1416.

to material that is in the public domain, the metaphor seems more fitting for an analysis of the progress of science and sits far less comfortably where writers are concerned.

For a writer the 'public domain' is not a high cliff from which to survey the world of literature but the mulch on the forest floor of creativity through which we chew our way, insect-like. It is the sea within which we swim as we develop our ideas, the source of our metaphors, the wellspring of analogy, homage and parody – the dumpster on the sidewalk of the road to successful imagination, ready to be dived into. Because it encompasses all that is free, and freely available, to plunder, take from, work with and even, on occasion, reproduce verbatim, the public domain defines an intellectual commons where all can walk free, one whose bounty is available to all who would take it, without the limitations which constrain the exploitation of real-world common lands and result in tragedies such as over-fishing, land erosion and eco-catastrophe. In the intellectual commons the overuse of a metaphor may make it stale and unattractive, but the allegorical grass constantly renews itself and can be grazed by many sheep.

3   THE DIMINUTION OF THE PUBLIC DOMAIN

Since it is important to all creative writers, there would seem to be a pressing need to create, defend, grow and cultivate this commons and ensure that its boundaries are drawn more widely not less; yet everywhere around us we see newly imposed limits on its scope. Material is removed from the public domain by new laws which extend copyright, while our ability to use what we find there is limited by restrictive licenses which replace copyright law with contractual terms and conditions that pay no heed to the need to balance the interests of creators and the public sphere. The interests of right-holders are given precedence, despite the lack of any clear evidence that rigid and extensive copyright protection has a positive impact on the volume or quality of creative output.

Sometimes the new dispensation aspires to levels of such foolishness that there must be a real danger that a performance art project is being misinterpreted. For example, in late 2005 it was announced that patent agent Andrew Knight is attempting to patent a movie plotline in the USA and may then sue film-makers who replicate, even inadvertently, his ideas.[8,9]

Sometimes it is more clearly dangerous, as with the way that laws designed to protect the interests of right-holders allow them to wrap digital rights

---

[8]   Andrew Knight's website is at www.plotpatents.com.
[9]   OUT-LAW News (2005), 'Zombie story seeks US patent', available at www.out-law.com/page-6303, 4 November.

management (DRM) systems around published material and then prosecute those who circumvent the DRM even if the purpose for which the material is to be used is itself perfectly permissible. In this way copyright law is superseded, and rights which might be granted under the law are removed and replaced by far more restrictive licences, which are themselves protected by rigid legislation that allows no fair dealing defence.

4   COPYRIGHT AND CONTRACT

According to Waelde and McGinley, 'the law mediates between absolute property rights and the commons';[10] but it does not have to be copyright law that performs this function, and we are increasingly moving towards a situation where copyright is replaced by click-through end-user licences for digital content, using contract law to establish the absolute property rights that copyright law was originally invented to deny to publishers. We may be seeing the end of the model established almost 300 years ago in the Statute of Anne of 1710.[11]

This situation is already widespread when it comes to recorded music and film. DVD movies are protected using a rights management system called CSS, the content scrambling system. It is therefore illegal to copy a DVD since doing so requires you to break CSS, and laws like the US Digital Millennium Copyright Act protect these 'technological protection measures'. When you buy a song from Apple Computer's iTunes Music Store, it comes locked with a digital rights management system called 'Fairplay', developed and owned by Apple. In order to buy from iTunes you have to agree not to attempt to remove this protection,[12] and indeed the US Digital Millennium Copyright Act, UK copyright law and statutes in many other jurisdictions make it illegal so to do. Unfortunately Fairplay is supported only by Apple's iPod music players, so you cannot play songs you have bought on other players, like a Sony or iRiver, unless you are willing to break the law.

This is not really about copyright law, but it limits purchasers' use of licensed material and makes it, for example, impossible to assert one's right to resell books and music that have already been paid for. It often means that a reader

---

[10]   Waelde, C. and McGinley, M. (2005), 'Public Domain; Public Interest; Public Funding: focussing on the "three Ps" in scientific research', 2:1 *SCRIPT-ed* 83 @: www. law.ed.ac.uk/ahrb/script-ed/vol2-1/3ps.asp.

[11]   The Statute of Anne was 'An Act for the Encouragement of Learning, by Vesting the Copies of Printed Books in the Authors or Purchasers of such Copies, during the Times therein mentioned'. A fascimile of the Act can be found at www.copyrighthistory. com/anne.html.

[12]   For example by using Jhymn, available at hymn-project.org/jhymndoc/.

cannot cut and paste from an out-of-copyright edition of an e-book since the publisher has decided to apply DRM restrictions. If you buy a Microsoft Reader e-book of Jane Austen's *Persuasion* from eBookmall[13] to read on your handheld computer, then you will not be able to copy and paste from it into your school essay, or print it for convenient reading in the bath, whatever rights you may have under the Copyright Designs and Patents Act 1988. For, while copyright may expire 70 years after the death of the author, the digital rights management licence endures.

While this is a minor inconvenience for a writer, the wider issue of the gradual replacement of copyright by contract is much more serious, since the licence terms a reader agrees to could easily be extended to cover the use of characters, locations or even plotlines, whatever copyright law might dictate.

This would matter less if the public domain was otherwise in rude health, but it is not. In the United States at the moment no US-published books have entered the public domain since 1998, and no more will until 2019.[14] The reason is the Sonny Bono Copyright Term Extension Act,[15] which saved Disney the embarrassment of seeing Mickey Mouse come out of copyright.[16] Orphan works, where the copyright status is unclear, are a particular concern. In 2005 James Boyle and Jennifer Jenkins at the Center for the Study of the Public Domain at Duke University argued that there is a 'film preservation emergency' simply because 'legal uncertainty, and the strict liability scheme laid down by the current copyright system operate to discourage exactly those acts copyright should be encouraging: restoration, exhibition, use in teaching, the presentation of new edited versions and so on.'[17] This has probably led to the destruction of many

---

[13] See www.ebookmall.com/ebook/4787-ebook.htm, which points out that for your $2.99 you get a book that comes with the following restrictions: No printing, No copy and paste.
[14] According to Stanford University Libraries website, 'Copyright has expired for all works published in the United States before 1923. In other words, if the work was published in the U.S. before January 1, 1923, you are free to use it in the U.S. without permission. As an example, the graphic illustration of the man with mustache was published sometime in the 19th Century and is in the public domain, so no permission is required to include it within this book. These rules and dates apply regardless of whether the work was created by an individual author, a group of authors or by an employee (the latter sometimes referred to as a "work made for hire."). Because of legislation passed in 1998, no new works will fall into the public domain until 2019 when works published in 1923 will expire.' Available at fairuse.stanford.edu/Copyright_and_Fair_Use_Overview/chapter8/8-a.html.
[15] For the full text, see www.techlawjournal.com/courts/eldritch/pl105-298.htm.
[16] See for example Teather, D. (2002), 'Copyright Case Threatens Disney', available at business.guardian.co.uk/story/0,3604,653128,00.html.
[17] Boyle, J. and Jenkins J. (2005), 'Access to Orphan Films', www.law.duke.edu/cspd/pdf/cspdorphanfilm.pdf, March 2005.

irreplaceable reels of early film, as the acetate stock decays before permission is available to transfer it to modern stock and exploit it commercially.

This may not seem to matter, since hundreds of films are distributed and thousands of new books are published every year, and writers seem to have no difficulty in coming up with new plots, storylines, characters and prose, even if little of it rises above the level of a Dan Brown pot-boiler. It is difficult to be sure what we are missing because of the limited use that can be made of other people's work until decades after their death, and those who argue for lower limits on copyright, like Stanford law professor Lawrence Lessig and the Creative Commons organisation he has inspired,[18] have a hard job demonstrating what positive things would result if we had a more extensive, and more accessible, public domain.

5 'NEW' CREATIVITY

Fortunately there are examples available, largely because many creative people have decided to disregard current copyright law, and reuse and remix work which is still protected. In this grey area a thousand flowers can bloom, although there are armies of corporate lawyers equipped with tanks of defoliant ready to move into action once they spot a splash of colour in the monochromatic world of the right-holder.

Perhaps the clearest demonstration of the creative opportunities that are denied us because of a restrictive attitude towards the public domain comes in 'slash fiction', named after a wide range of homoerotic stories inspired by a supposed Kirk/Spock relationship (hence the 'slash') in the *Star Trek* universe.[19] Slash fiction started out in fanzines, but grew up as a literary form once the Internet became a viable medium for self-publishing during the 1990s. While fans had been writing their own SF stories set in other writers' worlds for many years, their circulation was limited, so they barely entered into public consciousness and were not thought worth suppressing by the right-holders.

---

[18] See the Creative Commons website at www.creativecommons.org/ and Lessig, L. (2000), *Code and Other Laws of Cyberspace,* New York: Basic Books; Lessig L. (2002), *The Future of Ideas: The Fate of the Commons in a Connected World,* Random House USA Inc, Vintage; Lessig, L. (2004), *Free Culture: How Big Media Uses Technology and the Law to Lock Down Culture and Control Creativity,* The Penguin Press.

[19] According to the Wikipedia, which may be assumed to be a reliable source for such a topic of geek interest, slash fiction goes back to at least 1974 when 'A Fragment Out Of Time' was the first known Star Trek slash to be published in a fanzine, anon (2005) Wikipedia entry on Slash Fiction, available at en.wikipedia.org/wiki/Slash_fiction.

Today the genre goes far beyond the erotic, to incorporate many other types of writing – although the recasting of *Harry Potter* is still defiantly adult-only.[20] It also goes beyond words, with inspired movies like *Revelations* set in the *Star Wars* world[21] and even *The Codex*,[22] one of many dramas set in the *Halo* world that was made entirely by controlling characters in the *Halo* game world on Microsoft's Xbox Live, recording the resulting animation and providing music and voiceover to create a 'machinima'[23] or machine-generated animation.

In music we have mashups, a musical form that takes different songs and mixes them together to create something new. Perhaps the best know is *The Grey Album*, created by DJ Danger Mouse by combining the Beatles' *White Album* with Jay-Z's *The Black Album*,[24] but recent work like Dean Gray's *American Edit* is equally inventive and its creators have been pursued with equal vigour by record company lawyers.

The interest in these new forms of creativity and the enthusiasm with which they are circulated would seem to indicate that the current conception of what constitutes fair use may be too limited, stifling creativity where it should not be, and this in turn should lead us to reflect on the need to enhance the public domain. All of the examples quoted are unlicensed under current copyright law. George Lucas's Lucasfilm, holder of the *Star Wars* copyright, is tolerant of *Revelations* and other *Star Wars* creations[25] because it believes they enhance

---

[20]   For example, the material to be found at www.livejournal.com/community/hpslash/.

[21]   See www.panicstruckpro.com/revelations/.

[22]   See www.thecodexseries.com/.

[23]   According to www.machinima.com/article.php?article=186, Machinima is 'a new form of filmmaking that uses computer games technology to shoot films in the virtual reality of a game engine. Rather than picking up expensive camera equipment, or spending months painstakingly tweaking even more expensive 3D packages, Machinima creators act out their movies within a computer game. We treat the viewpoint the game gives them as a camera – "Shooting Film in a Virtual Reality", as we've been known to put it in their more slogan-high moments – and record and edit that viewpoint into any film we can imagine.'

[24]   Details are available from the Illegal Art website, www.illegal-art.org/audio/grey.html. DJ Danger Mouse remixed the vocals from Jay-Z's *The Black Album* and the Beatles' *White Album* and called his creation *The Grey Album*. He sent out around 3000 copies and was soon served with a cease-and-desist notice from EMI, who own the rights to the *White Album* master. Danger Mouse complied with EMI's order but the album is still widely available from other websites.

[25]   As seen in a *USA Today* article from November 2005 by Antony Breznican, where it is noted that 'Lucasfilm encourages fan films, but the makers are not allowed to sell them. They can, however, give the shorts away for free', Breznican, A. (2005), '"Star Wars" fan has "Revelations"', available at www.usatoday.com/life/movies/news/2005-05-11-star-wars-fan-film_x.htm, 11 November 2005.

the brand value, but *Harry Potter* material is stifled and record companies take every legal effort available to clamp down on mashups.

We should expect writers, whether of fact or fiction, to argue that the freedom to draw on other's ideas needs to be not only permitted but actively defended. All writers accept that there are limits on their freedom to draw on others' creations, whether words, phrases, characters or scenarios, but they might prefer such use to be constrained by artistic sensibility and a fear of losing status through accusations of plagiarism rather than by a rigid application of copyright law. After all, it would be a brave writer indeed who republished a 100-year old story under their own name and hoped to get away with it in the age of Google.

However for the moment we must deal with copyright law as it is, a situation that was well expressed by Siva Vaidhyanathan in an interview with the online magazine *Stayfree*,[26] when he pointed out that 'the deal with copyright is that we grant a temporary monopoly in order to allow the publisher to charge monopoly prices for a limited period of time. And what we get by giving the publisher that right is access to the work.'[27]

The limited, state-backed monopoly on the use of inventions, whether literary or practical, which copyright and patent law provide must balance the interests of right-holders and the wider society, and attempts by copyright holders to reify this legal abstraction and recast a time-limited monopoly on certain forms of exploitation into a fully-fledged property right break this bargain. The music and movie industries, and the publishers with them, see no reason why their exploitation rights to the output of their creative artists should vanish after an arbitrary time set in law, since nobody says that their ownership of a building or a printing press or a physical CD is time-limited. Musicians feel they can legitimately ask why ownership of the right to copy and sell a recording made 50 years ago should expire.[28]

This is, of course, to completely mis-state the nature of copyright, but we need to be careful in our arguments against reification. If we wish to call for a new bargain between creators and the public, we must not rely solely on the argument that intellectual property is non-rivalrous and hence distinct from

[26] Siva Vaidhyanathan is assistant professor of Culture and Communication at New York University and the author of the excellent book (2001), *Copyrights and Copywrongs: The Rise of Intellectual Property and How It Threatens Creativity*, New York: New York University Press.

[27] Vaidhyanathan, S. (2005), interview in *Stayfree*, available at www.stayfreemagazine.org/archives/20/siva_vaidhyanathan.html.

[28] Richard, C. (2004), Submission to the European Commission on working paper SEC (2004) 995, forum.europa.eu.int/Public/irc/markt/markt_consultations/library?l=/copyright_neighbouring/legislation_copyright/cliff_richard_enpdf/_EN_1.0_&a=d.

physical property – that taking away your car is not the same as copying your text. One reason it is dangerous to use this as the main focus of argument is that in many contexts there is just as much loss of commercial value when intellectual property is shared as there is with physical goods: if I have my own copy of a Kate Bush song, I do not need to buy it from iTunes. Indeed, despite Jefferson's comment, if I light my taper at yours,[29] I have taken something away from you – not the light of your own candle but your ability to sell me a torch. A better argument is the one made by Vaidhyanathan when he says:

> [Y]ou have to get back to that point that copyright is not natural, it's something that we the people decided to give to a certain class of people in exchange for something. And so if we're not giving what we promised to this group of people, we need to ask whether the system is properly balanced.[30]

New technologies and the new environment within which writers work have had a significant impact on this, and the balance point is clearly shifting. We see this shift clearly in the continuing campaign against Google's Book Search, previously known as Google Print.[31] Publishers may have a well-defined business model but Google seems to have found a new way of making money from the books that are published by others. In order to do this Google has to make a full-text scan of every book so that it can be electronically searched, but this is not made visible to the searcher, who gets only the publication details of the book and enough material to see the context. It is an effective catalogue, and seems likely to lead to more obscure books being consulted by researchers. It may also lead to greater sales of less obvious books and the more effective exploitation by the book trade of what Kevin Anderson calls the 'long tail'.[32]

Google will make money from this, because it will advertise on the search and results pages, but it is not making money by selling the books or indeed by making online copies of the books available. It is a new area, one that is not properly addressed by today's copyright law because nobody imagined it when the law was drawn up, but in the USA publishers are already suing Google in an attempt to extract their share of the new value. They can do this because in order to make

---

[29]   'He who receives an idea from me, receives instruction himself without lessening mine; as he who lights his taper at mine, receives light without darkening me', Thomas Jefferson to Isaac McPherson, 13 Aug. 1813, 13:333–35, in A.A. Lipscomb and A.E. Bergh (eds) (1905), *The Writings of Thomas Jefferson*, 20 vols, Washington: Thomas Jefferson Memorial Association.

[30]   Vaidhyanathan, S. (2005), interview in *Stayfree*, available at www.stayfreemaga-zine.org/archives/20/siva_vaidhyanathan.html.

[31]   Google Book Search is at books.google.com/.

[32]   Anderson, K. (2004), 'The Long Tail', available at www.wired.com/wired/ar-chive/12.10/tail.html, October.

its searchable index Google has to store a digitised copy of the text in an electronic retrieval system. This is clearly a licensable act under existing copyright law, and since Google does not have a licence for many of the publishers whose books it is scanning it would seem to be in breach of the law, even though the way it is proposing to use the index is not itself an infringement of copyright.

Things can go two ways here. In one world Google loses, or succumbs and pays for a licence from the publishers it deals with, and copyright law is more firmly entrenched as a property right. In the other, Google's argument that the law does not cover their use, or that it is legitimate under fair use/fair dealing exemptions, is accepted and the publishers acknowledge that owning a copyright does not automatically entitle you to a share of any transaction or operation involving the books or records. After all, the second-hand book trade goes on without protection money being paid to publishers.

6 A PUBLIC DOMAIN FOR CREATIVE WRITERS

The size and usefulness of the public domain depends entirely on the limits placed on the monopoly granted to creators by copyright law, and if copyright law is strengthened or the term extended, or if copyright is gradually replaced by more restrictive contract law, this will have a direct effect on the freedoms enjoyed by creative writers. What use is a public domain that has a high electric fence around it, with gated entry and armed guards patrolling to ensure that nothing is taken out and exploited elsewhere? The key point of the public domain for a writer is that it can be mined, exploited, changed, abused and – through the application of creative energy and inspiration – turned into our own property, to be exploited anew.

The idea that we can take from the public domain and assert ownership over the product of our labour is important. When Baz Luhrmann remade *Romeo and Juliet* with Leonardo di Caprio, or Gil Junger used *The Taming of the Shrew* as the basis for his film *10 Things I Hate About You*, neither director created something that remained in the public domain; they made something that was their own and therefore became entitled to the protection of copyright so that they could exploit it as they saw fit and even – shocking though this may be – make money out of it.

Writers, like most other creators, rely on copyright for their income and do not want everything they create to be in the public domain. Nor do they want anything created from materials in the public domain automatically to belong there too.[33]

---

[33] As the GNU General Public License does with free software, where all derivative works must be made available under the same licence. But, of course, free software is

They want to be able to strip-mine, take ideas and characters and plots, and sometimes whole worlds or stretches of text, and own them for themselves. Just as value comes from the application of effort to raw materials in manufacturing, so new value comes from the application of intellect to the raw materials of plot, character and incident.

For writers there is a danger that material in the public domain will be locked away and made inaccessible by changes to the law and by technical protection measures. In that case those who want to write will face the same problems as film-makers, having to clear every mention of a brand, check whether each allusion is allowable and worry in case their chosen metaphors and analogies put them on the wrong side of the corporate right-holders, clearing every idea, storyline and characterisation before publication, simply to avoid the danger of legal challenge and satisfy the requirements of litigation-averse publishers. This is not the world writers want, but the limits being put on the public domain today, and the ease with which politicians pass new laws that keep material from ever falling out of copyright, make this more and more likely.

One way to make life easier for writers would be to rethink the way in which we establish which works are in the public domain and therefore can be used without clearance. Lawrence Lessig has written extensively about the way that the removal of the need to register copyright in the United States from 1989 created problems for those who wish to work in the commons of the public domain,[34] and his argument is worth reinforcing. Even if there is no initial requirement to register, we would benefit greatly from a limited initial term of copyright followed by an extension, even one as generous as the current dispensation, only if registration formalities are completed. The main advantage would be that those works older than the current initial term – Lessig proposes 14 years, but the system would still work if it were 20 or even more – would be in the public domain unless they were registered, so the effort needed by a writer to demonstrate that the material they wish to use is not restricted becomes far more manageable, and, since the presumption is that unregistered work older than a certain date is out of copyright, the balance shifts in favour of the author of new or derivative work rather than that of the right-holder.

It is clearly important to preserve and grow the public domain, but writers need far more than the ability to make use of material which is verifiably out of copyright and therefore available. We must preserve the grey areas in which fair dealing and sometimes unfair dealing allow us to take, use, seek inspiration

---

made possible by copyright, and once the term of copyright on Linux or other GPL'd software expires then everyone, from Microsoft down, will be able to use the source code for whatever purposes they wish.

[34]   See for example his arguments for the 'Eldred Act', www.lessig.org/blog/archives/EAFAQ.html.

from, parody, play with and occasionally traduce, undermine and destroy the work of others. Writers want to cut and paste, copy and burn, read, and riff off – and then to sell. Writers also want the full protection of the law for the products of their own creative activity, at least for a short while, for we are unreasonable creatures, and we will rail against any abuse or even use of our own work just as we plunder from others, old and new.

While writers are willing to grapple with uncertainty, and to take risks with their sources of inspiration, the real danger of enforcing copyright through technology, with digital rights management systems and watermarking and even automatic plagiarism detection, is that it replaces the messy application of a human-made law with the rigid determinism of a rule-based system. This inevitably limits creativity in a number of ways. It will not stop the purely original artist or writer, but these are in short supply and cannot hope to furnish our world with its cultural and artistic requirements. Most of us steal unashamedly from the work of others, at least when it comes to the lowest levels of inspiration, and we need the flexibility which today's imperfect law offers to allow us space to work, breathe and seek inspiration.

Perhaps we should be thinking of how to extend the scope of permissible use of materials that are still in copyright, to allow the same freedoms as we enjoy with public domain works to extend towards the present, at least in a managed way. This would help, for example, in cases where literary executors choose not to make material available at any price. *Sylvia*, the recent film of the life of Sylvia Plath, was made without a line of poetry from either Plath or her husband Ted Hughes because their estates did not approve of the way they were portrayed. Of course, there is no simple resolution to this problem. It may be hard to see what justification can be made for allowing the estate such power over the scriptwriters, but a compulsory licensing system or a solution similar to that found with recorded music, where the collecting societies provide standard non-discriminatory licences, would bring its own problems. After all, a writer may feel that the use of their work by someone who they oppose politically or creatively amounts to derogatory treatment and infringes their moral rights, whatever the copyright situation may be.

7 CONCLUSION

Writers need more than the commons, valuable though it is. It will never be enough to limit our plundering to the public domain, and we should beware a more careful definition of what is inside or outside copyright, just as we resist attempts to replace copyright with contract, since even if the result is a general growth in what is available we will lose the ability to argue each case as it suits us or to exploit the grey, uncertain areas of copyright law to creative ends.

Yet, even while the public domain is clearly important, we should not shine too much light on the ways creative writers use other people's material, seek too much clarity about the law or ask too many difficult questions about the legitimacy of reuse or where inspiration crosses the line into plagiarism. As with sausages and laws, it is better not to look too closely at the way novels are made, and seeking too much clarity about the nature, extent or content of the public domain may not be in the wider interests of writers, however much the lawyers may welcome it.

10. The public domain and the economist

Manfredi M.A. La Manna

1 INTRODUCTION

The initial brief for this chapter – to examine from an economist's perspective the triad of open access, open science and open source – was daunting in two different ways. First, there is now an economics literature on this triad large and varied enough to make a survey article barely feasible within the space constraint and thus ultimately unsatisfactory, as interesting policy issues and personal experiences would have to be left out. Secondly, the public domain is an area where economists tread very carefully and rather uncomfortably, as they have to walk (or is it surf?) without the aid of some of their most trusted points of reference, such as well-defined property rights and individual incentives.[1]

I have thus redefined my brief, confining it to the examination of the relationship between the public domain and scholarly and scientific communication with special reference to one case-study which throws up interesting questions on the wider issues of open access, open science and open source: the case of economics journal publishing.

2 THE WEB AND THE DISSEMINATION OF RESEARCH OUTPUT: A PERFECT MATCH?

A key feature of 'research output' that distinguishes it from the rest of the material available on the Internet is that any piece of research, in order to qualify as proper 'output', has to go through a well-defined process of quality control and certification: the peer review mechanism. Although readers of this book are probably well acquainted with the concept, it may be useful to take as an example a piece of economic research and follow it through its three basic stages of development: (1) the *working paper*: this is the first draft circulated informally

---

[1] For a recent analysis, see Lerner, J. and Tirole, J. (2004), 'The Economics of Technology Sharing: Open Source and Beyond', NBER Working Paper 10956, December.

to a set of potentially interested fellow researchers and/or published (typically online) as a departmental/research centre discussion paper; (2) the version submitted to a journal (henceforth referred to as the *pre-print*); and finally (3) the *published article*.

This is indeed the *iter* followed by a piece of research in *any* academic discipline, but the meaning, status and timing of each phase show vast differences across disciplines.[2] I shall argue that these differences are extremely significant and indeed are at the root of some of the key problems that beset the relationship between the diffusion of academic research and the public domain.

On the face of it, the almost universal access to the Internet by researchers (definitely in the developed world and increasingly in developing countries) may seem to provide the ideal solution to the problem of dissemination of research. What could be simpler than using the Web to deposit and retrieve research output, without restrictions, tolls and barriers? In fact, if one examines more closely the incentives underlying the actions of researchers as *producers*, *monitors* and *consumers* of research output, the case for what is commonly called 'open access' appears irresistible:

- as producers, academic researchers supply their output without any expectation or prospect of *direct* economic gain (in terms of royalties and so on); indeed, sometimes potential authors *pay* submission fees in order to have their paper screened and reviewed by their peers. The main incentive is to maximise the *impact* of their research, by having it disseminated as widely as possible, hence gathering citations and peer-recognition, which eventually turns into career advancement, greater likelihood of research funding, and so on.
- as monitors (that is, as referees and editors), researchers provide their services either for free or for monetary rewards that are substantially below the opportunity cost of their time and effort. Again the incentives are not directly pecuniary and are provided by increased prestige within the profession/discipline. In the jargon of academic production, referees and especially editors act as 'gate-keepers', regulating access to, and defining the boundaries and direction of, the frontiers of the discipline.
- as consumers of research output, academics demand the widest and fastest access to publications.

---

[2]   For an interesting overview of the refereeing process (especially with relation to the public domain), see Rowland, F. (2002), 'The Peer-Review Process', *Learned Publishing*, 15 (4), 247–58. For a study on differences across disciplines regarding access to, and publication of, research output, see JISC Disciplinary Differences Report, August 2005, available at www.jisc.ac.uk/uploaded_documents/Disciplinary%20Differences%20and%20Needs.doc.

Thus the key aspects of the production, regulation and consumption of academic research, namely the lack of (direct) pecuniary gain, the collegiality of efforts and the desire for the widest and fastest dissemination appear to match perfectly the ethos of the Internet within the context of the 'public domain'.

This congruence of incentives and ethos is at the foundation of the open access movement, which advocates toll-free universal access to all scientific and academic output produced without any expectation of direct pecuniary reward. In fact, so perfect is the match that any external observer might have predicted that open access to all research produced not for pecuniary gain but for peer recognition would have taken place well before the advent of open source, where software with a market of potentially paying customers is instead made available by developers both to fellow developers and to users without any *direct* pecuniary gain. On the contrary, it can be argued that the open source movement has made far more significant inroads into the market of commercial software than open access into the field of scientific communication (I shall return to the relationship between open source software and open access to research output later in this chapter).

The reasons for this paradox and thus for the apparently inexplicable lack of widespread success for the open access campaign can be found in the specificities of scientific communication across different disciplines.

3   THE WEB AND OPEN ACCESS: A CAUTIONARY TALE?

In this section I shall try to examine how the specific interactions between the various phases of a typical piece of research (working paper, pre-print and published article) and between the various roles of researchers (producers, monitors and consumers of scientific communication) may explain why the road to open access is far more tortuous than some of the more evangelical advocates of open access are prepared to admit.

For reasons that will become apparent shortly, in the case of economics the main motivation for producing a *working paper* is (a) to establish priority of discovery, and (b) to elicit comments from peers. Although there is quite wide variation here, it is not uncommon for a working paper to be in circulation for quite some time before being turned into a pre-print and even to appear in different versions. The main reason for this lag is that the author's main aim is to produce a submission as polished as possible and to aim it at the highest-ranking journal with reasonable chances of being published. In order to achieve this aim, potential authors have a strong incentive to disseminate their work as widely as possible so as to signal their presence in a particular field, making their peers aware of their contributions, and expecting their peers to return the favour. It is crucial to realise that in this specific phase toll-free dissemination is feasible, desirable and virtually cost-free; and thus it is not altogether surprising that, as far as working papers are concerned, almost universal free access is a reality in economics. A good example is RePEc,[3] an open-access repository of over 164 000 working papers in economics. In spite of repeated assertions to the contrary by open-access advocates who should know better, the wide availability of working papers in economics is *not* synonymous with open access, as the latter refers to the free availability of the text *of the published article*.

To explain the difference between working papers and published articles we have to consider the role of editors and referees in economics. For a rather complicated series of reasons (to do with the nature of the discipline, which has become increasingly mathematical and specialised, and with the emergence of over-strict refereeing norms and conventions), refereeing in economics is a very protracted and generally painful process, involving successive rounds of resubmissions and substantial lags, and, on average, ends with the rejection of the submitted version.[4] Economics is one of the very few disciplines where rejection rates above 90 per cent are common among the highest-ranked journals. Indeed, even success at the lowest rung of the peer-recognition ladder – the acceptance of a paper for a conference – is far from certain, with some conferences having rejection rates (50–60 per cent) that in other disciplines are restricted to high- to medium-ranking journals. The experience of having one's papers rejected is a recurrent and widespread occurrence and even future (and current!) Nobel laureates are not immune.[5] One significant effect of the refereeing ethos in economics is the lag between submission and publication, which very rarely is less than two years and may be as long as seven years, a delay that is unheard of in many other disciplines, where submission-to-acceptance lags are measured in months. There is however a positive side to this lag, namely that, on average, the accepted version (which may have gone through several revisions and resubmissions) is typically rather different from the initial one. The same cannot be said of other disciplines where the referee-

---

[3]   At repec.org.

[4]   In two companion articles published in the (top-ranked) *Journal of Political Economy* ('The Slowdown of the Economics Publishing Process', 110 (5), 947–93; 'Evolving Standards for Academic Publishing', 110 (5). 994–1034) Glenn Ellison provides both a fascinating insight into the inner workings of some of the top-ranked journals in economics and an explanation for the progressive slowing down of refereeing.

[5]   I very much doubt that there are many disciplines that have produced as long a list of rejected 'classic articles' as that compiled in the field of economics by Gans, J.S. and Sheperd, G.B. (1994), 'How Are the Mighty Fallen: Rejected Classic Articles by Leading Economists', *Journal of Economic Perspectives* 8 (1), 165–79.

ing process (and here I oversimplify somewhat) has more of a binary nature, whereby a submission is checked for novelty and correctness and approved or rejected on that basis.

In economics the refereeing lag is a sociological problem, not a technological one: the advent of electronic submission and the use of software for manuscript reviewing (both increasingly popular in economics, but by no means universally adopted) seem to have had only a marginal impact. The lack of urgency applies also to the final stage of the process, when the lag between the final version being accepted for publication and the actual publication may extend to several months.

So, to recap the story so far: in economics the initial incarnation of a piece of research (the working paper) and the final one (the published article) perform significantly different roles in the chain of research communication and thus interact with the public domain in different ways. The working paper is used as a means to stake the priority of the author's contribution and to advertise his/her presence in the field. As a consequence, the speed and reach of the dissemination are essential, and it is no surprise that a very efficient mechanism for the posting, archiving and retrieving of working papers has developed wholly within the public domain. As far as the published article is concerned, the priorities are wholly different: speed is definitely unimportant and even reach is not of direct relevance. The paramount preoccupation of the published author in economics is the *prestige* of the publication. There are about 300 journals in economics (broadly defined), not only with a huge variation in their prestige but also in a very strict and codified ranking order. In economics there exists a very close correlation between the peer recognition of a researcher and the publication record of the said researcher in an extremely narrow set of top-ranked journals. Considering that in economics citations tend to accumulate over time often with a very slow start (unlike other scientific disciplines, where the citation impact is highest in the first couple of years after publication), articles are judged almost exclusively by the prestige of the journal they are published in, and not by short-term citation impact. A number of important consequences follow, as far as the relationship between the published economist and the public domain is concerned.

Although begrudged by many economists, the stranglehold of the top 5 per cent of journals on the journal market is a deeply entrenched phenomenon which has been strengthened in the last few years by the appearance of formalised research assessment mechanisms. The arrival and success of the Internet has had no impact whatsoever in terms of facilitating entry of new journals into the top echelons of the economics journal hierarchy.

Contrary to the mantra infinitely repeated by some advocates of open access that the sole/main/paramount aim of researchers is to maximise the impact of their published research, economists appear not to be at all bothered by the size of the potential readership of the journal, as long as it is a prestige journal. This should not be surprising. Once I asked the most strident and uncompromising of all open access advocates – Professor Stevan Harnad – where he would choose to deliver a paper if forced to choose between an audience comprising the 5 per cent top researchers in his discipline and an audience with all the rest. He could but admit that he would choose the former, but, of course, stressed that in the post-Gutenberg era it should be possible to reach a universal audience. This, in my view, is a fundamental misunderstanding of the role and status of journals in the Internet era (at least in disciplines such as economics).

4   OPEN-ACCESS PUBLISHING: A VIABLE ROUTE?

One of the routes to toll-free access to refereed academic work is by submitting one's research output to open-access publishers, where the costs of refereeing, online publishing, and distribution are not levied on the readers but on the authors (or rather on their institutions). The fact that open-access journals in economics are a minuscule fraction of the total and likely to remain the hobby-horse of a tiny minority disposes of open-access publishing as a viable strategy – at least for disciplines like economics. The reason is easy to see.

Let me start with an analogy. At a recent 'celebrity' event one of the many assembled paparazzi had the bright idea of furnishing himself with a step-ladder to gain a better view. Very quickly all other fellow photographers scrambled to equip themselves with step-ladders, too, thereby achieving the suboptimal equilibrium of everybody retaining their relative position but at a cost. The statement that in the Internet era there exist more efficient mechanisms to disseminate peer-reviewed scholarly and scientific work than reliance on a system of toll-access, while being objectively correct, is as useful as a policy prescription as the suggestion to the paparazzi of my example that they should come down from their inefficient step-ladders. No paparazzo would and should follow the advice (in itself very sound and well intentioned) unless he/she can assure him/herself that all others would follow suit.

It could be argued (correctly, as it turns out) that my analogy is imperfect in so far as, assuming that somehow all paparazzi could be persuaded to get rid of their step-ladders, each one of them would still have the incentive to acquire one, as it would give him/her an advantage over his/her rivals. In the case of research publishing, on the other hand, if somehow all researchers decided to move to the promised land of toll-free open access, there would be no incentive to restore inefficient toll barriers. While correct, this argument fails to grasp the deep-rooted nature of the problem of the *transition* to open access, which can be summarised in a single word: *coordination*.

The devastating effects of the *coordination trap* were made dramatically evident by the Public Library of Science debacle. Very briefly, what happened was that nearly 34000 scientists (mainly from the bio-medical sciences) signed a petition-ultimatum whereby each signatory threatened not to submit their work for peer review to any journal that did not undertake to grant (delayed) open access to the published articles.[6] The initiative received wide media coverage and, as any economist would have predicted, ended in a humiliating retreat: publishers called the scientists' bluff and, when the threatened deadline arrived, the great majority of the signatories meekly backed down and duly submitted their work to non-open-access publishers.[7]

The PLoS story shows that the existence of a better and feasible alternative (open access) to the status quo (toll-access) in itself does not imply that the transition to the superior equilibrium is feasible. Indeed, unless there exist credible mechanisms whereby individuals can commit (that is, force) themselves to the better alternative, the tyranny of the status quo will prevail.[8]

In conclusion, if one looks at the range of open-access journals one cannot but be struck by two overwhelming facts: (i) in spite of being probably the most efficient way of disseminating peer-reviewed research, open-access journals constitute a tiny minority of the universe of refereed publications; and (ii) even within the minority of open-access journals, there are significant differences across disciplines.

5 SELF-ARCHIVING: A PANACEA?

This leaves self-archiving of *the accepted version of the article* as the only potentially feasible route to open access. By examining the logic of self-

---

[6] 'We pledge that, beginning in September 2001, we will publish in, edit or review for, and personally subscribe to only those scholarly and scientific journals that have agreed to grant unrestricted free distribution rights to any and all original research reports that they have published, through PubMed Central and similar online public resources, within 6 months of their initial publication date.' Predictably, the PLoS website (www. plos.org) does not dwell on the failure of its Open Letter.

[7] I was told by a leading open-access publisher in biomedical sciences that out of the 34000 PLoS signatories the number of scientists who followed through with their 'threat' and did submit their work to open-access publishers instead could be counted on the fingers of *one* hand.

[8] The PLoS story has an interesting coda: some of its leading lights, following the failure of the petition, decided to become open-access publishers themselves and, thanks to a $10m donation from a charitable foundation, have launched a handful of open-access journals. Unfortunately, in the absence of philanthropists willing to donate billions of dollars, this is not a template that can be reproduced for all scholarly and scientific communication.

archiving, it may be possible to identify some of the fundamental problems of the relationship between the public domain and scientific and scholarly communication.

Another analogy may be useful here. In the UK telephony market (and probably elsewhere in the world) there are companies that offer completely free calls to fellow subscribers, that is, if you subscribe to company A, all your calls to all of company A's other subscribers are gratis.

Now consider the following statement: 'If all potential customers subscribe to company A, then the free-calls-to-fellow-subscribers outcome is not a sustainable equilibrium'. This statement is not a hypothesis nor does it require empirical corroboration. It is the only logical conclusion from the premises. I would argue that precisely the same argument applies to the statement, repeated ad nauseam by proponents of the self-archiving route to open access, that '100 per cent open access can be achieved overnight by all researchers self-archiving all their accepted articles'.

I would argue that one of the main reasons why economists (and possibly the majority of researchers, except for some sub-disciplines such as high-energy physics and some fields of mathematics and computer science) are reluctant self-archivers is that they regard the above strategy as inherently self-defeating as a long-term policy for the attainment of open access.

The reason is obvious: the accepted (as yet unpublished) version of an article, once self-archived in a repository whence it can be searched and retrieved, is at least as good a substitute for the published article in so far as its content is identical but it is, by definition, made available *before* the published version, and therefore, being available at a zero price, necessarily drives the *economic* price of the published article to zero, thereby making publication unsustainable (even if the article is priced *at cost*). The argument, however, is made subtler and more complicated by the fact that articles are not published individually but are bundled into journal issues, which in turn are bundled into annual subscriptions, which in turn are bundled into multi-journal 'packages'.

This complication explains the apparently paradoxical unholy alliance between the most radical proponents of self-archiving as a route to open access, on one side, and some of the most rapaciously commercial multinational publishers, on the other. 'Self-archivangelists' rank publishers according to how 'permissive' the latter's policies are in terms of allowing authors to self-archive the first submission (good), the final submission (very good) or the published version (divine). The sad irony is that self-archivangelists proudly announce a victory for the cause if a publisher joins the list of the 'good' guys or moves up the scale of self-archiving permissiveness, blissfully unaware that this, far from being a sign of success for the self-archiving cause, is evidence that academic journal publishers rightly perceive the self-archiving strategy as inherently unsustainable, thereby making a 'liberal' stance on their part not only a cheap PR stunt but also a diversionary tactic to prevent or delay badly needed regulation of their very profitable industry.[9]

The relationship between self-archiving as a dissemination strategy on the one hand and academic economists *as a profession* on the other is, in my view, a good example of how complex and subtle is the nexus between the public domain and scientists and scholars more generally.

As we have seen above, economists have been among the first and most enthusiastic self-archivers as far as early (that is, *as yet un-refereed*) research work is concerned. Therefore the commonly advanced suggestion that the lack of a self-archiving 'culture' may be due to inertia, lack of technical skills and so on clearly does not apply to economics as a discipline. So, why is it that economists, who, by training and inclination, ought to be keen on exploiting the benefits of cost-free wider dissemination, have shown so far no strong inclination to adopt *as a professional norm* the policy of self-archiving accepted articles (refereed pre-prints)?

The main reason, as I argued above, is that self-archiving is considered a policy for the dissemination of refereed research that cannot be sustained in the long term. It is not at all surprising that a discipline that, for good or ill, relies almost exclusively on the refereeing customs and ethos of a handful of journals at the top of a strictly codified hierarchical publication structure as its mechanism for apportioning recognition and prestige should promote behaviour that does not threaten in any way the long-term survival of 'the ranked journal'. Indeed, as we are going to see in the next section, this 'protectionism' extends to other areas of the relationship between academia and the public domain.

6 OPEN SCIENCE, THE PUBLIC DOMAIN, AND ECONOMICS AS A DISCIPLINE

In line with the strategy deployed in this chapter, namely to try to extrapolate from a specific case some conclusions of potentially more general applicability, in this section I wish to focus on one particular aspect of the relationship between open science[10] and the public domain. I would argue that the very specific

---

[9]   For evidence and analysis of the highly inefficient but extremely profitable market of academic journals in economics, see La Manna, M. (2003), 'The Economics of Publishing and the Publishing of Economics', *Library Review*, 52 (1), 18–28.

[10]   One of the main preoccupations of open science advocates (especially in the biomedical sciences) is the free access to datasets on which research papers are based. Although in economics, too, researchers tend to be rather protective of any datasets they may have collected, often at some considerable cost, the editorial policies of journals are moving in an open-science direction. The top-ranked *American Economic Review*,

case of what we might call 'refereeing technology' in economics journals is worth exploring.

It could be argued that the advent of the Internet provided not only the means for wider and faster dissemination for traditionally refereed research output but also the opportunity of improving the very process of peer review and its relationship with the academe and the general public.

At a rather superficial level the Internet allows journal editors to make the pre-Web system of refereeing more efficient by replacing paper transactions with online communication, with obvious gains in terms of speed, ease of retrieval and so on. In this respect, it is somewhat surprising to note that economics journals have been singularly slow in adopting even simple and well-established best practices such as the electronic submission of manuscripts. In spite of the wide availability of both commercial and open-source software for the electronic reviewing of manuscripts, again economics journals have not been at the forefront. Perhaps this slow start could be ascribed to the general phenomenon of institutional inertia that surrounds the adoption of new technology and indeed there are some encouraging signs that at long last economics journals are slowly joining the 21st century.

There is, however, one important aspect of the quality-control process where economics shows no sign whatsoever of using *new* opportunities offered by online technology – I refer here to wider and more innovative peer review on the one hand and to interactions with the readership on the other.

Although economics is by no means an isolated phenomenon in its rejection of these new technological opportunities (which is common to most scientific disciplines), one would have expected economics journals to avail themselves of any available chance both to enhance refereeing as a process and to raise the status of referees. What are the innovations in refereeing that the Internet has made possible and that are apparently steadfastly eschewed by journals? I shall list briefly some of them:

- especially in disciplines such as economics where (repeated) resubmissions are the norm, the value added by peer review to the quality of the published article can be enhanced by allowing direct (but anonymous) contact between author and referees;
- online refereeing offers a simple and effective solution to the long-standing problem of unbundling *assessment* from *evaluation*. Let me explain. It could be argued that referees perform two main tasks: (i) they assess

---

for example, explicitly states that it will publish papers 'only if the data used in the analysis are clearly and precisely documented and are readily available to any researcher for purposes of replication'.

submissions in terms of a number of criteria, such as originality, correctness, technical/methodological advance and so on and (ii) they evaluate
submissions by assigning weights to, and trade-offs between, various assessment criteria. It is perfectly possible (and in the case of economics
very likely[11]) that some referees, while very scrupulous and accurate in
their assessment, may apply the 'wrong' criteria, that is, may attach excessive importance to certain criteria to the detriment of others. Online
submission assessment/evaluation forms make it possible to distinguish
between the two tasks (assessment and evaluation), thereby making better
use of referees' reports.

- online refereeing software makes very easy the relative and absolute
  evaluation of referees, thereby raising the status of referees themselves.
  Editors who wished to signal to the profession the performance of their
  outstanding referees (according to a set of publicly announced criteria)
  could easily do so.

More importantly, appropriate use of online technology could turn journals
from one-directional documents into interactive knowledge exchanges.[12] What
I mean here is that instead of viewing the published article as the terminal point
of a uni-directional transfer from the author, through the review process, to the
reader, one could envisage an interactive process whereby readers can interact
both with the author *and* with the referees, thereby turning the published article
into an intermediate stage in the process of knowledge exchange. To consider
but a simple example, readers could provide their own assessment and evaluation, using the same online forms designed for referees, thereby providing
potentially very useful feedback on the quality (and bias, if any) of both the article and the refereeing process.

In my experience of promoting more efficient publishing modes to the economics profession, I have come across not just indifference to the suggestion
of moving economics towards more innovative refereeing and interaction between authors, referees and readers but mainly outright *hostility*, especially from
the community of past and current editors of both well-established and new
journals. The reason, I would surmise, is yet again the fact that the availability
of technologies and practices that could be regarded as superior alternatives to
the status quo is no guarantee that such technologies and practices will be
adopted, unless they fit the ethos and incentives of the would-be adopters: the

---

[11] See, for example, Ellison, G., 'Evolving Standards', op. cit.
[12] See La Manna, M. and Young, J. (2002), 'The Electronic Society for Social Scientists: from Journals as Documents to Journals as Knowledge Exchanges', *Interlending
and Document Supply*, 30 (4), 178–82.

desire to protect a peer-review mechanism grounded on the journal as the 'focus of energy' and 'nexus of interactions' may and does easily turn into a justification for resisting *any* efficiency-enhancing reform by the stakeholders in the status quo.

7   CONCLUDING REMARKS ON OPEN SCIENCE/ SOURCE/ACCESS AND SCHOLARLY COMMUNICATIONS

This chapter has taken as its point of departure the remarkable and yet largely neglected similarities between the open source movement and the process of peer review of research output.[13] In both cases, (i) substantial amounts of time and effort are devoted to activities yielding no direct financial reward; (ii) the main motivation is peer recognition and prestige; (iii) the outcome is a *joint* production of the original authors/developers and their referees/fellow developers; (iv) both producers and users have a common interest in the widest dissemination of new ideas.

In view of these remarkable similarities, then, how can one explain the substantial difference between the success of open source in the software market and the failure (or, more charitably, the lack of progress) in achieving open access to scientific and scholarly research output?

The answer, I have argued, is two-fold. First, there is no single homogeneous 'research output': a typical piece of research goes through different phases where the incentives of the parties involved may be different and it may be perfectly individually rational to combine open access at one stage (such as the working paper stage) and toll-access at a different stage (the published article) if the latter is more congruous with the aims of the stakeholders (prestige for the authors, preservation of a hierarchical mechanism of peer review and 'gatekeeping'). Secondly, the relationship between open access and 'the researchers' varies according to the *specific role* played by the players in the process who are producers, assessors and consumers. Again, there are important trade-offs here: while the researcher as consumer would clearly benefit from having toll-free access to all published articles, the researcher as producer and assessor may perceive open access *to the published output* as a threat to the viability of the

---

[13]   The otherwise exhaustive analysis of 'commons-based peer production' by Y. Benkler (2002), 'Coase's Penguin, or, Linux and *The Nature of the Firm*', *Yale Law Journal*, 112, 369–446, hardly mentions the similarities between open source and academic peer review. Similarly, Lerner and Tirole (2004) also treat the relationship between open source and academia in a paragraph or two.

(not cost-free) process of peer review, namely the mechanism that guarantees the evaluation and eventually certifies the prestige of research.

This 'unpacking' both of research outputs and of multi-role researchers renders policy-making more complex to design and difficult to implement but all the more necessary and urgent: precisely because individual players may have conflicting incentives and, more importantly, because there exists a gap between individual and collective incentives, there is ample scope for welfare-enhancing government intervention. Such intervention is likely to be discipline-specific and would involve a subtle mixture of competition policy, advocacy, training, changes in grant-awarding rules, and so on.

11. The public domain and public sector information

Richard Susskind OBE

1 INTRODUCTION

This chapter concerns public sector information (PSI). Broadly speaking, PSI is information that is created within or on behalf of public sector bodies. In the Internet age, PSI is a form of intellectual property that is rapidly increasing in significance – economically, socially and legally. This chapter seeks to place PSI in its broader context of UK information policy; to explain the overlap between the PSI and the freedom of information regimes; to clarify the scope, sources and value of PSI; to chart the evolution of government policy, legislation and regulation in relation to PSI; to offer a critique of the current position (as at February 2006); and to illustrate some of the central themes through a brief case study relating to statutory material.

2 BACKGROUND

Governments have always been in the business of managing information – as creators, controllers, distributors, and more. As a holder of information, until a decade ago, the state had two main roles in relation to information. First, there was the responsibility to ensure that information on matters of national security was held securely and beyond the reach of potential miscreants. Second, there was the job of ensuring that full records of public affairs were maintained, archived and made accessible to authorised persons. At the same time, much public information enjoyed a form of intellectual property protection known as Crown copyright, which meant that the reproduction of public information generally required permission and that any licence to reproduce would often have been provided at a cost.

Over the past decade, there has been a clear shift in UK government policy in relation to information generated from within or on behalf of the public sector. In summary, the UK government has shown commitment to making official information more easily accessible. There are two main strands of thinking here.

One is that government should be more open: this has given rise to the freedom of information (FOI) regime. The other strand is that PSI can and should be *re-used* where benefits can accrue. For example, geographical, meteorological, statutory and census data, although captured by government departments for use in the course of their regular activities, can also be used to good effect by others, such as publishers, traders, educators and citizens. To be re-used, the information may well need to be reorganised and improved upon – either by government departments themselves or by private sector organisations. Perhaps the most dramatic illustration of re-use is the claim that the geographic information of Ordnance Survey, the UK's national mapping agency, even in 1996, underpinned £79–136 billion worth of the UK's goods and services.[1] In commercial terms, PSI is not trivial.

Intuitively, in relation to the re-use of PSI, two broad challenges emerge. The first is to make sure that core public sector information is made available, under appropriate conditions, to intermediaries who can add value to it. The second challenge is more radical – it is about information management and knowledge management on a grand scale. It is about ensuring that the valuable collective knowledge and experience (the 'intellectual capital') of public sector workers is captured and re-used. Today it is barely managed and is under-exploited. In a sense, knowledge has become disposable. Strong arguments can be made that systematic recycling is instead required.

These two challenges have been articulated and identified by the Advisory Panel on Public Sector Information (APPSI), of which the author is the present Chair.[2] Indeed, the work of APPSI has informed much of the analysis and evaluation of this chapter. APPSI is a non-departmental public body, established by the Cabinet Office in April 2003. When first set up, it was known as the Advisory Panel on Crown Copyright. The current terms of reference of the Panel are as follows:

- to advise Ministers on how to encourage and create opportunities in the information industry for greater re-use of public sector information;
- to advise the Director of the Office of Public Sector Information and Controller of Her Majesty's Stationery Office about changes and opportunities in the information industry, so that the licensing of Crown copyright and public sector information is aligned with current and emerging developments;
- to review and consider complaints under the Re-use of Public Sector Information Regulations 2005 and advise on the impact of the complaints procedures under those Regulations.

---

[1]   See (1999), *The Economic Contribution of Ordnance Survey GB*, Oxera.
[2]   www.appsi.gov.uk.

Formally, the Panel reports to Ministers annually. Informally, the Panel's strapline is 'realising the value of public sector information'. This intentionally trades on two different meanings of 'realising'. The Panel's focus is on identifying, articulating and raising awareness of the value of PSI as well as on encouraging its exploitation.

3   THE OVERLAP BETWEEN PSI AND FOI

One potential misunderstanding needs extended clarification at the outset. The law, policy and practice on PSI are commonly confused with those of freedom of information (FOI). It is important to understand the relationship between PSI and FOI.

Considerable effort has being expended by the UK Government in the implementation both of the FOI Act[3] (which came into force on 1 January 2005) and of the EU Directive on the Re-use of Public Sector Information 2003/98 (the PSI Directive, which came into force on 1 July 2005 in the form of the Re-use of Public Sector Information Regulations 2005). This work is not restricted to England and Wales: in respect of Scotland, although some of the issues raised in this chapter are devolved matters (see, for example, the Freedom of Information (Scotland) Act 2002), it is suggested that the central messages apply equally to Scotland and that, as far as possible, the Scottish and English approaches to PSI can and should fully align.

The FOI Act confers a general right of access to information held by public authorities; the PSI Directive and Regulations seek to establish a minimum set of rules governing the re-use of PSI (although UK officials are keen to maintain a distinction between access and re-use, the distinction is not always watertight). Although the subject matter (public information) and the broad scope (public bodies) of these instruments are similar, the underpinning policies are quite different. The FOI Act seeks to promote greater transparency and openness in the conduct of public affairs, while the PSI regime recognises the value, and aims to encourage the commercial exploitation, of public information. The focus of FOI is on enhancing individuals' rights in a democratic society. At the heart of the PSI Directive is the smoother running of the internal market – the stimulation of the European information industry to compete more effectively in the global marketplace.

The implementation of the FOI Act is the responsibility of the Department for Constitutional Affairs (DCA)[4] and the FOI Act itself is regulated by the

---

[3]   The Environmental Information Regulations 2004 are also implemented with the FOI Act.

[4]   www.dca.gov.uk.

Information Commissioner.[5] The implementation of the PSI Directive was the joint responsibility of the Department for Trade and Industry and what was Her Majesty's Stationery Office (HMSO), while its ongoing regulation is within the province of what is now known as the Office of Public Sector Information (OPSI).[6] (OPSI was created, in large part and in effect, to regulate the re-use of PSI; HMSO has been subsumed within OPSI.)

The FOI Act and its implications are fairly widely appreciated across both the public and private sectors. In contrast, the PSI Directive and Regulations and their ramifications are hardly recognised, other than by a few departments and agencies and by the private sector information industry. This is understandable: officials have been addressing FOI since 1997 as a major manifesto commitment; PSI is a relatively new topic of concern.

Underpinning this chapter is the belief that the PSI regime may be as fundamental in its impact as the FOI regime. In the PSI Directive, 're-use' is defined very widely, referring to any use 'for commercial or non-commercial purposes other than the initial purpose within the public task for which the documents were produced'. A central theme of this chapter is that the PSI Directive and Regulations can and should lead to a systematic and pervasive effort to harness and recycle the collective intellectual capital of the public sector. Crucially, this may be driven from beyond the public sector – for example, by private sector companies (such as electronic publishers) invoking the provisions of the PSI regime.

FOI and PSI together will be the fundamental building blocks of so-called 'information age government'. This is not merely about making formal government publications available online. It is about capturing, nurturing and maintaining almost all of the information generated by public sector bodies as a common and easily accessible good for all of society. At a policy level, these developments will combine to bring about an entirely new landscape for the management and control of information in the public sector. It is far from clear that most senior officials and politicians are yet alive to the cumulative shift in policy and practice. Nor is there evidence of analysis of the long-term implications of these changes.

Although the histories, underlying policies and implementation regimes of the FOI and PSI initiatives are quite different, their effects on public bodies overlap considerably. In practical terms, much of the same PSI is subject to both regimes, although the obligations imposed and entitlements conferred differ. And, although they are not co-extensive, both instruments apply broadly to UK public sector bodies.

---

[5]   www.informationcommissioner.gov.uk.

[6]   www.opsi.gov.uk.

FOI and PSI implementation will require public bodies to change the way in which their information systems are set up; to change some of their working practices; indeed to change their very culture. Whereas, in the past, there was a presumption in favour of PSI being for official use only, these two regimes combine to reverse that position, and public bodies will need to change accordingly, although the demands imposed by each regime will be subtly different.

Over the past two years, UK officials from DCA and OPSI have met regularly to ensure coherence between the ongoing management and regulation of the FOI and PSI regimes. Given the substantial overlaps just noted, this engagement is entirely sensible.

4   THE SCOPE, SOURCES AND VALUE OF PSI

Focusing now on PSI, several questions call for consideration. What sorts of information fall within its ambit? Where can this information be found? Of what value is PSI? These questions are considered below.

With regard to its scope, much debate and discussion concentrates on the challenge of making core PSI (such as government statistics and geographical data) available to intermediaries, especially the information industries, so they can add value to it and commercially exploit it. While the systematic and fair re-use of PSI in this way remains a central issue, it can be argued with considerable force that much more generic and, in turn, beneficial exploitation of the intellectual assets of the public sector is both possible and desirable.

In this light, PSI can be viewed as the most valuable body of intellectual capital in the UK. It encompasses most of the work product of public sector workers; the bulk of the data and information gathered in the course of public service; vast amounts of knowledge and expertise that are synthesised and created; the collective wisdom and ideas of a vast group of remarkably able individuals in the public domain; the reports, analysis, research and development, policy papers and recommendations generated within the public sector; and much of the work commissioned by central and local government from external organisations, consultants and specialists. The scale and extent of this information is seldom appreciated by ministers, officials and commentators alike. There is a wealth of intellectual property here. One of the great questions of our time is: how can this resource be exploited for the benefit of citizens and society?

Where is this vast corpus of information held? PSI is currently held in formal official publications that are made available online; in public sector IT-based document management systems, of a more or less sophisticated kind; in government knowledge management systems, some nascent, others more advanced;

in e-mails on PCs and networks and backed up variously; in filing cabinets; and, as ever, in people's heads.

Mining the jewels from these various locations is a formidable task, not least because public sector information systems, both manual and electronic, are generally at an early stage of evolution. It is commonly hypothesised that PSI, as a generic resource, is currently managed in a haphazard manner and that re-cycling of PSI is exceptional rather than prevalent. It is further hypothesised that the current information systems and enabling technologies in general use in the public sector are not yet rich enough to support the full-scale exploitation of PSI that the many champions are envisaging.

To begin to test these hypotheses, APPSI commissioned two pieces of re-search, which were undertaken by HMSO: on information management within central government and on knowledge management within central government.[7] These studies, together with related discussions and consultations, suggest that there is indeed much information and knowledge management activity within government – for example, the work by the National Archives on electronic document and records management, the numerous discrete knowledge manage-ment initiatives in various departments, the valuable attempt to introduce an e-government metadata standard and OPSI's important Information Asset Reg-ister. Nonetheless, despite these and other developments, APPSI sounded the following notes of caution.

First, document management technology within the public sector (systems that help name, store, retrieve and control all computer-based files, but most significantly word-processed documents and the ever more pervasive e-mail) is several years behind good practice in the private sector. The concern here is that full exploitation of PSI will depend on the presence of advanced systems – docu-ment management systems – for identifying and making available information in electronic form. Without such systems, exploitation of PSI will always be disappointingly incomplete.

Second, many, but not all, information and knowledge management initiatives within the public sector are almost exclusively inward-facing, that is, devoted to improved performance and efficiency internally. Yet these same efforts could valuably also have an external dimension – for example, a knowledge manage-ment project devoted to identifying and maintaining a database of useful reports for re-use internally could and should be extended to embrace materials that could also be exploited externally.

What of the value of PSI? This is another pivotal question. Regular and sys-tematic collection of statistics and qualitative data on licensing, use and re-use of PSI is essential for two reasons. In the first instance, by requiring accountabil-

---

[7] See APPSI's first annual report (2004), at www.appsi.gov.uk.

ity and transparency in relation to value, costs and price, this should encourage progress to be made by government departments and agencies towards achieving government objectives on liberalising access to and encouraging greater re-use of PSI. Second, the availability of metrics should provide a range of quantitative indicators to measure progress towards the Government's objective of opening up opportunities for greater re-use of government information by the private and voluntary sectors of the economy.

Remarkably, APPSI found that there are no robust, quantifiable data available on the value and contribution of Crown copyright in particular, and PSI in general, to the UK economy. This is a major concern to the Panel, as it is seen as a serious obstacle to measuring the success of the government's objectives.

5   THE EVOLUTION OF GOVERNMENT POLICY

Taking a step back now, it is instructive to trace the development of government policy in relation to PSI. The last decade has witnessed enormous change, to some extent catalysed by the advent of the Internet, which is steadily, fundamentally and globally changing the relationship between the individual and the state.

Before the 1990s, most government was closed government – official information was made available, largely, on a need-to-know basis. Restricting the flow of information was clearly central to totalitarian rule, for example. But benevolent democracies also held back, adopting a paternalistic posture, releasing information sparingly. Perhaps it was not in people's interests to know too much. Anti-paternalists claim the problem was, rather, that there were no effective channels for fuller information flows between citizen and government. But this changed in the 1990s with the coming of the Internet. Suddenly information could be shared widely and cheaply. And in 1996 and 1997 the Conservative and Labour Governments stated their commitment to providing official information on the Web. Why? Was it that the Internet made it all but impossible for government to resist greater openness? Or was there, coincidentally, some new political will to make public affairs more transparent? Either way, open government arrived.[8]

---

[8]   The path to open government can be traced through various government papers, including: *Your Right to Know: the Government's proposals for a Freedom of Information Act* (Cm 3818, 1997); *Crown Copyright in the Information Age* (Cm 3819, 1998); and *The Future Management of Crown Copyright* (Cm 4300, 1999). For an excellent summary of the development of government thinking, see Saxby, S. (2005), 'Crown Copyright Regulation in the UK – Is the Debate Still Alive?', *International Journal of Law and Information Technology*, **13** (3), 299.

There are two types of open government. A reactive open government, when faced with a request for access to official information, will respond favourably. Request leads to access. In contrast, a proactive open government believes that an integral part of the job is to make all information created in the process of governing available to the people. Proactive open government is much more than meeting, more or less willingly, a request for access. Instead, it is regarding the provision, usually online, of all official information as part of the very business of government. Withholding information is looked upon as exceptional and requiring justification.

The UK Government is currently moving from being reactively to proactively open. One sign of this is the drive to provide more useful and better stocked websites. Another is that, under freedom of information legislation, all public authorities must maintain publication schemes which indicate what information will be made available proactively. However, full-scale proactivity will require a positive effort on the part of public authorities actually to maximise the value of their information. A vital step in this direction was the adoption, at the end of 2003, of the EU Directive on the re-use of public sector information (the PSI Directive), which was implemented in the UK on 1 July 2005.

The PSI Directive creates a new, harmonised regime for the re-use of PSI, broadly defined as any information held by public sector bodies. Research carried out in 2000 by Pira International for the European Commission compared the size of the US information industry with its European counterpart, and found that the US industry was up to five times larger than Europe's, even though the two economies were almost equal in size.[9] The Commission believes that the difference is due, in part, to the much more liberal rules on re-use of federal information in the USA. The Recitals to the PSI Directive make clear the Commission's view that a harmonised regime will provide a springboard for the development of a more successful information industry in Europe.

After extensive consultation, the Government decided to implement the PSI Directive through the Re-use of Public Sector Information Regulations 2005, which came into force on 1 July 2005. It was also decided that there was a need for a dedicated body to be the principal focal point for advising on and regulating the operation of public sector information re-use. OPSI was established for that purpose. Amongst other responsibilities, it develops information policy, sets standards and provides a practical framework of best practice for opening

---

[9] For reference see (2004), 'Exploiting the Potential of Europe's Public Sector Information', *European Commission, Directorate General for the Information Society, Unit Information market* (E4), available at europa.eu.int/information_society/policy/psi/docs/pdfs/brochure/psi_brochure_en.pdf.

up and encouraging the re-use of PSI. HMSO continues to exist and now performs its central tasks, operating from within OPSI.

The Regulations establish a framework for the effective re-use of public sector information based on principles of fairness to both the public sector and re-users. A public sector body (PSB) that creates or produces information must operate in a manner that is transparent, non-discriminatory, consistent, and in line with established best practice. PSBs are also required to have procedures in place to deal with complaints.

The Regulations introduce the category of 'complainant'. A complainant can be a public or private sector body or an individual who wants to make a complaint that a PSB has not complied with the Regulations. A complainant who has exhausted the PSB's internal complaints procedure can refer the matter to OPSI.

Where either party is dissatisfied with the conclusions reached by OPSI, they may request that it be reviewed by APPSI. A specially constituted board of APPSI (the Review Board) will consider eligible complaints. Additionally, where a complaint relates to the licensing of Crown copyright undertaken by OPSI, Her Majesty's Stationery Office (HMSO) or the Office of the Queen's Printer for Scotland (OQPS), the complainant may refer the complaint directly to APPSI. In exceptional circumstances, parties may request that a complaint is dealt with directly by APPSI.

It is early days yet for the Regulations; too early, in fact, to evaluate their impact so far.

6 CRITIQUE

Should UK citizens and business be pleased with progress? Is the Government moving in a sensible direction and, if so, is the rate of progress acceptable? Once again, the answers to these questions here are based on the ongoing work of APPSI, as laid out most definitively in the Panel's first and second annual reports.[10] The critique that follows relates to the period ending February 2006.

6.1 Overall ...

As said above, OPSI plays the leading role in formulating, implementing and regulating government policy on the re-use of PSI. APPSI has been impressed with the professionalism and energy of OPSI. Working closely with the DTI, OPSI implemented the PSI Directive very effectively. OPSI led two consultation

---

[10] www.appsi.gov.uk.

exercises, clarified and evolved PSI policy, oversaw the drafting of the PSI regulations and did so during the rather difficult pre-general election period. At the same time, OPSI runs a website that enjoys over 20 million hits each month and, as such, is the most visited government site in the UK.[11] Its Click-Use Licence scheme is an easy and effective system that permits the re-use of a wide range of core government information, while its Information Asset Register is a promising but, as yet, under-exploited listing of information resources held by the Government. All of that said, it is not clear to APPSI that the work of OPSI attracts sufficient support from ministers beyond the Cabinet Office. APPSI recognises that PSI is not seen (yet) as an issue of direct relevance to the general public but the Panel believes that it is vital to the economy of the country.

6.2 Awareness of the Importance of the Re-use of PSI is Low

It is not just ministers who are uninterested or unaware. Other than amongst government experts, digital content providers and information specialists, general awareness of the potential impact of the re-use of PSI is very low. How widely is it appreciated, for example, that, in 1996, 12–20 per cent of the UK's goods and services economy (to the value of £79–136 billion)[12] was underpinned by geographical information provided by Ordnance Survey, or that the public sector is the UK's largest producer of information, contributing to the nation's £18.37 billion information industry?[13] It is APPSI's experience that such statistics surprise all but a handful of senior officials and business people.

During 2005, to some extent, the Government's freedom of information (FOI) initiative may well have eclipsed the parallel work on the re-use of PSI. FOI was well publicised and, as said, there is often some confusion about the overlaps between the FOI regime and the PSI Directive. In principle, they are distinct – FOI is about access to information, while PSI is about re-use. In practice, the two can easily be confused. It may be that, as FOI handling becomes established, there will be scope now to build on the success of that initiative. As APPSI recommended in its first annual report, the re-use of PSI can complement FOI, and work to promote the two in tandem is encouraged. In any event, awareness-raising on PSI re-use remains a major challenge.

To respond to this challenge, APPSI has recommended that, just as the Government is now successfully stimulating interest and action in respect of the

---

[11] www.opsi.gov.uk.

[12] See note 1.

[13] See (2002), 'Publishing in the Knowledge Economy: Competitiveness Analysis of the UK Publishing Media Sector', research conducted by Pira International for the DTI and the UK Publishing Media.

FOI regime, similar effort should be expended in relation to the re-use of PSI. To complement awareness-raising, it is also important that the Government clarifies various confusions (such as the distinctions between 'access to PSI', 're-use of PSI' and 'use of PSI', and between 'core data' and 'value-added data'), so that newcomers and practitioners in the field are not deterred by what may seem to be confusing terminology. Although the Government and the digital content industry speak confidently about PSI and its re-use, the reality is that the field is complex, diverse and perplexing.

6.3   Government Policy is Too Fragmented

Generally, there can be little doubt that the Government is committed to the re-use and the maximisation of the value of PSI. Indeed, as suggested, since 1996 there has been increasing liberalisation, such that it has become steadily easier to identify and gain access to relevant official information. APPSI has welcomed the overall direction of that policy. However, it has regretted to find that, on closer scrutiny, the policies pursued in this area by individual departments do not always align with one another.

While it is clear that there is general commitment to deriving value from the re-use of PSI, it is not clear who the Government would want to benefit. In broad summary, and to mention but four perspectives: the Cabinet Office promotes the re-use of PSI to enhance the knowledge economy and the quality and range of government services; HM Treasury is particularly keen on leveraging PSI to generate revenue or reduce the costs of government; the DCA is seeking to create more transparent government through freedom of information legislation; and the DTI wishes to enhance the competitive positioning of the UK information industry. None of these objectives, in isolation, is incoherent. However, taken together, these various approaches can and often do conflict with one another. Certainly, they do not cohere and form a single, consistent set of policies on PSI which can be readily understood by the citizen.

And there is further confusion in government policy. Although copyright is the principal legal tool for managing the re-use of PSI, the same copyright regime does not apply across the public sector. For example, Crown copyright applies only to Crown bodies. Some central government bodies, which might be taken by the layperson to be Crown bodies, are not Crown bodies for technical legal reasons; and different rules on the re-use of PSI apply to each. By way of further illustration, local authorities are subject to laws of copyright but not to Crown copyright and so, again, the rules that apply to them are not the same as those that apply to Crown bodies. Even more surprisingly, the output of the Houses of Parliament is subject to a distinct set of provisions – Parliamentary copyright, which, although administered by OPSI, is governed by distinct rules.

A coherent system that would make sense to the citizen would surely have the same set of copyright provisions applying equally to all public bodies, whether local or central government, Crown body or otherwise. APPSI has therefore concluded in this context that the government's policy on PSI is unacceptably piecemeal, fragmented by diverging departmental policy objectives and a clear absence of so-called 'joined-up' thinking. There was some progress in this area during 2004 and 2005. One of APPSI's recommendations was that a joint working party be set up to bring together the Department for Constitutional Affairs (DCA), the Department of Trade and Industry (DTI) and OPSI to work on PSI matters. This has happened and it is understood that the meetings are productive.

APPSI directly addressed the issue of coherence of government policy in its second annual seminar in Oxford (in March 2005), entitled 'Managing public sector information more coherently'.[14] The National Archives (TNA) were represented at that event at a senior level and a solid relationship between TNA, OPSI and APPSI began to be forged.

It can be concluded that policy-making and thinking about the management of PSI at the centre of government is becoming more coherent. It still falls short of the single, cost-efficient, coherent long-term policy and strategy that APPSI recommended in 2004 but OPSI, DTI, TNA and DCA, for example, are recognising and managing the overlaps more effectively. However, some significant tensions remain, not least on the economic front – whether PSI re-use is, crudely, for the benefit of government, intermediaries or end-users remains unclear. Nor can this be settled until there is greater clarity about the government's future intentions with regard to the commercial exploitation of PSI, as discussed below.

Furthermore, thinking and practice still seem insufficiently joined up within departments and agencies and in local government. Public bodies should regard record-keeping and document management, FOI and the re-use of PSI as a single management challenge. Feedback to APPSI is that, on the ground, public sector information management is instead rather fragmented.

With these shortcomings in mind, it is relevant to note that, for the longer term, APPSI has recommended that a group of senior officials from across relevant government departments formulate one single, cost-efficient, coherent long-term policy and strategy for information management within the UK public sector. This would embrace not only FOI and PSI but also electronic records management, e-government, knowledge management within government, data protection, Environmental Information Regulations 2004, national statistics and, importantly (given its considerable scope and potential), the redevelopment of

---

[14] See APPSI's second Annual Report at www.appsi.gov.uk.

the Government's Information Asset Register. This work would include consideration of whether there is merit in all information management being brought under the umbrella of a single department.

6.4   Government's Commercial Exploitation of PSI Needs Greater Scrutiny

It is difficult to evaluate the Government's current approach to the commercial exploitation of PSI because, surprisingly and as already mentioned, there seems to be little robust financial data about the actual or potential value of PSI, or about the revenues and profits that PSI yields across the public sector. Individual sectors and agencies can and do provide statistics but there is insufficient data *across* government and the public sector. Nor indeed does it seem clear to the government how PSI can or should be measured.

Moreover, academic and theoretical thinking about the economics of PSI is still at an early stage. There are no well-established schools of thought or neat, standard models upon which analysts and the Government can rely. Accordingly, commentators should be wary of any dogmatic thinking about what might be claimed to be the best way to maximise the value of PSI. The Government, too, might usefully keep an open mind.

The current position is that most public bodies charge for the supply of PSI at marginal cost. However, some government departments or agencies (or parts of departments or agencies), known as trading funds, are permitted to operate like private sector businesses. The licensing of PSI by the current trading funds generates significant revenues that finance their daily governmental operations. APPSI has not yet found itself in a position to comment definitively as to whether this current position is optimal for now or the future. Its early thinking was that it was broadly supportive of the general approach and it saw value in preserving trading funds (not least to maintain incentives to innovate). But it was also of the view that the scope of trading funds' activities and the extent to which they competed with the private sector needed serious further analysis.

In its first annual report, APPSI made recommendations in this connection. First, the Panel urged the government to be more systematic and rigorous in its measurement of PSI activity. Looking to the longer term, such measurement needed to include not just PSI re-use but also the value of the fuller exploitation of public sector *knowledge* systems. It also recommended that the Government should establish benchmarks and targets for the steady increase in re-use of PSI. These should include figures in respect of added-value services provided by commercial re-users who exploit PSI. The result should be a PSI sector that is more measurable and accountable than today. In its second annual report, APPSI noted with 'much regret' that its recommendations of the previous year, urging more systematic measurement and establishing benchmarks and targets for PSI re-use, had seemed to have been given little priority.

Interestingly, in the intervening year, some APPSI members encountered a growing uncertainty about the economic models underpinning the trading funds – those public bodies that, in licensing PSI, are permitted to operate more like private sector businesses. Accordingly, in its second annual report, APPSI also recommended that the Government undertake or commission a sustained and detailed study into the economics of government information, including but not limited to the activities of those trading funds whose main business is the collection, maintenance and dissemination of PSI. In turn, it was believed that this work would require more rigorous measurement of PSI re-use than had been undertaken in the past. Coincidentally, or perhaps not, the Office of Fair Trading is now conducting a market study on the commercial use of public information which should address some of these vexed questions about the economics of PSI.[15]

6.5   PSI should be of Value to End Users as well as to Intermediaries

When APPSI was first set up, much of the emphasis was on making sure that core public sector information was made available, under appropriate conditions, to intermediaries who could add value to it. A second more radical challenge has emerged, and this has been mentioned periodically in this chapter. It concerns information management and knowledge management on a very large scale across government. It is about ensuring that the valuable collective knowledge and experience (the 'intellectual capital') of public sector workers is captured and re-used. As has been said, today it is barely managed and is underexploited; knowledge has become disposable; more systematic recycling is required. In this context, APPSI has supported recent calls for a government minister to be given explicit responsibility for the proactive management of knowledge within the public sector. APPSI has encouraged ministers to identify one amongst their number to take explicit responsibility in this area. As yet, by way of response, there has been silence.

---

[15]   www.oft.gov.uk/business/market+studies/cases.

7   CASE STUDY – STATUTE LAW

Some of the themes of this chapter can be illustrated, by way of conclusion, through a case study relating to the availability and accessibility of statute law.[16]

Traditionally, which for current purposes can be taken to mean 'before the Web', to gain sight of statutory material, a reader had to visit a library, or purchase a hard copy of the instrument in question, or perhaps buy a textbook in which the law in question had been reproduced (by permission of the Crown). This state of affairs attracted all sorts of criticisms. How could citizens be presumed to know all of the law, it was often asked, even though its contents were rather inaccessible? And, when the Internet came along, why was statutory material not available on what was then called the 'information superhighway'? In 1996, at proof stage, the current author inserted a footnote in his book, *The Future of Law*: 'As this book went to press, however, the government announced (on 9th February 1996) what appears to be a sensible change in policy in relation to the electronic reproduction of legislation, although it is too early to know what the practical effects might be.'[17]

One practical effect, of course, is that huge quantities of legislative material (primary and secondary legislation) are now made available online, at no cost to users. This is now a key public service, provided by OPSI in the form of *HMSOnline* at their much-used website, www.opsi.gov.uk.

Fundamentally, for the purposes of this chapter, however, the shift in government policy relating to legislation enabled the development of a very significant online legal information service, one that highlights some of this chapter's themes about the re-use of PSI. The service in question is the British and Irish Legal Information Institute (BAILII).[18] Run as a modestly funded charity, BAILII provides the largest, free-of-charge online collection of British and Irish primary legal materials (legislation and case law). In 2005, when it celebrated its fifth birthday, the service covered seven jurisdictions and held 400 000 searchable documents with about 15 million internal hypertext links. The links were vital, enabling users to jump, for example, from law reports into specific sections of legislation. BAILII deploys Australian technology contributed originally by AustLII,[19] an institute that has also championed the remarkable WorldLII.[20] The

[16]   For a more general discussion of this subject, see Leith, P. and McCullagh, K. (2004), 'Developing European Legal Information Markets based on Government Information', *International Journal of Law and Information Technology*, **12** (3), 247.

[17]   Oxford University Press, 1996, p. 20, footnote 1.

[18]   www.bailii.org.

[19]   www.austlii.org.

[20]   www.wordlii.org.

latter's mission is to offer free and independent access to the law of many legal systems (currently 55 jurisdictions). Underpinning these various services is the conviction – encapsulated in the slogan 'free the law' – that legal materials should be directly accessible to all citizens at no cost to them.

BAILII is an early and fine example of the re-use of PSI. The raw material, in the form of statutes and law reports, was brought together and subjected to remarkable technology that was developed by academics. A new, extremely valuable information resource was thereby created and is now available to all. More than this, where BAILII has been of immense significance, the service has actually brought about a shift in the Government's approach to statutory material and law reports – a shift from being reactive to being proactive. Source materials for inclusion in BAILII, whether legislation or law reports, are now provided as a matter of course; it is part of the process of government (of DCA and OPSI). BAILII is not just about making legal information available to citizens and to lawyers, which of itself is of immense significance. More than this, it is a very early example of a fundamental shift in the nature of government, a shift towards thorough-going proactive government.

In many ways, the BAILII experience foreshadows a great many of the other efforts across government to try to re-use and harness PSI more widely. To re-use it, as can be seen from BAILII, it may indeed be necessary to reorganise PSI, or add to it or refine it. This additional value might be added by public sector bodies or by private sector organizations (such as publishers), or by charitable bodies or academic organisations. Or the work might be carried out in the spirit of an 'open source' venture.[21] In any event, what is fundamental is the Government's active support and involvement.[22]

---

[21] See Weber, S. (2004), *The Success of Open Source*, Cambridge, MA: Harvard University Press.

[22] For sake of completeness, one further, related, government initiative should be mentioned – the Statute Law Database (SLD) project. The Statutory Publications Office, an office within the Department for Constitutional Affairs, is producing a Statute Law Database of United Kingdom legislation. This currently contains the text of all Acts that were in force on 1 February 1991 and all Acts and printed Statutory Instruments passed since then. It also contains local legislation, both primary and printed secondary. The key feature of the system is that it will offer a historical view of primary legislation for any specific day from the base date of 1 February 1991 and any prospective legislation. This project has been running for over a decade. It will be interesting to see, given the thrust of the PSI regime and given the general trend to make PSI freely available, whether the government seeks to charge for the provision of that service, even that part that is argued to be value-added. There could be some heated discussions about this!

12. Audiences in tradition: traditional knowledge and the public domain

Johanna Gibson

1 INTRODUCTION

Indigenous and traditional knowledge has emerged as critical subject matter in international trade and development. While presenting significant commercial and research potential in various areas of knowledge and technology – including medicine, agriculture and creative industries – such cultural resources are also intrinsic to the integrity and identity specific to local and traditional communities. Historically, the appropriation of that knowledge was 'justified' as legitimate spoils of colonial, scientific and anthropological endeavour, where the knowledge (like any other aspect of the environment 'discovered' through colonial exploration) was itself deemed 'natural', part of humanity's global heritage, and for the benefit of all. Indeed, the subjugation of the knowledge and cultures of colonised peoples to the 'superior' knowledge of the coloniser can be identified as a critical aspect of the imperialist process.

Similarly, within current concerns over expanding intellectual property rights, access to knowledge, and the vitality of the 'public domain', the debate over traditional knowledge seems to be dominated by the prior and governing concerns of a global knowledge of a global public. In other words, traditional knowledge was, and to an extent continues to be, interpreted within the dominant legal and social discourse as common heritage rather than creative or personal knowledge.[1] The knowledge of traditional and indigenous communities is

---

[1]   Gray, S. (1996), 'Squatting in Red Dust: Non-Aboriginal Law's Construction of the "Traditional" Aboriginal Artist', 14(2) *Law in Context* 29, 30. Note also the rejection of this management of traditional knowledge as public domain goods, with respect to crop genetic resources, particularly in the context of the International Treaty on Plant Genetic Resources for Food and Agriculture, in Brush, S.B. (2003), 'The Demise of "Common Heritage" and Protection for Traditional Agricultural Knowledge', conference paper, Biodiversity, Biotechnology and the Protection of Traditional Knowledge, St Louis, MO, 4–5 April. See also the discussion of this Treaty and the potential impact on traditional knowledge in genetic resources in IISD (Summer 2003), 'Traditional Know-

presented as a nostalgic and archaic object, created for the benefit and sharing of all.[2] The question of access to those resources is legitimated and prioritised over the question of cultural integrity, rather than recognised as being perhaps just one aspect of the interests at stake.

Concerning this notion of common heritage (within the expanding concept of the global public, to which the discussion will return), the denial of 'ownership' has been systematically refuted in diverse forums, including the institutionalised debate within the World Intellectual Property Organization (WIPO) Intergovernmental Committee on Intellectual Property and Genetic Resources, Traditional Knowledge and Folklore (IGC). Calls have been made for the protection of traditional knowledge, not only as a matter of property but also, and more critically, as a matter of intrinsic importance to the dignity and cohesion of traditional and indigenous communities. However, particularly in the case of the institutionalised and legitimated debate on these questions (namely, the debate within WIPO), proposals for protection continue to resonate within intellectual property systems, informed particularly by the potential value of trade in traditional knowledge. One critical aspect of the debate is the situation of traditional knowledge within the public domain that is qualified by modern intellectual property systems.

---

ledge and Patentability' IISD Trade and Development Brief, No. 7. See also the discussion in Taubman, A., 'The Public Domain and International Intellectual Property Lay Treaties', Chapter 4 in this volume.

[2]   Chander and Sunder discuss this romanticisation of traditional knowledge and identify the polarisation (and, as such, hierarchisation) of knowledge from the north and south as private (commercial, useful) and public (archaic, natural) respectively, Chander, A. and Sunder, M. (2004), 'The Romance of the Public Domain,' 92 *California Law Review* 1331. See also the discussion in Nwokeabia, H. (2001), 'Why Industrial Revolution Missed Africa: A "Traditional Knowledge" Perspective', Economic Commission for Africa, ECA/ESPD/WPS/01/02, 15, where the author identifies a similar polarisation of useful (commercial) private knowledge and insignificant (non-commercial) traditional or public knowledge: 'Because of the insignificance of African traditional knowledge on the livelihood of the owners, comparative to the European counterparts in the Western perception and intellectual property laws, African TK is regarded as information in the "public domain," static and freely available for use by anyone.' See also the concerns raised in Coombe, R.J. (1998), 'Intellectual Property Rights, Human Rights and Sovereignty: New Dilemmas in International Law Posed by the Recognition of Indigenous Knowledge and the Conservation of Biodiversity', 6 *Indiana Journal of Global Legal Studies*, 59, 15. Dutfield also notes a cultural bias in the way in which the public domain is applied to traditional knowledge, Dutfield, G. (2002), 'Protection of Traditional Knowledge and Folklore: A Review of Progress in Diplomacy and Policy Formulation', in UNCTAD/ICTSD, *Capacity Building Project on Intellectual Property Rights and Sustainable Development*, October, 47, note 90.

2   PUBLIC KNOWLEDGE – NO SPACE FOR TRADITION

The notion of the 'public domain' as defined, understood and applied within intellectual property frameworks,[3] continues to legitimate ongoing appropriation of traditional knowledge as 'archaic' public goods. Construing traditional knowledge as public goods in this way, it is sometimes argued to be legally (and morally) impossible to exclude access. Thus arguments for access to traditional knowledge are seemingly ethically privileged over arguments for recognition of the importance of traditional knowledge as cultural resources, by virtue of the construction of the public domain around the 'good' of traditional knowledge rather than the diversity and internal governance of community.[4]

Somewhat supporting this presumption with respect to traditional knowledge (of public access and public goods), international standardisation of intellectual property protection has been criticised as a potentially unjust generalisation of protection, almost inevitably in conflict with the needs of traditional knowledge holders.[5] First, there is an increasing emphasis on the economic analysis[6] and conceptualisation of the knowledge according to a Western norm of efficiency and certainty in international trade,[7] as disengaged from the personal under-

---

[3]   Tauli-Corpuz notes that the development of the concept of the public domain is tied to the development of intellectual property rights, Tauli-Corpuz, V. (2005), 'Biodiversity, Traditional Knowledge and Rights of Indigenous Peoples' IPRs Series No. 5, International Workshop on Traditional Knowledge, 21–23 September, UN Department of Economic and Social Affairs, Division for Social Policy and Development, Secretariat of the Permanent Forum on Indigenous Issues, PFII/2005/WS.TK/5, 11. See also the concerns of the Tulalip Tribes of Washington in their Statement to the Fifth Session of the IGC: Tulalip Tribes (2003), Statement by the Tulalip Tribes of Washington on Folklore, Indigenous Knowledge, and the Public Domain, 9 July, WIPO Intergovernmental Committee on Intellectual Property and Genetic Resources, Traditional Knowledge and Folklore, Fifth Session, Geneva, 5–17 July.

[4]   For further discussion on the notion of resources as a means of individual communities, as distinct from discrete products or goods to be identified through trading relationships, see Gibson, J. (2005), *Community Resources: Intellectual Property, International Trade and Protection of Traditional Knowledge*, Aldershot: Ashgate (hereafter Gibson (2005)).

[5]   Dutfield notes this conflict between intellectual property regimes in developing and developed countries and capacity building in developing countries in Dutfield, G. (2003), *Intellectual Property Rights and the Life Science Industries: A Twentieth Century History*, Aldershot: Ashgate, p. 29.

[6]   The globalisation of intellectual property rights has been identified as emphasising the economic analysis of rights, in which a Western perspective dominates the international standards. For a discussion of this emphasis in the context of the TRIPS negotiations, see Gervais, D. (2003), *The TRIPS Agreement: Drafting History and Analysis*, 2nd edn, London: Sweet & Maxwell.

[7]   The drive towards greater efficiency is coupled with notions of increased certainty

standing and investment of the community. The assimilation of traditional knowledge within intellectual property models suggests, therefore, a (n implicit) deference to international trade relationships. Secondly, the interests of communities in preserving and managing resources on a cohesive local basis,[8] while respecting the global diversity of communities and their self-governance, is at best compromised and at worst rendered impossible under this generalising economy of commodities.

Indeed, the very construction of traditional knowledge as 'public' common knowledge within the public domain is built upon essentially commercial concerns for that public. The public domain is, in and of itself, a question of commercial construction, composed as it is of those goods for which the monopoly (as an assessment of the value in time required to recover the 'costs' in the risks of creativity and innovation) has expired. It is therefore implied that the commercial utility of anything within the public domain has passed, while the value and priority continues to attach to knowledge that is protected by intellectual property rights.[9]

Traditional knowledge recognised and governed as resources of and by the community, and acknowledgement and application of the specific 'public domains' that operate within specific communities, are thus rejected, as it were, both by the commercial interests seeking access to the creation of intellectual property rights and by certain aspects of campaigns for greater public access. Rightly or wrongly, the focus created by the 'public domain' debate is defined by 'commercial' reasons in the broader sense, because of the way in which the public domain is itself constructed, interpreted and applied. Thus the public domain is a strategic factor not only in arguments for access but also in industry rhetoric, to support commercial interests seeking access to traditional knowledge and genetic resources as public resources.

There appears to be an uneasy relationship between traditional knowledge and access debates, despite the concerns regarding expanding intellectual prop-

---

and risk-management. The notion of 'risk' and international regulation of knowledge and information is considered in more detail in Gibson (2005).

[8] For instance, with regard to the current process of implementation of the Convention on Biological Diversity (CBD), see most recently the press release issued by the CBD, where Ahmed Djoghlaf, Executive Secretary to the CBD, recognises the role of local traditional communities in that technical governance process and at the physical *in situ* conservation recognised in the Convention text and at the meetings of the Conference of the Parties, CBD (2006), 'Indigenous and Local Communities Have Important Role to Play in Implementation of Biodiversity Convention', press release, 6 January.

[9] Nwokeabia, H. (2001), 'Why Industrial Revolution Missed Africa: A "Traditional Knowledge" Perspective', Economic Commission for Africa, ECA/ESPD/WPS/01/02, 15.

erty rights almost uniformly shared by both interests. Paradoxically, the traditional knowledge holders are sometimes vilified by access groups as seeking an expansion of intellectual property rights, a construction which arguably misreads and misrepresents the fundamental terms of the debate. As the universal public domain is created, therefore, and traditional knowledge situated within that fictive space, the relevance of local or traditional cultural identity and understanding is disorganised. That is, the application of the label of public domain to traditional knowledge assists in the organisation of all knowledge without reference to indigenous or local tradition. In other words, a 'public' of users is created without any reference to conflicting (historically and otherwise) cultural and ideological circumstances for the production of that knowledge. In particular territories where there is ongoing conflict between indigenous peoples and invaders (including, for example, Australia, Canada, the United States and New Zealand) this interpretation of traditional knowledge as public domain knowledge conjures a uniform public of both colonisers and colonised in what is arguably an ongoing imperialist process upon the assimilation of knowledge. The circumstances for knowledge production, the cultural and political identity attaching to that knowledge and the practices associated with that knowledge are 'forgotten' in this process,[10] which depends upon the extraction of traditional knowledge as 'products'.

What is critical in distilling the terms of the debate is an examination of the way in which references to the public domain operate in the construction of the users (including the construction of traditional peoples as any other users with respect to their 'public' traditional knowledge) as a passive audience, as consumers, and indeed as somehow opposite to the business of creativity.[11] The very nature of the Western concept of the public domain is such that intellectual property ownership is prior to the debate. Users are somewhat diminished as coming after intellectual property and, to a certain extent, 'created' by intellectual property in so far as they arise as an audience of the knowledge products within the creative economy of intellectual property. This process of distancing and disengagement from the creative enterprise is critical to the construction of the passive and anonymous user or consumer of the personality of the creator.

---

[10]   In this construction of the public the figure of the 'global' user becomes clear and one which almost depends upon an obscuring of the cultural diversity otherwise at work in the production of knowledge.

[11]   Alastair Hannay makes similar comments on the notion of the political public, where he argues that the public merely has 'a watching brief' in modern political debate, Hannay, A. (2005), *On the Public*, London: Routledge, p. 67. In modern intellectual property law debates, Hannay's concept is useful in understanding the way in which NGOs are able to participate formally within the debate and the extent to which that participation (and representation) is recognised.

Active users are thus not conceivable and any 'creativity' in that use is not rec-
ognisable within the paradigm. Intellectual property right-holders, by the same
process, are constructed as the initial or primary public invested in participation
in the debate.[12] Arguably, intellectual property rights are somewhat conceived
as a prerequisite for participation, a requirement of the 'political' participation
in the debate in that they indicate an 'investment' in the civilised organisation
of the public.[13]

3   THE PUBLIC DOMAIN AS PROTECTION

As noted earlier, international discussion towards the resolution of these apparently competing interests has been placed formally under the administration of
WIPO's Intergovernmental Committee on Intellectual Property and Genetic
Resources, Traditional Knowledge and Folklore (IGC).[14] To date most applications of protection have been merely defensive, through exclusions from the
creation of intellectual property and the 'appropriation' of traditional knowledge
within the private domain of a particular commercial interest.[15] In this way,

---

[12]   In practical terms this is often realised in the form of a certain authority or qualification granted to right-holders within the debates, whereby the arguments of publishers
are sometimes interpreted as more credible and informed and the interests of consumers
in those debates somewhat distanced. This was a criticism made by consumer groups of
recent government consultations in Europe (for instance, see the Access to Knowledge
campaign archives concerning the Creative Economy UK EU Presidency Conference,
London, 5–7 October 2005).

[13]   In this respect, intellectual property rights and the risks undertaken in their creation
(as creators and as investors) are almost privileged with respect to the ethical position
of the various interests. For instance, see the 'unreasonableness' applied to positions
contrary to intellectual property rights in Sell, S.K. (1999), 'Multinational Corporations
as Agents of Change: the Globalization of Intellectual Property Rights', in Cutler, A.C.
et al. (eds), *Private Authority and International Affairs*, Albany: SUNY Press,
pp. 174–5.

[14]   The WIPO Intergovernmental Committee on Intellectual Property and Genetic
Resources, Traditional Knowledge and Folklore (IGC) was established in the 26th (12th
Extraordinary Session) of the WIPO General Assembly, held in Geneva, 25 September
to 3 October 2000, to consider and advise on appropriate actions concerning the economic and cultural significance of tradition-based creations and the issues of conservation,
management, sustainable use and sharing of the benefits from the use of genetic resources
and traditional knowledge, as well as the enforcement of rights to traditional knowledge
and folklore. For a review of the progress of the IGC, see Gibson, J. (2004), 'Intellectual
Property Systems, Traditional Knowledge, and the Legal Authority of Community', **26**
(7) *European Intellectual Property Review* 280; and Gibson (2005), Chapter 4.

[15]   Examples of defensive mechanisms include moves towards the documentation of
traditional knowledge, for example, to assist its recognition as prior art (see the extensive

mechanisms to ensure the status of traditional knowledge as knowledge in the public domain (such as prior art databases,[16] digital libraries[17] and the concept

---

report on registers and databases in Alexander, M. et al. (2003), 'The Role of Registers and Databases in the Protection of Traditional Knowledge: A Comparative Analysis', Report, Tokyo: UNU-IAS; see also the discussion in Gibson, J. (2004), 'Intellectual Property Systems, Traditional Knowledge, and the Legal Authority of Community', 26 (7) *European Intellectual Property Review* 280, and Gibson (2005), Chapter 4, of the developments in international patent classification tools for traditional knowledge, as part of the discussions of the Special Union for the International Patent Classification, the exclusion from trade mark registration of marks likely to cause cultural offence (for instance, the specific application of trade mark law in New Zealand, as discussed in Chapter 4), and certification marks. For a discussion of authenticity and certification marks in the Australian context, see Wiseman, L. (2001), 'The Protection of Indigenous Art and Culture in Australia: The Labels of Authenticity', 23 (1) *European Intellectual Property Review* 14; Gough, R. (2000), 'Label of Authenticity', 13 (1) *Intellectual Property Law Bulletin* 9; Wells, K. (1996), 'The Development of an Authenticity Trade Mark for Indigenous Artists', 21 (1) *Alternative Law Journal* 38; Golvan, C. and Wollner, A. (1991), 'Certification Mark to Protect Art', 4 *Australian Intellectual Property Law Bulletin* 104. Defensive mechanisms form a major part of discussions in the IGC (discussed further in Gibson (2005), Chapter 4). Similarly, the 2004 United Nations Development Programme (UNDP) Human Development Report also unreservedly recommends documentation, maintaining that it is frequently essential to achieve protection and 'does not prejudice rights', UNDP (2004), 'Cultural Liberty in Today's Diverse World', in *Human Development Report*, New York, p. 95. However, documentation is not unproblematic in its application. See further Gibson (2005), Chapter 4.

[16]   For example, note the Traditional Ecological Knowledge Prior Art Database of AAAS, which has met much criticism. See also the discussion of traditional knowledge as prior art in Ruiz, M. (2002), 'The International Debate on Traditional Knowledge as Prior Art in the Patent System: Issues and Options for Developing Countries', Trade-Related Agenda, Development and Equity (TRADE) Occasional Papers, No. 9, Geneva, South Centre.

[17]   For example, note the Traditional Knowledge Digital Library (TKDL) for Indian systems of medicine, which has met both positive (see Sen, N. (2002), 'TKDL: A Safeguard for Indian Traditional Knowledge', 82 (9) *Current Science*, 1070) and negative receptions (see Sharma, D. (2002), 'Digital Library Another Tool for Biopiracy', Mindfully.org, 29 May; Jayaraman, K.S. (2002), 'Biopiracy Fears Cloud Indian Database', *Science and Development Network*, 5 December). For more on the TKDL see CIPR (2002), Commission on Intellectual Property Rights, *Integrating Intellectual Property Rights and Development Policy*, London, p. 81. See the extensive report on databases and registers undertaken for the UNU-IAS by Alexander, M. et al. (2003), *The Role of Registers and Databases in the Protection of Traditional Knowledge: A Comparative Analysis*, Report, Tokyo: UNU-IAS. See also the concerns regarding documentation and misappropriation in Tauli-Corpuz, V. (2005), 'Biodiversity, Traditional Knowledge and Rights of Indigenous Peoples', IPRs Series No. 5, International Workshop on Traditional Knowledge, 21–23 September, UN Department of Economic and Social Affairs, Division for Social Policy and Development, Secretariat of the Permanent Forum on Indigenous Issues, PFII/2005/WS.TK/5.

of *domaine public payant[18]*) have been presumed to be logical and relevant means of protection.[19] However, such approaches prioritise a certain user public without giving effect to customary systems of governance and maintenance of cultural integrity with respect to that knowledge.[20] Thus, in many cases, it is accepted that traditional knowledge can nevertheless be understood as 'public knowledge,' as it were, without recognising community authority with respect to the way in which that knowledge is accessed, disseminated and used.

Indigenous and traditional groups have made strong arguments against this rendition of their knowledge, throughout the international discussions and in various arenas. In a recent Joint Statement to the 23rd session of the Working Group on Indigenous Populations,[21] the Indigenous World Association and Indigenous Media Network raised several concerns about the concept of the public domain and about the articulation of protection through the application of public and private databases:

> [W]e stress that there are striking similarities between seizing our territories and the taking of our knowledge by defining it as part of the public domain. Both are based on the notion that they constitute *res nullius*, the property of no one, and can be treated as such. Placing our knowledge into the public domain turns it into a freely available resource for commercial utilization. Thus, it also creates the pre-condition for using

---

[18] The *domaine public payant* (a paying public domain) involves the collection of funds from those seeking access to the knowledge within. Such funds would ordinarily be used towards programmes within the communities of the traditional knowledge holders involved. See the discussion in Gervais, D. (2001), 'Traditional Knowledge: A Challenge to the International Intellectual Property System', Fordham University Conference on International Intellectual Property Law & Policy, New York City, 20 April, p. 13. See also Dutfield, G. (2002), 'Protection of Traditional Knowledge and Folklore: A Review of Progress in Diplomacy and Policy Formulation', UNCTAD/ICTSD Capacity Building Project on Intellectual Property Rights and Sustainable Development, October, p. 34. See also the discussion on the *domaine public payante* in Davies, G., 'The Public Domain and the Public Interest', Chapter 5 of this volume.

[19] Downes, D. (1997), 'Using Intellectual Property as a Tool to Protect Traditional Knowledge: Recommendations for Next Steps', CIEL Discussion Paper, November. See also the discussion in Chapman, A.R. (2001), 'Approaching Intellectual Property as a Human Right', 35 (3) *Copyright Bulletin* 4.

[20] Tauli-Corpuz explains: 'We have developed nuanced systems and mechanisms which enable us to safeguard and protect our knowledge and to define how, when and to whom it can be shared with. The public domain concept has not taken these into consideration', Tauli-Corpuz, V. (2005), 'Biodiversity, Traditional Knowledge and Rights of Indigenous Peoples', IPRs Series No. 5, International Workshop on Traditional Knowledge, 21–23 September, UN Department of Economic and Social Affairs, Division for Social Policy and Development, Secretariat of the Permanent Forum on Indigenous Issues, PFII/2005/WS.TK/5, 11.

[21] Commission on Human Rights, Sub-Commission on the Promotion and Protection of Human Rights, Working Group on Indigenous Populations.

non-indigenous Intellectual Property Rights (IPR) regimes to patent 'inventions'
based upon our knowledge ... We therefore strongly reject the application of the
public domain concept to any aspect related to our cultures and identities, including
human and other genetic information originating from our lands and waters.[22]

Significantly, this Joint Statement likens the construction of traditional knowledge as public to the imperialist conquering of territory during colonisation, as
suggested earlier. Knowledge is a critical tool not only historically in forces of
colonisation but also in a contemporary context through the prioritisation of
particular economic constructions of innovation, models of knowledge production, and presumptions of how and why we create.

These concerns are supported in the reports and studies of non-governmental
organisations (NGOs). For instance, the policy discussion paper of the United
Nations Commission on Trade and Development (UNCTAD) and the International Centre for Trade and Sustainable Development (ICTSD) Joint Project on
IPRs and Sustainable Development identifies the following:

[F]or many traditional peoples and groups, certain expressions and works are central
to their cultural identity and should therefore never be fully released into the public
domain, at least not to the extent that others would be free to do whatever they like
with them. This is not to say that copyright protection should therefore be permanent
for culturally significant expressions and works, but that copyright law should not be
seen as the appropriate approach for each and every kind of cultural work.[23]

Evident in these discussions is the key concern that while traditional knowledge
is presumed to be sacred and cultural knowledge, for which certain 'exclusions'
from intellectual property protection would be adequate,[24] this kind of defensive

---

²²   Indigenous World Association and Indigenous Media Network (2005), Joint Statement, Commission on Human Rights, Sub-Commission on the Promotion and Protection
of Human Rights, Working Group on Indigenous Populations, 23rd Session, 18–22 July,
3, Review of Developments Pertaining to the Promotion and Protection of the Rights of
Indigenous Peoples, Including their Human Rights and Fundamental Freedoms: Principal
Theme, 'Indigenous Peoples and the International and Domestic Protection of Traditional
Knowledge', Item 4(b) of the provisional agenda, 13 July, E/CN.4/Sub.2/AC.4/2005/
CRP.3.
²³   UNCTAD/ICTSD (2003), 'Intellectual Property Rights: Implications for Development', Policy Discussion Paper, UNCTAD/*ICTSD* Capacity Building Project on
Intellectual Property Rights and Sustainable Development, August, p. 120.
²⁴   The basis of this approach is the argument that cultural symbols would be appropriately protected through recognition as 'national' emblems or royal insignia, and thus
excluded from trade mark registration. For example, the Zia Indians of New Mexico
sought to make symbols unable to be trademarked: Lopez, R. (1999), 'Tribes seek
trademark protection for sacred symbols', *Revista Magazine*, 9 July. However, this approach fails to capture a broad quantity of knowledge (words, for example) as well as
ignoring the fact that communities wish to retain (and should be entitled to do so) the

archiving and 'safeguarding' continues the historical and classical anthropological effect[25] upon indigenous and traditional communities, documenting knowledge as a kind of 'ethnographic present.'[26] While defensive approaches are an aspect of mechanisms of protection, they risk an ongoing paternalism and persistent historicising of the value of knowledge.

Furthermore, this conceptualisation of protection maintains the underlying presumption, with respect to the processes of innovation and creativity within indigenous and traditional communities, that such processes are processes of the 'global' public, rather than creativity of the community. As such, the innovation is not recognised for the purposes of the 'self' of intellectual property, and so the knowledge is not recognised as personal to the community. Rather, the knowledge is distanced as an end in and of itself and as a right of the public domain.

Repeatedly implied in this approach, and in the construction of traditional knowledge as public domain knowledge, is an informal distinction between the validation of conventional knowledge production and the invalidation of traditional forms of innovation.[27] As a result, that innovation is not recognised for

---

right to license material where appropriate (as became apparent to the Zia Indians). Ignoring this right continues the presumption that traditional knowledge is historical and 'antiquated' knowledge in the public domain. Protection therefore proceeds from the notion of preservation of that history, rather than genuine recognition of customary management by living communities.

[25] This is of course with reference, in particular, to 19th-century anthropology and the perceived relationship with colonial efforts, as distinct from contemporary critical anthropology which seeks to problematise and dismantle dominant relationships between the privileged anthropological eye and the natural, organic, anthropological object. For instance, see the work of critical anthropologists, including Clifford Geertz, James Clifford, Marilyn Strathern and Vered Amit. In particular, see Strathern, M. (1999), *Property Substance and Effect: Anthropological Essays on Persons and Things*, London: Athlone Press; Geertz, C. (1973), *The Interpretation of Cultures*, London: Fontana; Geertz, C. (1983), *Local Knowledge*, New York: Basic Books; Clifford, J. (1986), 'On Ethnographic Allegory', in J. Clifford and G.E. Marcus (eds), *Writing Culture: The Poetics and Politics of Ethnography*, Berkeley: U. of California, pp. 98–121; Amit, V. and Rapport, N. (2002), *The Trouble with Community: Anthropological Reflections on Movement, Identity and Collectivity*, London: Pluto Press. See also the concerns with the relationship between imperialist endeavour and anthropology in Masolo, D.A. (1994), *African Philosophy in Search of Identity*, Bloomington: Indiana UP; and Mudimbe, V.Y. (1988), *The Invention of Africa*, Bloomington: Indiana UP.

[26] Note James Clifford's comments on the tendency of early anthropology to presume and idealise an 'ethnographic present' as 'a static, pre-contact, traditional culture', in Clifford, J. (2003), *On the Edges of Anthropology: Interviews*, Chicago: Prickly Paradigm, p. 9.

[27] Note the earlier discussion on the polarisation of valuable (commercial) knowledge and expired (traditional) knowledge through the operation of the public domain.

the purposes of the 'personality' of intellectual property and, categorised within the public domain, communities are denied full governance with respect to that knowledge. In other words, 'traditional knowledge' is 'historical', not only for the purposes of anthropological record and in the context of a kind of knowledge imperialism, as it were, but also for the purposes of contemporary governance of knowledge resources within the community itself. For protection to be relevant, the community must begin to realise 'authority' over that knowledge other than as an anthropological object itself. Thus defensive forms of protection that rely upon situating traditional knowledge within the public domain are limited. Indeed, such protection constructs the community in question as merely another anonymous individual within a greater public, for which access is thus facilitated through the public domain. In other words, the very 'protection' offered by the public domain relies upon the legitimation of the appropriation of traditional knowledge as its starting point.

Where traditional knowledge is deemed 'unoriginal', and thus in the public domain, conventional standards of intellectual property cannot protect the personal attachment of the community to that knowledge. Rather, intellectual property laws facilitate the disengagement of the community, its distancing from the knowledge, and its anonymity within a global audience seeking access to that knowledge. Access and appropriation is legitimated under these systems, notwithstanding that such appropriation may constitute an offensive use, taking from the community in question through the inappropriate application and dissemination of knowledge (for instance, cultural symbols, dress, and artistic methods).[28]

Even current trends[29] towards requiring the disclosure of origins in traditional knowledge somewhat simplify the critical relationship between the community and its knowledge resources, and the offence and harm caused by the assumption that such taking is fundamentally just.[30] Protection offered by geographical

---

[28]   Owen Morgan provides a useful analysis of the relevance of offence in his discussion of the taking of Maori words and the legislative response in the New Zealand Trade Marks Act 2002, Morgan, O. (2003), 'The New Zealand Trade Marks Act: No Place for Offence', Occasional Paper No 2/03, Intellectual Property Institute of Australia, University of Melbourne. See the discussion of cultural offence in WIPO/GRTKF/IC/6/6 (30 November 2003), p. 24. See also the references to offence caused by the patenting of traditional knowledge in CIPR (2002), Commission on Intellectual Property Rights, *Integrating Intellectual Property Rights and Development Policy*, London, pp. 81–3.

[29]   In particular, see the development of protection on an international level in the documents of the WIPO IGC. All documents of the WIPO IGC are available at www.wipo.int/tk/en/igc/documents/index.html.

[30]   In other words, the taking will occur in the context of scientific progress and the advance of civilisation, and so on, making it appear to be inherently just. Thus discussions are invariably towards a way to facilitate cooperation with that taking, in the form

indications, trade marks and so on are not readily available other than through efforts to 'exclude' certain material from trade mark registration[31] or to anonymise communities within national publics (as in the use of geographical indications). Any efforts within these models (including disclosure of origin, certification and authenticity marks, and so on) depend upon a presumption of the importance of safeguarding the knowledge as cultural artefact, rather than recognising community and respecting and giving effect to customary law.

4   THE PUBLIC IN THE DOMAIN

The process by which traditional knowledge is rendered part of the public domain raises questions beyond the mere criteria by which intellectual property is recognised. The public domain, as it operates within an increasingly globalised system of intellectual property protection, imagines a 'global' public, as it were. That is, the 'public' about which the institution of intellectual property is articulated is a kind of culturally and socially universalised, uniform, international public. This is a highly strategic aspect of the rhetoric of intellectual property in that the public domain and this 'universal public' assimilate the 'public' of traditional communities within this model and indeed without their consent. Further, comparable concepts of the 'public domain', as in place within diverse traditional or tribal communities, are obscured by the simplification of this 'global' public domain, which makes possible an ahistorical universalised public out of diverse cultures, individuals and groups. It brings colonised and coloniser together in the competitive territory of the public.

In this way, the construction of the public by intellectual property laws is indeed not, as it were. Thus the notions of 'public domain' and 'public interest' as they may operate within the rhetoric of the more corporate 'intellectual property' are not properly public at all in so far as individuals are (as are traditional and indigenous communities) anonymised and alienated within that public. That is, the 'public' is not a functioning public.[32] The users of the public domain are not a functioning public, but a public created out of the structures

---

of traditional knowledge protection. Bruno Latour challenges the way in which scientific discourse draws upon this revolutionary difference between tradition and modern science in Latour, B. (1987), *Science in Action*, Cambridge, MA: Harvard UP, Chapter 6.

[31]   Problems persist in relying on exclusions of emblems and symbols, in that these must be fixed and repeatable for protection. Such defensive mechanisms cannot capture methods in cultural expressions (such as dot painting).

[32]   Hannay, A. (2005), *On the Public*, London: Routledge, p. 7. Hannay explains, in the context of political participation (but the comments can be extended to an interpretation of the way in which the regulation of intellectual property rights modifies and creates the creative public), that the public is not functioning in that its members are not active

presented by the intellectual property framework that anticipates their identity or representation, that brings the public into view. In fact, this mythical public is extremely strategic. It is made possible by the regulation of the public domain by intellectual property laws – that is, how, what, when and where the public may use certain intellectual property rights; how the public may use knowledge; how the public may create. Furthermore, the regulation of the public domain is highly commercial, focused upon the questions of the market and the assessment of the value to be realised, in calculations of the duration of the monopoly to be applied. These parameters for the creation of the global public domain are indeed quite irrelevant or incomparable to those that may regulate the public domains of various traditional and indigenous communities.

Indeed, within this anonymous public the active user is somewhat compromised, subjugated to the personality of the creator. Controversially, perhaps, unlimited access to knowledge may simply reiterate this subjugation. To a certain extent, limits upon the abstraction and construction of knowledge within these polarising Western concepts of the public domain and privatised intellectual property rights unsettle the dynamics of the dominant rhetoric without necessarily reinforcing the language of limits at work in intellectual property paradigms. In the case of traditional knowledge, therefore, free access to traditional knowledge through its situation within the public domain may simply constitute an imposition of regularity and universality through a standardising of cultural diversity that is in fact facilitated by the overarching cultural institution of intellectual property. In this way, the Western concept of the public domain, as it operates within the language of international intellectual property systems, puts the audience in its place, demarcating the territory of knowledge and the personality (the recognised 'creators', the intellectual property right-holders) of the authority over that territory. It is thus critically necessary to come to terms with the way in which traditional knowledge governance is beyond the simplistic conditions set forth by attempts to assimilate traditional knowledge within intellectual property protection. The terms of the debate are concerned with what amounts to a paradoxical process of privatisation of traditional knowledge as public domain knowledge,[33] with the stakeholder becoming the anonymous 'public', in effect presuming to speak on behalf of traditional knowledge holders.

The public domain, therefore, is a kind of property of the private individuals, the private creators, who are necessarily members of the public and creators of the means (intellectual property) by which the public domain (and thus the

---

participants in the political process. Similarly, the 'public' constructed with respect to the public domain alienates users from the creative process.

[33]   For instance, in the articulation of the relationship between intellectual property rights and human rights, this is particularly clear. See Chapman, A.R. (2001), 'Approaching Intellectual Property as a Human Right', **35** (3) *Copyright Bulletin* 4, 10.

public itself) is recognised and valued. Indeed, the debate over the protection of traditional knowledge is frequently dominated by industry representatives. Intellectual property ownership is almost a guarantee of entry into the debate over what is necessarily a question of communities and cultural rights, customary law, and diversity in knowledge traditions. The public, the users, are created by intellectual property, they come later than intellectual property, subsequently to it, and thus they are frequently marginalised in the creative economy of intellectual property systems. The public domain, in this way, is a spectacle; the users are merely the witnesses, spectators, audience of that spectacle. The public domain is becoming increasingly privatised in an extension of the private sphere of intellectual properties.

In an important way, intellectual property laws and concepts depend upon the distance that is generated between the 'public' thus created and the knowledge in the public domain, the distance between creators and users that dominates the current debates over access and protection. The 'use' and access sought by the public is somewhat displaced from the personality of the public, the unaccountable witness. In other words, where the risk involved in creativity is recognised and evaluated in terms of commercial parameters (such as the calculation of the appropriate duration of monopoly in order to make the financial return necessary to encourage and support that risk), the public is unaccountable with respect to that risk. In this way, the participation of the public (the user) is 'de-valued' (as mere witness, spectator) in the creative economy. Intellectual property recognises, identifies and regulates the creativity and originality of the knowledge. The public, as audience, necessarily cannot participate in that performance but is, rather, constituted by it; the public is a consumer of that performance, a topic of the commercially constructed public domain. This distance in turn makes the notion of the witnessing 'public,' the 'global' public, possible, and further indoctrinates the public as audience and as distinct from the creative process.

6   CONCLUSION: THE TRADITION IN KNOWLEDGE

It would appear, therefore, that ongoing attempts to assimilate traditional knowledge within intellectual property frameworks arguably presume entirely different concerns from those at stake for traditional knowledge holders. As one commentator maintains, 'we are not asking that our knowledge be protected by the IPR system. We would like to protect these using our own systems.'[34] In particu-

---

[34]   Tauli-Corpuz, V. (2005), 'Biodiversity, Traditional Knowledge and Rights of Indigenous Peoples', IPRs Series No. 5. International Workshop on Traditional Knowledge,

lar, through an examination of the application of the public domain in this context, the anonymity of the community through the very processes involved very much undermines the vital aspects of that knowledge that are integral to community identity, cultural integrity, and ongoing knowledge diversity and social life within traditional and indigenous groups.

The notion of the public domain allows intellectual property laws to regulate and classify the knowledge and indeed the public itself that is constituted by traditional and indigenous communities if that knowledge is to be articulated and understood through such systems. Through this process, the communities themselves are rendered mere witnesses of their knowledge, mere users, mere public. There is no accountability to traditional knowledge forfeited in the public domain. The knowledge is anonymous and with anonymity comes a lack of accountability, a relinquishing of responsibility, and a disregard for the tradition and understanding that contextualises that knowledge. The knowledge is presented without background, without responsibility, and without tradition. It is accessed without qualification, and the community is rendered selfless:

> There is no public domain in traditional knowledge ... Even knowledge shared and used widely does not fall into the public domain. When knowledge is shared, it is shared among those who are trusted to know their roles and responsibilities in using the knowledge ... Misuse, even when used by others outside of the tribe, or by tribal members who are outside of the control of customary authority, can cause severe physical or spiritual harm to the individual caretakers of the knowledge or their entire tribe from their failure to ensure that the Creator's gifts are properly used. For this reason, misappropriation and misuse is not simply a violation of 'moral rights' leading to a collective offense, but a matter of cultural survival for many Indigenous peoples.[35]

Traditional knowledge is knowledge *with* responsibility.

21–23 September, UN Department of Economic and Social Affairs, Division for Social Policy and Development, Secretariat of the Permanent Forum on Indigenous Issues, PFII/2005/WS.TK/5, 11.

[35]   Tulalip Tribes (2003), Statement by the Tulalip Tribes of Washington on Folklore, Indigenous Knowledge, and the Public Domain, 9 July, WIPO Intergovernmental Committee on Intellectual Property and Genetic Resources, Traditional Knowledge and Folklore, Fifth Session, Geneva, 5–17 July.

13. Scientific research agendas: controlled and shaped by the scope of patentability

Helen Wallace and Sue Mayer

1 INTRODUCTION

Recent controversies surrounding intellectual property rights (IPRs) and patenting have included whether discoveries about nature, such as gene sequences, should be patentable; whether innovation is stimulated or stifled by the extension of IPRs; and how benefits should be shared in situations where biological material or knowledge from a particular area underpins the claimed 'invention'. These debates have focused on how the monopolistic rights granted in 'patents on life' restrict scientists' or patients' access to new biological discoveries or their applications and whether they disproportionately reward companies which claim patents based on the results of shared scientific discovery or indigenous knowledge.[1]

In this chapter, we explore a different and neglected issue which concerns the effects of patenting on the scientific research agenda. We argue that scientific knowledge that can be made the subject of a patent application is being favoured above the acquisition of other knowledge. It is thus not only *access* to biological discoveries that is controlled and shaped by the patent system, but what constitutes scientific knowledge itself. Because knowledge in the 'knowledge-based economy' is defined by what can be patented and marketed, the 'public domain' of knowledge about human, animal and plant biology is not just becoming less public; it is also changing shape. We argue that this is having a negative effect on innovation in public health and agricultural systems which may have greater benefits overall for health and food security. This focus on the generation of

---

[1] For a general discussion on patenting and drugs see Dutfield, G., 'A Rights Free World – Is it Workable, and What is the Point?', in Chapter 15, and for a discussion on public engagement with the science agenda Bruce, A., 'The Public Domain: Ideology vs. Interest', Chapter 14 of this volume.

knowledge which is monopolisable above that which is communal is likely to have particularly damaging effects in developing countries.

2 SHAPING RESEARCH AGENDAS

Scientific research policy in the UK[2] and Europe[3] has an emphasis on science and technology as the engines of economic development and wealth. Knowledge, not just new products or processes, is now seen as an important tradable commodity of the new 'knowledge economy'. Four factors have been identified as shaping the agricultural research agenda in the UK[4] and these are common to other areas of research, namely:

1. advancing knowledge and technology and maintaining the science base;
2. wealth creation and international competitiveness;
3. government policy, regulation and legislation – to provide for evidence-based decision making;
4. public priorities and aspirations for science – including building public confidence in science.

Although research councils, such as the Medical Research Council (MRC) and the Biotechnology and Biological Sciences Research Council (BBSRC), also have priorities that include promoting health or sustainable agriculture, these are shaped within the overarching demands of wealth generation.

As part of this economic shaping of the scientific research agenda, scientists are being urged to build partnerships with the private sector and to have intellectual property protection for their knowledge to facilitate its transfer and use by business. In this way, access to, and control of, the knowledge moves from the public to the private domain. To facilitate this generation of knowledge that is utilisable by industry, both in health and agriculture, there is an emphasis on

---

[2] HM Treasury, Department of Trade and Industry, Department for Education and Skills (2004), *Science and Innovation Investment Framework 2004–2014*, London: The Stationery Office, available at www.hm-treasury.gov.uk/spending_review/spend_sr04/associated_documents/spending_sr04_science.cfm.

[3] European Commission (2004), Communication from the Commission, 'Science and Technology, the Key to Europe's Future – Guidelines for Future European Union Policy to Support Research', Brussels, COM(2004) 353 final.

[4] Agriculture and Environment Biotechnology Commission (2005), *What Shapes the Research Agenda in Agricultural Biotechnology?*, London: Department of Trade and Industry, p. 5, available at www.aebc.gov.uk/aebc/reports/research_agendas_final_report.pdf.

'technology platforms',[5] including biotechnology and nanotechnology. These are technologies which are seen as being at the cutting edge of innovation and applicable across many industrial sectors. Building such 'technology platforms' is also being promoted as a mechanism for economic improvement in developing countries.[6]

3 PATENTING AND SCIENTIFIC RESEARCH

The demand that scientific knowledge must have intellectual property protection if it is to be suitable for stimulating innovation and wealth generation is having important implications. Without such IP protection, it is considered that businesses will be unwilling to invest in further development because of the risk that other companies will use or 'copy' the knowledge for their own product development. Having a period where a company has a monopoly over the commercial exploitation is seen as a fair reward for disclosure of information about an invention.

The advent of biotechnology and the new commercial opportunities it offered posed difficulties for the patent system initially. Discoveries about nature, which gene sequences could be argued to be, were not considered the provenance of patents which were intended to be reserved for novel inventions that had commercial uses. As a result, the scope of patentability has been forced to increase so that gene sequences, micro-organisms, cells, plants and animals produced through genetic modification are now the routine subject matter of patent applications. Nanotechnology does not require similar adjustments to be made, but there are concerns about the breadth of early patents in the field.[7] As with biotech patents[8] these will raise concerns about whether the privatisation of the basic knowledge will facilitate or hinder innovation.

Because of the emphasis that is being placed on commercial exploitation of scientific research, including when it is paid for by the public purse, and the

---

[5]   European Commission (2004), 'Technology Platforms: from Definition to Implementation of a Common Research Agenda', European Commission, Directorate-General for Research, Brussels, ftp://ftp.cordis.lu/pub/technology-platforms/docs/tp_report_defweb_en.pdf.

[6]   United Nations Task Force on Science, Technology and Innovation (2004), 'Innovation: Applying Knowledge in Development', Geneva: United Nations, www.unmillenniumproject.org/documents/Science-complete.pdf.

[7]   ETC Group (2005), 'Nanotech's "Second Nature" Patents: Implications for the Global South', Ottowa: ETC Group, available at www.etcgroup.org/documents/Com-8788SpecialPNanoMar-Jun05ENG.pdf.

[8]   Nuffield Council on Bioethics (2002), *The Ethics of Patenting DNA*, London: Nuffield Council on Bioethics.

accompanying demands that the outcomes in terms of knowledge be amenable
to monopolisation, the scientific knowledge we are generating may not deliver
public health or sustainable agricultural systems. We now explore this in more
detail for each of these areas.

4   PRIORITISING PATENTABLE KNOWLEDGE: IMPLICATIONS FOR HEALTH

Although the aim of improving health is ostensibly given priority by the MRC,[9]
the secondary aim of improving 'economic competitiveness' drives much of the
research agenda. Along with the other research councils, the MRC has been required by the Government's Office of Science and Technology to develop a
delivery plan, setting out how it will achieve its targets for improving the economy through science and technology. It also has a strategic objective 'to
encourage commercial exploitation for the benefit of national health and wealth',
working primarily through its knowledge transfer company, MRC Technology
Ltd, which manages its patent portfolio.[10] Although encouraging commercial
exploitation can help beneficial treatments to reach patients, there is also a
danger that it skews health research priorities. This is partly because the most
profitable interventions (new pharmaceuticals) are not necessarily those which
make the most difference to public health, and partly because for-profit health
research prioritises the best markets, not the people most in need.

UK health research spending by pharmaceutical and biotechnology companies is about £3 billion a year, more than three times government spending
figures. The market-driven biases within pharmaceutical research are well
known, including the neglect of developing-country diseases,[11] the emphasis on
'me too' drugs rather than genuinely new products[12] and the increasing medi-
calisation of ordinary life in order to expand markets.[13] Unsurprisingly, a 2002

[9]   Medical Research Council (2005), Annual Report and Accounts 2004/05, London:
The Stationery Office.
[10]   Ibid.
[11]   Global Forum for Health Research (2004), *Monitoring Financial Flows for Health
Research*, Geneva: Global Forum for Health Research, available at www.globalforum-
health.org/Site/002__What%20we%20do/005__Publications/004__Resource%20flows.
php.
[12]   (2002), 'America's Other Drug Problem: a Briefing Book on the Rx Drug Debate',
Public Citizens' Congress Watch, Washington, DC, available at www.citizen.org/docu-
ments/dbbapril.pdf.
[13]   Moynihan, R., Heath, I., Henry, D. and Gotzsche, P.C. (2002), 'Selling Sickness:
the Pharmaceutical Industry and Disease Mongering', *British Medical Journal*, **324**,
886–90.

study by the King's Fund found that, within the UK private sector, profit is the major driver of health research and is underpinned by the patent system.[14] However, the report also identified some major problems with the role of public sector funding. In particular, certain kinds of research attract little if any funding, either because results cannot be patented or because they are of little scientific interest. This conclusion is supported by a survey of UK research publications, which found that not more than 0.4 per cent of current academic and research output is relevant to public health intervention research.[15]

The implications for health of prioritising patentable knowledge are not limited to the neglect of many infectious diseases in developing countries. Tackling chronic diet- and tobacco-related diseases (such as heart disease, type 2 diabetes and some cancers) and the current epidemic of obesity is now a priority in both high- and middle-income countries. These are not 'neglected diseases', yet the 'wealth creation' model of science and technology favours some types of research over others and almost entirely ignores the enormous potential benefits of public health research to people in both developing and developed countries. Public health interventions could not only prevent much of the burden of chronic disease: according to a recent Treasury report, they could also save the National Health Service billions of pounds.[16] However, the report also concluded that:

> The major constraint to further progress on the implementation of public health interventions is the weakness of the evidence base for their effectiveness and cost-effectiveness. This is largely due to the lack of funding of public health intervention research, with funding from research organisations and the private sector very heavily directed towards clinical, pharmaceutical, biological and genetic research ... Substantial investment, or reprioritisation, is necessary if this imbalance in research funding is to be addressed.[17]

Patenting is only one of many factors driving the 'health research economy'[18] and its role in health research is clearly much broader than 'patents on life'. However, granting patent claims on human gene sequences allows 'genetic information' to become a commodity, bought and sold as a key part of the knowledge-based economy. A DNA sequence is not patentable without any knowledge of its function, but a claim that a sequence can diagnose or predict

---

[14]   Harrison, A. and New, B. (2002), *Public Interest, Private Decisions*, London: The King's Fund.

[15]   Millward, L.M., Kelly, M.P. and Nutbeam, D. (2003), *Public Health Intervention Research – the Evidence*, London: Health Development Agency.

[16]   Wanless, D. (2004), *Securing Good Health for the Whole Population*, London: The Stationery Office.

[17]   Ibid., p. 120.

[18]   Harrison, A. and New, B. (2002), *Public Interest, Private Decisions*, London: The King's Fund.

susceptibility to a specific condition (or conditions) is sufficient to render it patentable. In practice this means that 'genetic information' is treated as an invention and subject to intellectual property rights, although the nature of the invention may be disputed and unclear.[19]

The discovery of a new link between a gene and a disease has come to be seen as one of the most exciting and newsworthy aspects of medical research, and forms the basis of many patent applications. The main claimed uses of DNA patents filed between 1996 and 1999 were as research tools (27 per cent of DNA patents) and as diagnostics (18 per cent): many such patents had no immediate therapeutic value.[20]

Trends in genomic patenting are leading to more emphasis on the function of the gene and to patents based on bioinformatics and computer-generated 'genetic information'. However, identifying the function of a gene is often problematic and may differ radically from our commonsense understanding of what it is for an invention to be useful.[21] There is a growing recognition amongst geneticists that the majority of cases of common diseases are not genetically determined to any meaningful extent and probably involve numerous genetic and other (epigenetic) factors, each of small effect, together with major social and environmental influences.[22] This complexity is reflected in the fact that most statistical studies linking genes to common diseases later turn out to be wrong. For example, a 2002 paper found that of over 600 published positive associations between common gene variants and disease, only 6 had been consistently replicated.[23] Typically larger, later studies show weak or no association, compared to smaller, earlier research.[24] Yet patent claims are filed and granted based on early studies.

Patents based on false or exaggerated associations, or 'genetic misinformation', do not raise concerns about access or benefit sharing, unless they have alternative unknown uses to which future access is restricted by the patent. However, the implications of gene sequence patents go far beyond issues of who gains access to, and who profits from, new genetic tests and treatments. Granting

[19]   Paradise, J., Andrews, L. and Holbrook, T. (2005), 'Patents on Human Genes: an Analysis of Scope and Claims', *Science*, **307**, 1566–7.

[20]   Thomas, S.M., Hopkins, M.M. and Brady, M. (2002), 'Shares in the Human Genome – the Future of Patenting DNA', *Nature Biotechnology*, **20**, 1185–8.

[21]   Calvert, J. (2004), 'Genomic Patenting and the Utility Requirement', *New Genetics and Society*, **23** (3), 301–12.

[22]   Wright, A.F. and Hastie, N.D. (2001), 'Complex genetic diseases: controversy over the Croesus code', *Genome Biology*, **2** (8): comment 2007.1–2007.8

[23]   Hirschorn, J.N., Lohmueller, K., Byrne, E. and Hirschorn, K. (2002), 'A Comprehensive Review of Genetic Association Studies', *Genetics in Medicine*, **4** (2), 45–61.

[24]   Ioannidis, J.P.A. (2003), 'Genetic Associations in Large versus Small Studies: an Empirical Assessment', *The Lancet*, **361**, 567–71.

such patents on the basis of their future utility or industrial application is not simply a response to science, but is an attempt to predict the future of the science and thus drives it in particular directions.[25] The ownership of patents gives value to 'genetic information' and drives the formation of 'spin-out' companies from academic institutions, licensing deals between academia and industry and investment by industry and venture capitalists. The patenting of human DNA thus plays a central role in the 'biomedicalisation' and 'geneticisation' of health.[26]

5 PRIORITIZING PATENTABLE KNOWLEDGE: IMPLICATIONS FOR SUSTAINABLE AGRICULTURE

Formed in 1994 and replacing the Agriculture and Food Research Council, the BBSRC has an agenda which is explicitly driven in part by a commitment to a particular technology considered of commercial importance. The BBSRC's mission is focused on the gathering of knowledge and its exploitation to meet the needs of commercial users[27] and its 'Agri Food' research forms one part of its research portfolio to meet this mission. Patentable knowledge is given special status and support within the BBSRC. For example, the BBSRC has a Business and Innovation Unit which seeks to promote the use of intellectual property into products. It has schemes to encourage innovation and understanding of patent management, its research units have 'periodic assessment of their performance in knowledge transfer as an element for determining future funding levels' and it collects 'exploitation data' from university departments with high levels of BBSRC funding.[28] The BBSRC also accepts the cost that must be paid in terms of openness in scientific research, saying: 'in the area of adequately protecting intellectual property, judgement must be exercised; delays in the announcement of results or the publication of papers may be necessary to ensure that ownership of intellectual property has been secured.' It is against this background that the BBSRC shapes its research funding.

In crop and food research, genomics and its application in the form of genetic modification (GM) has come to be the focus of agricultural research in large part because knowledge about gene sequences and its use in making transgenic crops has been patentable. The advent of crop GM techniques arose at a time

---

[25] Calvert, J. (2005), 'Genomics and the Patent System: Debates over Function and Information', CARR/Egenis conference, Exeter, 10–11 March.

[26] Clarke, A.E., Mamo, L., Fishman, J.R., Shim, J.K. and Fosket, J.R. (2003), 'Biomedicalization: Technoscientific Transformations of Health, Illness, and US Biomedicine', *American Sociological Review*, **68**, 161–94.

[27] BBSRC (2005), 'Mission', available at www.bbsrc.ac.uk/about/mission.html.

[28] See www.bbsrc.ac.uk/business/ip/Welcome.html.

of changing political views on the purpose and position of science in society. Starting with the Thatcher Government, there has been a move away from near-market research being conducted in public institutes in the UK.[29] This has been accompanied by an increasing demand that basic science meets the needs of business and for greater links between public researchers and industry, in order that industry's needs are better understood and reflected.[30] These two forces have had a particular effect on agricultural research in the UK, the applied (or near-market) nature of which meant that much was no longer considered appropriate for public funding. Overall, and in a pattern which is reflected globally, there has been a shift from the majority of agricultural research being in the public sector to most being the private sector.[31]

In plant breeding there has been a particularly dramatic effect because, historically, plant breeding was conducted largely in the public sector, with several research institutes in the UK producing and gaining revenue from plant variety sales.[32] Today, there is very little public sector plant breeding taking place in the UK.[33] The move away from plant breeding by public institutions opened up a space for private companies to expand their plant breeding operations. Crop genetic modification was seen as offering the best means of crop improvement and, to facilitate this, companies required intellectual property rights protection in the form of patents. Patents give much wider monopoly rights than the more traditional plant breeders rights, where plant varieties can be used by others to produce new varieties. The advent of patents on plants has contributed to the take-overs and mergers which have led to consolidation of the seed industry.[34]

Broadening the scope of patentability, to include not only genes and genetic information but also plants and animals, has facilitated the restructuring of plant

---

[29] HM Government, (1993), *Realising our Potential: A Strategy for Science, Engineering and Technology*, Cm 2250, London: The Stationery Office.
[30] Agriculture and Environment Biotechnology Commission (2005), *What Shapes the Research Agenda in Agricultural Biotechnology?*, London: Department of Trade and Industry, available at www.aebc.gov.uk/aebc/reports/research_agendas_final_report.pdf.
[31] Klotz-Ingram, C. and Day-Rubenstein, K. (1999), 'The Changing Agricultural Research Environment: What Does It Mean For Public–Private Innovation?', *AgBio Forum*, **2**, 24–32.
[32] Agriculture and Environment Biotechnology Commission, (2005), *What Shapes the Research Agenda in Agricultural Biotechnology?*, London: Department of Trade and Industry, available at www.aebc.gov.uk/aebc/reports/research_agendas_final_report.pdf.
[33] Dale, P. (2004), 'Public-good Plant Breeding: What Should Be Done Next?', *Journal of Commercial Biotechnology*, **10**, 199–208.
[34] Commission on Intellectual Property Rights (2002), *Integrating Intellectual Property Rights and Development Policy*, London: Department for International Development.

breeding for agriculture and a redirection of research priorities for the public sector. The focus of basic agricultural research in the UK has been the underpinning of genomics research to meet the needs of companies wishing to exploit the commercial opportunities opened by GM crops. The majority of GM crop development is restricted to that which will be most useful in industrialised agriculture[35] and the control over access to germ plasm that patenting allows has effectively also hindered those remaining researchers in the public sector gaining access and conducting research for different goals.[36] However, a much more neglected consequence is that other research into agricultural systems for crop or animal production has had little or no attention, as the knowledge cannot be taken into the private domain through patenting.

Although the aim of the UK's basic research over the past decade has been to meet the demands of private sector interests, in some respects this has failed, partly because the knowledge generated from the model species, *Arabadopsis*, has not been directly relevant to crop species.[37] The proposed response to this is to maintain a genomics focus but with more research directly on crop species. Other, systems-based research to improve agriculture largely remains outside mainline research.

6   CONCLUSIONS

Although patents are primarily used to protect inventions from imitation and to secure markets, companies increasingly have other motivations for patenting, including blocking competitors; increasing the company's reputation and value; exchanging value with partners, licensees and investors; and controlling internal performance and motivations.[38] Beginning in the US in the 1980s, universities have also been encouraged to treat knowledge as property and to file patents, including patents on human DNA.[39]

---

[35]   Nuffield Council on Bioethics (2004), *The Use of Genetically Modified Crops in Developing Countries: a Follow-up Discussion Paper*, London: Nuffield Council on Bioethics.

[36]   Knight, J. (2003), 'Crop Improvement: A Dying Breed', *Nature*, 421, 568–70.

[37]   'Review of BBSRC-funded Research Relevant to Crop Science: a Report for BBSRC Council', April 2004, www.bbsrc.ac.uk/about/pub/reports/crop_sci_review 12_05_04.pdf.

[38]   Blind, K., Edler, J., Frietsch, R. and Schmoch, U. (2003), *Erfindungen kontra Patente*, Karlsruhe: Fraunhofer-Institut fur Systemtechnik und Innovationsforschung [summary in English].

[39]   Krimsky, S. (2003), *Science in the Private Interest*, Lanham, MD: Rowman & Littlefield.

In the UK, as in many other countries, patenting applications and income from intellectual property have now become measures of university success[40] which underpin policy-makers' attempts to shift towards a 'knowledge-based' economy.[41] Thus the commodification and prioritisation of 'genetic information' (and misinformation) via patent claims also plays a key role in the 'geneticisation' of both health and agriculture and the health and agriculture research agendas. In health, genetic risk factors, unlike social, economic or environmental ones, can be patented and thus have become the focus of research. The potential contribution of this approach to reducing the incidence of common diseases is questionable[42] and the problem is compounded by genetic tests being largely unregulated, so 'genetic information' can be marketed even when it is not valid or useful.[43] In agriculture, GM crops can be patented, which has helped drive agricultural research into the private domain, changing the research priorities from public good to market potential. The value of GM crops in sustainable agriculture in both the developed and developing worlds has been widely contested.[44] However, it is evident that the interests of high-input farming of commodity crops have been prioritised over those of poor, organic and low-input farmers in decisions about crop development.[45]

Treating knowledge as property raises questions not only about who gains access to this knowledge and who benefits from its use and sale, but also about how patentable knowledge (including 'genetic information') is defined and prioritised above other forms of knowledge. Other authors have discussed the implications for 'indigenous' versus 'scientific' knowledge[46] and potential im-

[40]   HM Treasury, Department of Trade and Industry, Department for Education and Skills (2004), *Science and Innovation Investment Framework 2004–2014*, London: The Stationery Office, available at www.hm-treasury.gov.uk/spending_review/spend_sr04/associated_documents/spending_sr04_science.cfm.

[41]   Department of Trade and Industry (2003), *Creating Wealth from Knowledge*, London: The Stationery Office, www.dti.gov.uk/about/fiveyearprogramme.pdf.

[42]   Baird, P. (2001), 'The Human Genome Project, Genetics and Health', *Community Genetics*, **4**, 77–80.

[43]   Wallace, H. (2005), 'Who Regulates Genetic Tests?', *Nature Reviews Genetics*, **6**, 517; Baird, P. (2002), 'Identification of Genetic Susceptibility to Common Diseases: the Case for Regulation', *Perspectives in Biology and Medicine*, **45**, 516–28.

[44]   Cf. Garcia, M.A. and Altieri, M.A. (2005), 'Transgenic Crops: Implications for Biodiversity and Sustainable Agriculture', *Bulletin of Science, Technology & Society*, **25**, 335–53; Shelton, M.A. (2003), 'The Role of Plant Biotechnology in the Worlds' Food Systems', *Economic Perspectives* **8**, 23–5.

[45]   Nuffield Council on Bioethics (2004), *The Use of Genetically Modified Crops in Developing Countries: a Follow-up Discussion Paper*, London: Nuffield Council on Bioethics.

[46]   Harry, D. (2005), 'Acts of Self-Determination and Self-Defense: Indigenous Peoples' Responses to Biocolonialism', in Krimsky, S. and Shorett, P. (eds), *Rights and*

pacts on the freedom of scientists to exchange genetic information.[47] However, the issue of how patenting is shaping not only what science is public but what science is done has tended to be neglected.

The perceived economic value of patenting DNA sequences is one factor which leads to the identification of individual gene function, and genetic associations with disease, being prioritised over and above other potentially more useful knowledge. Public, as well as private, research funding decisions focus on wealth generation and economic competitiveness as part of government efforts to generate a 'knowledge-based economy'. But, in so doing, they redefine what counts as academic knowledge and neglect both biological complexity and the research needs of public health and sustainable agriculture.

More public involvement in research funding decisions is needed so that the knowledge-base itself is not distorted by commercial incentives,[48] including gene patenting. In addition to the important debates about the impacts of intellectual property rights on access to and control of new technologies, we should ask whether the current intellectual property regime creates the right incentives for knowledge and innovation that meet global needs in terms of health and food security, particularly the needs of poor and disadvantaged populations.

Liberties in the Biotech Age: Why We Need a Genetic Bill of Rights, Lanham: Rowman & Littlefield.

[47] For example Barton, J.H. (2002), 'Patents, Genomics, Research, and Diagnostics', *Academic Medicine*, **77**, 1339–47.

[48] Mayer, S. (2003), 'Science Out of Step with the Public: the Need for Public Accountability of Science in the UK', *Science and Public Policy*, **30**, 177–81.

14. The public domain: ideology vs. interest

Ann Bruce*

1 INTRODUCTION

This chapter considers the issue of science in the public domain and reflects how different interests and ideologies are dealt with in this context. I take the 'private' domain to represent the situation where the decision-making influences rest primarily with bodies of scientific and other 'experts' acting in private, for example, in government advisory committees. In this model only the specific scientists involved are deemed to have 'competence' in the area of science, to give advice on risks, likely consequences and future prospects. Over the last decade or so, this model of decision making has been increasingly challenged. There have been growing demands to recognise the role of a wider range of people and publics to influence decisions in science, and I take this to represent the move of science from the 'private' to the 'public' domain.

Why has this happened? Part of the answer is a perceived crisis in confidence in established scientific advice. The House of Lords Select Committee on Science and Technology (2002) describes it as follows:

> Public confidence in scientific advice to Government has been rocked by a series of events, culminating in the BSE fiasco, and many people are deeply uneasy about the huge opportunities presented by areas of science including biotechnology and information technology, which seem to be advancing far ahead of their awareness and assent.[1]

There are therefore two aspects to this pressure to move science into the public domain: ensuring that scientific evidence is used appropriately to make decisions

*   Acknowledgements: with thanks to the many colleagues and especially Joyce Tait, Graeme Laurie and Donald Bruce for their comments on this chapter and to ESRC for funding research on disputes in areas of genomics. The views expressed in this chapter and responsibility for the content, however, rest solely with the author.
[1]   Section 1:1.

for the public benefit and ensuring the direction of scientific research itself is for public benefit.

2   PUBLIC ENGAGEMENT

Public engagement has become a strong theme in science policy. A recent public engagement initiative from the Office of Science and Technology describes the aims of public engagement as follows:

> The aim is for our society to have confidence in the decisions that are made in the development, governance, regulation and use of science and technology. To achieve this, the public should be given the opportunity to engage in dialogue about the ethical, safety, health and environmental implications of new areas of science and technology.[2]

2.1   The *GM Nation?* Debate

Perhaps the best way to understand the move of science from the private to the public domain is to take an example: the UK national debate about genetically modified (GM) crops which took place in 2003, chosen because it reflects a recent situation where scientific evidence alone was seen as an insufficient basis for policy decisions and where a rather novel and extensive attempt was made to include public concerns in the decision-making process. The Government initiated a series of assessments on different aspects of GM crops prior to making a decision as to whether to allow commercial cultivation of any varieties of GM crops. The different strands included an economic assessment, an evaluation of the state of the science, a series of field trials to evaluate the impact of more wide-scale cultivation of GM crops and a public debate – *GM Nation?* I will focus primarily on the *GM Nation?* debate as the stream most obviously in the public domain, although we should note that the economic and science strands also included elements that could be described as being in the public domain, for example, a forum for Internet discussion.

The *GM Nation?* debate had several different components. First, a series of closed foundation workshops sought to elicit how lay publics conceptualised GM-related issues to set the scene for subsequent dialogue. A website, stimulus material and questionnaire were produced for use in discussion in three tiers of public meetings. Tier 1 public meetings consisted of six centrally organised national and regional events around the UK. Tier 2 discussions were organised as a partnership between councils and other public organisations and the central

---

[2]   www.sciencewise.org.uk/default.cfm last accessed 22/11/05.

organisers. Tier 3 events were open for anyone to organise but a 'tool kit' was provided for them centrally.[3] Lastly, focus groups of representative samples of the public were convened twice, before and after participants were encouraged to access information on the issues around GM crops. *GM Nation?* is probably the largest and most ambitious example of organised debate about science in the public domain ever undertaken in the UK and it has put the UK at the forefront of innovative approaches to public engagement about science in Europe. *GM Nation?* also involved a substantial commitment in financial resources, over £0.5m,[4] although this was still inadequate in the view of many, including the House of Commons Environment, Food and Rural Affairs Committee (2003).[5]

How did this dialogue exercise come about and what were the motivations for it? One description of the *GM Nation?* debate talks about this being 'evidence of attempts by government to develop a flexible regulatory architecture designed to resolve contemporary tensions within the nexus of science, technology, social values and market needs',[6] indicating that this was part of policy-makers' response to a contentious area of regulation. The *GM Nation?* debate was instigated by the UK Government following recommendations from the Agriculture and Environment Biotechnology Commission (AEBC). This Commission was set up by the UK Government in 2000 as part of a new regulatory framework for biotechnology and with the purpose of providing advice on ethical and social implications and public acceptability of new developments.[7] Following a review of the Commission in 2004, it was disbanded in 2005, for reasons which are discussed later in this chapter. A sub-committee of the AEBC had oversight of the *GM Nation?* debate, although the debate itself was run by COI (Central Office of Information) Communications, an agency of the UK Government.

It is worth asking why the Government went to unparalleled lengths to consult the public when, in the event, it apparently chose to ignore the overwhelming

[3]   Department of Trade and Industry (2003), *GM Nation? The Findings of the Public Debate*, available at www.gmnation.org.uk/docs/gmnation_finalreport.pdf.

[4]   Ibid.

[5]   House of Commons Environment, Food and Rural Affairs Committee (November 2003), *Conduct of the GM Public Debate*, Session 2002–03, 18th Report, London: The Stationery Office.

[6]   Horlick-Jones, T., Walls, J., Rowe, G., Pidgeon, N., Poortinga, W. and O'Riordan, T. (2004), 'A Deliberative Future? An Independent Evaluation of the "GM Nation?" Public Debate about the Possible Commercialisation of Transgenic Crops in Britain', *Understanding Risk Working Paper*, 04-02, p.14, see www.sci-soc/SciSoc/Library/Governance.

[7]   Williams, N. (2004), *Organisational and Performance Review of the Agriculture and Environment Biotechnology Commission,* the InHouse Policy Consultancy, hereafter Williams (2004).

response it received. The *GM Nation?* debate concluded that there was an largely negative attitude towards GM crops in the UK (although the representativeness of the respondents has been questioned[8]). The Government, however, decided to disallow commercial cultivation of two of the varieties of GM crop being considered, but to allow the cultivation of the third of the varieties under consideration. The company producing this third variety later chose to withdraw the crop from the market. The basis for the Government making its decision appeared not to be overtly the *GM Nation?* public debate but rather the results of the field trials which suggested the potential for environmental damage resulting from the cultivation of two of the crop varieties being considered (although others would argue that the environmental impacts were a reflection of the management practices used rather than the use GM crops *per se*[9]). Whilst the *GM Nation?* debate therefore did not appear to resolve the issue, it did appear to act to some extent as a cathartic exercise to allow dissenting voices to be heard, despite initial cynicism from many that the Government had already decided to allow commercialisation of GM crops. The meaning of the results of both *GM Nation?* and the field-scale trials continue, however, to be contested.

2.2 The Role of Evidence

One of the interesting features about the GM crops example described is what has happened to the role of evidence. Traditionally, decisions about matters to do with science could be expected to be heavily reliant on the basis of scientific evidence. However, what became clear in the GM crops debate was that evidence became contested, not just in the *GM Nation?* strand, but also in the science strand. Even apparently innocuous data, such as the amount of GM crops grown around the world, could easily become a cause for dispute. Do these figures imply that GM crops are a minority interest which no one really wants? Or do they suggest that everyone else is adopting GM crops with enthusiasm, leaving the UK lagging behind? For a government that stresses 'evidence based' policy and is concerned that 'what matters is what works' rather than to focus on ideology, dispute over evidence will be clearly difficult. So, what now counts as evidence and who decides that this is evidence?

---

[8] Op.cit. note 6.
[9] For example Innogen (2003), *Precaution and Progress: Lessons from the GM Dialogue*, proceedings of a conference held in Edinburgh, November.

3 VALUES

Attention has moved increasingly onto the question as to how the Government might prevent a similar difficult progress for other innovative technologies, nanotechnology for example. In an attempt to learn the lessons of GM crops, there have been increasing calls for more 'upstream' engagement with the public on matters of scientific development and a concomitant willingness by Government to encourage this engagement to happen. We are told that engaging the public at an early stage of scientific development, before there are any products from that innovation on the market, will mean that the values of the public will be incorporated within the technological process,[10] perhaps implying that this will result in successful and uncontentious introduction of new technologies into the public domain.

The focus on 'values' is an interesting one. From early in the 1990s and into the second millennium, Professor Joyce Tait had been studying the debates around pesticides and then GM crops as conducted by a number of different stakeholder groups, including various publics. Based on these experiences, she developed a scheme by which to consider the ongoing debates and noted that there appeared to be two different types of conversation taking place at the same time.[11] The louder debate was about risks and whether GM crops posed new threats to human health and the environment; but at the same time there was an underlying and initially quieter debate about issues such as what sort of agriculture do we want in the future? Do we want to continue intensification or do we want to reorient towards an arguably more holistic and sustainable, organically based agriculture? Professor Tait has termed these 'interest'-based arguments and 'value'- or 'ideology'-based arguments respectively, and has identified each with different characteristics. The interest-based arguments are potentially more amenable to resolution by provision of information or by compensation for those disadvantaged by the technology or negotiation of modifications. Interest-based arguments tend to be restricted to the specific issue being discussed. Value-based arguments on the other hand are more likely to spread to similar developments elsewhere, including world-wide. Provision of information may be viewed as propaganda, provision of compensation as bribery and negotiation as betrayal. Giving concessions is less likely to lead to mutual accommodation and more likely to lead to escalation of demands. These two

---

[10]   As suggested for example by Wilsdon et al., although others have made similar arguments: Wilsdon, J., Wynne, B. and Stilgoe, J. (2005), *The Public Value of Science – Or How to Ensure that Science Really Matters*, Demos.

[11]   Tait, J. (2001), 'More Faust than Frankenstein: the European Debate about the Precautionary Principle in Risk Regulation for Genetically Modified Crops', *Journal of Risk Research* **4** (2), 175–89.

types of argument are not mutually exclusive, both types of argument may be deployed in the context of a specific issue, but they are rarely equally strong.

The way in which regulation works tends in general to favour an 'interest' style of argument, for example in terms of risks. The UK and European Union have well-developed risk regulatory regimes. Furthermore, government bodies may be more comfortable with forms of argument that appear to allow transparent decision-making, preferably on a quantifiable basis, that could be duplicated by others.[12] The problem then arises when 'value' type arguments are deployed. The UK Government, for example, simply has not had clear mechanisms for deciding on issues such as 'what sort of agriculture do we want?' With early GM crop debates, what should arguably have been a discussion about acceptable levels of intervention in nature, the future shape of agriculture and the role of commercial companies in it, as well as a discussion about the risks of GM crops, became a discussion focused on the risks of GM crops, with each piece of evidence hotly contested by the different sides. The mechanisms developed for risk regulation suddenly became the battleground on which the future of GM crops would be decided, whether the regulatory system was capable of resolving this type of dispute or not. Similar arguments have been made about the patenting system, which has increasingly had to deal with ethical issues concerning patenting living organisms and genetic material, which it was never designed to do,[13] as was particularly apparent in 1994–98, during discussion around the European Directive on legal protection of biotechnological inventions.[14]

Several different approaches have been attempted to address value-laden issues in science. Prior to the setting up of the AEBC, the main forum for such issues was ad hoc committees of specialists, for example the Polkinghorne Committee Report on GM foods.[15] The AEBC was set up as part of the Government's response to criticism that these committees were fragmented and there was no overall body responsible for a strategic overview of developments in agricultural biotechnology and in a position to give advice on the ethical and social implications and social acceptability of these developments.[16] The AEBC consisted of a group of people with highly divergent views on agricultural bio-

---

[12]   Evans, J.H. (2002), *Playing God: Human Genetic Engineering and the Rationalization of Public Bioethical Debate*, Chicago and London: The University of Chicago Press.

[13]   Bruce, D.M. (1997), 'Patenting Human Genes – a Christian View,' *Bulletin of Medical Ethics*, January, 18–20.

[14]   EC/98/44.

[15]   Ministry of Agriculture, Fisheries and Food (MAFF) (1993), *Report of the Committee on the Ethics of Genetic Modification and Food Use*, Polkinghorne Committee Report, London: HMSO.

[16]   Williams (2004).

technology, and could be seen to act as a corrective to the perceived non-representativeness hitherto of the bodies set up to advise Government. However, this polarised make-up may have made reaching a consensus particularly difficult. The review of the AEBC[17] suggested that there was a tension inherent in the way in which the AEBC was set up and operated, such that it was expected to deliver both as an investigative/analytical body (as was the case with specialist ad hoc committees) but also as a stakeholder consultative/consensus-forming body. A criticism made of the need for time to develop a consensus within the AEBC was that this meant that advice came too late to fit into the policy-makers' framework.[18] Meanwhile, there was a move both within and outside the AEBC for more engagement with the public to resolve these contentious issues, and it is to considerations of this that I now turn.

4   A NEW APPROACH TO PUBLIC ENGAGEMENT?

There has been a shift in thinking about communication in the sphere of science from a 'deficit' model, where the diagnosis is that what is needed is to inform and educate the public about science and what this knowledge is producing, to a model of more dialogue. The assumption used to be that, once the public understood the science, there would be widespread acceptance of the products that science delivers (the 'public understanding of science' model). The belief was that much of the resistance to scientific developments was a failure to understand the science. The realisation with the GM debate was that often the people who were most against GM crops were also very knowledgeable about it.[19] More knowledge did not automatically result in more acceptance. The issue was other than just better understanding of the science (while not denying that this was also needed). A key report from the House of Lords in 2000, *Science and Society*,[20] shifted the mood away from scientists imparting information to an uninformed public towards more interaction and dialogue, with scientists listening to public views. This approach has now been reflected in the UK. Government policy, for example the 10-year investment plan for science and technology,[21] views public engagement as one of the key deliverables. Notice-

---

[17]   Ibid.

[18]   Ibid.

[19]   For example Martin, S. and Tait, J. (1992), 'Attitudes of Selected Public Groups in the UK to Biotechnology', in Durant, J., *Biotechnology in Public: a Review of Recent Research*, London: Science Museum.

[20]   House of Lords Select Committee on Science and Technology (2000), *Science and Society: Third Report*, London: The Stationery Office.

[21]   HM Treasury, Department of Education and Skills and Department for Trade and

ably, other deliverables stress the need for academic research scientists to work more closely with industry. This close link is in itself one of the causes of concern about what is driving science and whether industry is an accountable and appropriate forum for setting the direction of science. The 10-year investment plan does not, however, suggest how individual scientists or scientific organisations should meet these potentially conflicting objectives. It is also interesting to note that, just seven years before the key House of Lords report that stressed the need for science and society interactions, the same body produced a report advocating the relaxation of regulation on the release of GM crops, arguably a predisposing factor for the subsequent high-tension debates.[22]

What then will these public engagement activities deliver? The answer must be that we do not know. We have embarked on an experiment to engage with values as well as interests and increasingly to place direction of science in the public domain. There are a number of issues to be considered.

First, society is not homogeneous and societal values are diverse. The answer to the question 'Who is the public?' is likely to be that there are multiple publics, each with its different views. Much stress in public engagement activities has been to ensure that 'unheard' or marginalised voices, for example, from ethnic minorities or socially excluded groups, are heard. But in the likely event of disagreements, which values become dominant? Is it the ones that are most loudly expressed? This does not, however, mean that debates inevitably become irreconcilable:

> The coexistence of many different beliefs and traditions is a characteristic cultural condition of late modern societies. It could be argued that in such a society intrinsic views, strictly speaking, have ethical power only within the value systems of identifiable groups ... however, there is often considerably more scope for dialogue between supposedly incommensurable views than might be thought possible. Strongly held positions either way may be re-evaluated in the light of fresh angles, or by realising hitherto unappreciated implications. What becomes more difficult is when an issue becomes strongly politicised ... after a time it becomes almost impossible for one side to hear the other.[23]

To what extent can different values be reconciled with each other? For example, had GM crops been introduced on a small scale, in a targeted fashion, on specifi-

---

Industry (2004), *Science and Innovation Investment Framework 2004–2014*, London: HMSO, July.

[22]   House of Lords Select Committee on Science and Technology (1993), *Regulation of the United Kingdom Biotechnoloy Industry and Global Competitiveness*, London: The Stationery Office.

[23]   Bruce, D. and Bruce, A. (eds) (1998), *Engineering Genesis: The Ethics of Genetic Engineering in Non-human Species*, London: Earthscan, pp. 106–7.

cally identified crops only, and with monitoring for long-term effects, would this have made a difference to the debate? Engagement may be effective in un-covering underlying attitudes but may be incapable of mediating between them. Political decisions are still likely to be required.

The expectations of what public engagement can deliver vary. We can, for example, broadly identify the following types of engagement:

- Stakeholder engagement – including consumer groups and advocacy groups. This means to explicitly engage in negotiation between groups with different interest and value positions to arrive at a more broadly informed and potentially widely accepted decision.
- End-user engagement – taking into account expertise in the practical aspects of a situation, for example, involving slaughterhouse workers in looking at regulations relating to protection from BSE. This acknowledges that expertise can reside elsewhere than with scientific experts.
- Engaging uncommitted publics in already existing scientific developments. This may include involvement in different ways, for example:

  – to test out what kind of developments might be acceptable and use this information to inform policy;
  – to understand what issues are important to lay publics rather than specialists;
  – to engage in participatory democracy.

- Upstream engagement – to set the research agenda according to public values. This is often seen as a reaction to perceived excessive influence by commercial companies over what research is carried out.

Recognition of different roles for different parts of the public in different situations has been developed, for example, by the International Risk Governance Council. In their risk management model,[24] different involvement of different publics is advocated according to the extent to which the issue exhibits complexity, uncertainty and ambiguity (that is, ambiguity as to what is the real question being addressed). However, there are some bodies that appear to see engagement in scientific issues as a move towards 'participative democracy', resulting in a movement of power and decision-making 'to the people'.

The issue of power should not be lightly dismissed. All public engagement activities require some kind of intermediary to stimulate the discussion and to co-ordinate the development of a summary report. A great deal of effort has

---

[24] Renn, O. (2005), *Risk Governance – Towards an Integrative Approach*, White Paper 1, International Risk Governance Council, Geneva, September.

been invested in many cases to try to ensure that these processes are driven by the participants and not the facilitators. Nevertheless, the facilitators are potentially in a position of power. Many carry out excellent work, but there is no guarantee that this will always be the case – there is no 'quality standard' that identifies appropriate facilitators. We might not, for example, trust the output from an engagement exercise funded by a multinational company; but how much do we trust one funded by, say, an environmental NGO or a pro-life advocacy group? Each of these groups has a strong value position which they are likely to wish to further. It is possible that such groups can use an external facilitator who is unbiased and professional, but, like the results of scientific research funded by particular interests, the results of public engagement funded by interest groups may be contested. The issue of power has not gone unnoticed. A recent editorial in the journal *Research Fortnight* notes that 'It is evident that scientists are supposed to lose power, but who is supposed to gain it?'[25]

A further issue relates to the complexity of the scientific issues under debate. We do not know how science will progress and previous attempts at foresight have demonstrated that we are poor at predicting what the result of a particular piece of science is likely to be. Humans are enormously inventive and science developed for a particular purpose may end up being used in different and unpredictable ways once it enters the social sphere.[26] Science is also continually discovering new information – sometimes unexpectedly so. It is this uncertainty that causes some of the concerns about applying science – we do not know everything and there may be things that we do not even know that we ought to know that will make a material difference in the future. The corollary to this is, however, that any public engagement exercise cannot be a single event but needs to be an ongoing process to take into account new knowledge and information. The danger of making a decision based on early engagement focused on what may prove to be inappropriate developments is that future benefits may be forgone. As Adams points out, we take risks because we expect benefits in the future.[27]

Public engagement may be effective at providing information on values relating to whether to proceed with a scientific/technological development or not. However, it is currently a rather blunt instrument. Engagement is not yet well developed to provide information on a way forward rather than blocking a way forward. It is not well developed to consider the consequences of its views; for example, what would be the impact of banning GM crop cultivation in the UK?

---

[25] Bown, W.C. (2005), 'Time to Disengage', *Research Fortnight,* 14 September, 2.
[26] Williams, R. (2005), 'Compressed Foresight and Narrative Bias: Pitfalls in Assessing High Technology Futures', Innogen Working Paper 39.
[27] Adams, J. (2005), 'Risk', *New Scientist*, 17 September, 36.

Nor to consider the constraints under which policy-makers have to operate. In reality, UK actions on GM crops are subject to EU legislation in the area. At one level, the *GM Nation?* debate may be considered to have been irrelevant at the time when it took place. Under Directive 2001/18/EC, the UK was not necessarily free to exclude GM crops whatever the public thought about them. At a wider international level, the situation becomes even more constrained within the international trade rules of the World Trade Organization (WTO). The provision for excluding international trade in particular items under the Sanitary and Phytosanitary Measures and Technical Barriers to Trade arrangements do not generally allow exclusion for 'value' reasons, including issues such as animal welfare. Governments therefore face difficulties in taking account of the values of their publics, given the need to innovate for economic development and the restrictions incurred by being part of an international trading system.

5   CONCLUSION

In conclusion, the desire by many influential bodies to have decisions about scientific developments in the public domain is very clear. While this may not be true of some areas of development (for example, there is little public engagement about the development of information technology, where the market is dominant), it is unlikely that the pressure for public engagement about the values driving scientific developments, particularly in the biological sciences, will disappear. It is perhaps not surprising that in a late-modern society, where individual values dominate and there is an erosion of respect for authority figures, the purposes to which science is being harnessed and the values that drive these are being questioned, at least as much as the consequences of the research. It is unlikely that it will be sufficient to 'tick the box' of public engagement and then allow the scientists to go back to their labs to carry on business as usual. It also seems unlikely that merely undertaking a public engagement exercise will produce a swift resolution to the 'crisis' in the governance of science and result in an easier passage of scientific developments into the market place. More sophisticated solutions will be required. Recognising that debates around the direction of science are at least as much to do with values, power and different conceptions of the future as they are about safety and efficacy is a starting point for developing regulatory processes that can take these into account.

15. A rights-free world – is it workable, and what is the point?

Graham Dutfield

1 INTRODUCTION

1.1 A Rights-free World – an Appealing Prospect ...

Imagine a world without intellectual property: one in which information's alleged wanting to be free would at last be realised, standing on the shoulders of giants would be a right and not – at best – a wafer-thin experimental use exemption, and for those starved of science, culture and Coldplay's latest CD there *would* be such a thing as a free lunch.

It certainly *sounds* appealing. Surely we could then distribute AIDS treatments to the dying in Africa whether or not they have money to buy them. We would be able to ensure schoolchildren and university students in poor countries have access to the best and most up-to-date educational materials. Would not an intellectual property rights-free world also save developing-country farmers from having to buy expensive new seeds and pesticides? And, even if traditional knowledge continued to be available without charge, why complain if everything else is free?

Becoming intoxicated by this vision, would-be abolitionists would no doubt scorn the objections of those claiming that without intellectual property rights inventors would stop inventing, authors would stop writing, and musicians would down instruments never to pick them up again. Did not Homo sapiens' 'creative explosion'[1] predate the Statutes of Monopolies and Anne by 40 000 years, if not longer, and the birth of the Renaissance by at least two centuries?

---

[1] Or, more prosaically, the 'Upper Palaeolithic Revolution'. See Lewis-Williams, D. (2002), *The Mind in the Cave: Consciousness and the Origins of Art*, New York: Thames and Hudson, p. 40 and generally. Also, Pfeiffer, J. E. (1982), *The Creative Explosion: An Inquiry into the Origins of Art and Religion*, New York: HarperCollins.

1.2   ... But Would it Really be Better?

So a rights-free world sounds like a wonderful idea. But would it actually be better than the intellectual property rights-infested one we have today?

The ideal way to find out would be to squeeze into a time machine with us enough anti-intellectual property[2] politicians to form a parliamentary majority, return to 1623 and then 1710, outvote the MPs supporting the Statutes, come back, observe events from those years to the counter-present, somehow shift back to this version of today, and then compare the world it would have become with the one it did. Since we are some way from being able to perform such a technological feat but in the meantime have a book to publish, we had better think of alternatives.

2   USING COUNTERFACTUAL HISTORY

The rather controversial technique of counterfactual history may be worth a try. Essentially, this is a retelling of history that differs because we have made something happen that did not really, or something not happen that did, such as Napoleon winning at Waterloo or Hitler deciding not to invade the Soviet Union; or perhaps the Ancient Greeks passing a copyright law so we could then ask ourselves whether Homer would have been 'incentivised' to write a sequel to the *Odyssey* or a prequel to the *Iliad*. The idea is that such an alternative account of history's unfolding will help us to understand the real events better, their repercussions, and the implications of going down the particular paths that human societies followed from that event onwards, whether deliberately and with eyes wide open, or blindfolded and at the point of a gun – metaphorical or otherwise.

Let us try this with intellectual property. Since we lack space in this short chapter to consider the whole field of intellectual property rights, we will take as an example the patent system and the pharmaceutical industry. Even then, the best we can probably achieve is an informed speculation, and not really a history at all.[3]

---

[2]   Admittedly, the term 'intellectual property' was unknown before the 19th century. It seems in fact to have been introduced into the English language by Lysander Spooner, an American libertarian who argued that scientists and inventors should enjoy a permanent property right in their ideas (see Spooner, L. (1855 [1971]) 'The Law of Intellectual Property; or an Essay on the Right of Authors and Inventors to a Perpetual Property in their Ideas', in C. Shively (ed.), *The Collected Works of Lysander Spooner, Volume 1*, Weston: M&S Press; and Spooner, L. (1884) *A Letter to Scientists and Inventors on the Science of Justice, and their Rights of Perpetual Property in their Discoveries and Inventions*, Boston: Cupples, Upham and Co.).

[3]   For an exposition and defence of counterfactual history, once dismissed by E.H.

So the question to be asked is this: if there had been no patent system, would there have been fewer or more life-saving drugs than the ones that were developed and sold since the pharmaceutical industry emerged out of the dyestuff makers of the late 19th century?[4] As we will see, the answer is inconclusive but does at least help us to consider realistically what a rights-free world might achieve that a rights-having one is failing to do.

3   THERAPEUTIC REVOLUTIONS, DRUGS AND PATENTS

It almost goes without saying both that the pharmaceutical industry is crucially important for human welfare since it produces and trades in life-saving cures (among other things), and that it is considered to be the most dependent of all industries on patents. But does this dependence mean that drugs coming onto the market during the 20th century would be lower in quantity and quality if the system of patents for invention had never been invented?[5]

Before investigating this question, one must immediately accept the plausibility of the argument – propounded by industry – that without the incentive effect of enforceable patent rights, fewer new drugs could possibly have entered the market. After all, they are expensive to develop; so, in theory at least, only a time-limited restriction on competition can allow them to recoup their costs and make profits they can plough back into further drug development. If so, for developed countries at least, where price is not such an important issue as in poor countries, it may well be true that we would be far worse off without patents.

But how far have patents truly been responsible for creating the conditions leading to the discovery and development of new medicines, or – to look from a more negative perspective – for the paucity of new medicines compared with what a patent-free world could have achieved?

It is important first to acknowledge how far we have come since the pre-Second World War era. Until that time, the number of new chemical entities entering the market each year was small, the research-based pharmaceutical industry hardly existed and was mainly confined to Germany, and most of the drugs available would be considered primitive by today's doctors, pharmacists and patients. According to the medical journalist James Le Fanu,

---

Carr as 'a parlour game', see Ferguson, N. (1997), 'Introduction', in Ferguson, N. (ed.), *Virtual History: Alternatives and Counterfactuals*, London: Picador, pp. 1–90.

[4]   This history is told in Dutfield, G. (2003), *Intellectual Property Rights and the Life Science Industries: a Twentieth Century History*, Aldershot: Ashgate.

[5]   Originally patents were Crown-granted monopoly privileges that had nothing to do with inventions as the term is understood today.

The newly qualified doctor setting up practice in the 1930s had a dozen or so proven remedies with which to treat the multiplicity of different diseases he encountered every day: aspirin for rheumatic fever, digoxin for heart failure, the hormones thyroxine and insulin for an underactive thyroid and diabetes respectively, salvarsan for syphilis, bromides for those who needed a sedative, barbiturates for epilepsy, and morphine for pain.[6]

Yet 'thirty years later, when the same doctor would have been approaching retirement, those dozen remedies had grown to over 2,000.'[7] So clearly the drug-makers – as well as the universities and public sector research institutions also involved in pharmaceutical research and development – have been productive in the past 70 years even if they are experiencing a very lean patch at the moment (see further below).

Arguably, two of the most significant therapeutic advances in terms of productivity, profitability and their seminal impacts on drug research and development during the 20th century were the sulpha drugs and the antibiotics.

3.1   The Sulphonamides

The sulphonamide 'revolution' was founded on the working hypothesis, first formulated by Paul Ehrlich, that the ability of dye chemicals to stain microbes and tissues selectively might enable them to affect the metabolism of disease-causing microbes without damaging or killing friendly ones and tissues. The story begins in the late 1920s, when Gerhard Domagk at I.G. Farbenindustrie tested his company's dyes for therapeutic effects. In 1932 he discovered that a dye given the name of Prontosil Red inhibited streptococcal infections in mice.

In France, Roussel Laboratories soon took advantage of being able to copy Farben's French patent on Prontosil Red. This was because French patent law at the time allowed it to be protected as a dye but not as a medicine.[8] Subsequent research at the Pasteur Institute led to the discovery of a more effective substance, called sulphanilamide. This chemical was actually the active part of prontosil, released into the body as the dye was metabolised. Since sulphanilamide had been synthesised three decades earlier and described in a publication, it was unpatentable.

Soon after, a British company called May and Baker developed a related drug called M&B 693 that was more effective against streptococci as well as other

---

6   Le Fanu, J. (1999), *The Rise and Fall of Modern Medicine*, London: Little, Brown and Co., p. 206.

7   Ibid.

8   Sneader, W. (1985), *Drug Discovery: The Evolution of Modern Medicines*, Chichester, New York, Brisbane, Toronto, Singapore: John Wiley and Sons, p. 287.

organisms, including pneumococci, and was also less toxic.[9] Other similar substances were subsequently synthesised and found also to have therapeutic effects against a range of infectious diseases, including leprosy. These became known collectively as the sulphonamides, or sulpha drugs.

The sulpha drugs contributed enormously to future drug discovery. Research into the mode of action of sulphanilamide led to the formulation of a new working hypothesis that guided scientists in their design of new drugs for specific microbial targets: competitive antagonism. The idea is that certain chemicals play a vital role in metabolic processes that are specific to particular species of microbe. The possibility arises that structurally related chemicals can be designed which 'trick' the target microbe into taking them up and using them in place of the real substance. But, since they do not perform the same role, the process cannot take place, and the microbe is weakened or destroyed.[10] Adoption of this principle led to the development of several important drugs. These include para-amino salicylic acid (PAS), a treatment for tuberculosis; azathioprine, an immuno-suppressive drug; and the beta-blockers that were pioneered in the 1960s by James Black, then at ICI. A decade later, Black was responsible for another triumph of rational drug design, the anti-ulcerant cimetidine. Under the brand name of Tagamet, this drug generated massive revenues for Smith, Kline and French, where he was employed at the time.

All of the above happened. So let us consider what would have been different without patents being available, whether for products or processes. Most probably I.G. Farben would be a going concern, albeit a smaller one, and would still have tested old dyes and thus discovered sulphonamide. But would the sulphonamide revolution at that point have become stillborn? We have to remember that Domagk's discovery was a major scientific breakthrough that made it easier to discover many more drugs, some of which were chemically unrelated. Without patents, a lot of these would have been discovered anyway. A good example is PAS, which was discovered by a Danish doctor called Jorgen Lehmann. Without the promise of a patent, there is a good chance that secrecy and lead time would have been sufficient incentive for companies to have tried entering the market in sulpha drugs. Nonetheless, since many of the drugs that followed *were* patented and government drug approval regulations became more and more expensive to comply with, we would go too far by claiming without strong evidence that without patents the sulphonamide revolution would have been as fruitful as it was.

---

[9] Ibid., p. 288.
[10] Weatherall, M. (1990), *In Search of a Cure: A History of Pharmaceutical Discovery*, Oxford: Oxford University Press, pp. 152–4.

3.2 Antibiotics

The discovery of penicillin is normally traced to 1928, when Alexander Fleming found a mould displaying antibacterial properties in his laboratory. Little
progress was made for a decade.[11] This changed when Howard Florey and
Ernst Chain at Oxford University decided to study penicillin. With the Second
World War underway, the urgent need to scale up production was manifest to
the government, but domestic companies were unable or unwilling to invest
in the development of new technologies to mass-produce penicillin. Four US
pharmaceutical companies – Merck, Pfizer, Lederle and Squibb – became involved in penicillin research. Pfizer's patented deep fermentation technology
turned out to be especially productive and generated tremendous profits for
the company.

Penicillin was no one-off. Various types of penicillin and semi-synthetic analogues came on the market during the following decades, including those
effective against resistant strains of disease-causing microbes like staphylococ-
cus. And, while its discovery was accidental, penicillin inspired scientists to
search for other micro-organisms producing substances that are toxic for other
microbes but harmless to humans, or what became known as 'antibiotics'. The
result was the discovery and development of streptomycin, cephalosporin, tetracycline and a wide range of other antibiotics. It was largely out of the
investment of profits from the antibiotics revolution into research and development that today's research-based pharmaceutical industry emerged, especially
in the USA and Britain.

Seeing the possibility of making unprecedented profits from antibiotics
screened through increasingly routine procedures, the American pharmaceutical
industry faced the uncertainty that they could get patents for natural products
discovered through what had become routine screening procedures. But successful lobbying by the American pharmaceutical industry achieved the
incorporation in the 1952 Patent Act of helpful language in order to ensure that
antibiotics discovered through techniques of systematic screening could be
patented.[12] Essentially, the non-obviousness criterion was incorporated into
patent law in a particular way that meant 'patentability shall not be negatived
[sic] by the manner in which the invention was made'. This provision was meant
to keep the innovation threshold low. Subsequently, the US pharmaceutical industry, previously somewhat backward compared with its German and Swiss

---

[11]   Brown, K. (2004), *Penicillin Man: Alexander Fleming and the Antibiotic Revolution*, Stroud: Sutton Publishing; Macfarlane, G. (1984), *Alexander Fleming: the Man
and the Myth*, Cambridge, MA: Harvard University Press.

[12]   Kingston, W. (2004), 'Removing Some Harm from the World Trade Organization',
Oxford Development Studies, **32** (2), 309–20.

counterparts, became the world's biggest on the strength of the antibiotics revolution.

As with the sulphonamide revolution, in a world without patents the advent of the antibiotics era would still have happened. The exigencies of war made it essential for ways to be found to mass-produce penicillin, and to this end the US Government encouraged the main drug firms to collaborate. Indeed, a more interesting counterfactual speculation is that of whether the antibiotics revolution would have happened if Hitler had not invaded Poland and started the Second World War.

In the 1940s and 1950s there were almost too many antibiotics, at least for the convenience of industry. While it may be that without patents some if not many of these drugs would never have been discovered or at least have reached the market, the extent of the abuse of patent rights to prevent competitors from entering the market can draw us to another conclusion about whether we would have been better off without patents. This is that even if the incentive to invest in research and development were less in our patent-free world, the impossibility of using patents to create market entry barriers would have had a highly positive effect by encouraging possibly more innovative actors to join the competition.

As it happened, as firms began to discover and market increasing numbers of effective but similar antibiotics, there was a very real threat of price-reducing competition. This actually happened in the case of both penicillin and streptomycin. Companies found various ways to deal with the situation, including by aggressively asserting their patent and trade mark rights, restricting patent licensing, forming cartels and setting up large sales teams to market their drugs.

One of the most controversial instances of the use of patents to support anti-competitive behaviour by the industry took place during the 1950s when five companies formed an international antibiotics cartel. The story begins with the introduction of the broad-spectrum antibiotics, whose chemical structures were unknown when they first came to market but turned out often to be extremely similar to each other. The earliest of these products were Lederle's Aureomycin (introduced in 1948), Parke Davis' Chloromycetin (1949) and Pfizer's Terramycin (1950). The similarity of these products stimulated intense competition, which was reflected not just in increased marketing and advertising expenditures but also in a determination to elucidate the chemical structures of these drugs and to develop portfolios of related compounds. Pfizer's research proved the close affinity of Aureomycin and Terramycin and resulted in a very similar but more effective new substance, which was the first ever semi-synthetic antibiotic. This was patented and given the name 'tetracycline'. Lederle also discovered tetracycline by the same method and filed patent applications. Subsequently, Bristol and Hayden Chemical Corporation came up with tetracycline by another method and also applied for patents. Pfizer's and Bristol's patents were granted in 1955 after being initially rejected.[13]

The other companies' patent applications failed. However, it was extremely doubtful that either patent should really have been awarded; the companies themselves were apparently fully aware that they were vulnerable to legal challenge.[14] But, by agreeing to recognise Pfizer's patent and to limit competition, a group of five companies – Pfizer, Cyanamid (Lederle's parent company), Bristol, Squibb and Upjohn – cornered the tetracycline market and managed to ensure that the price of their closely related products remained high and almost equal for about a decade. According to Braithwaite, the situation suggested that the patent was providing 'a cover for conspiratorial behaviour to partition a market which in the absence of the patent would have been clearly illegal'.[15] Although the Government failed – despite its determined efforts – to prove that the companies had violated antitrust law or had defrauded the Patent Office, they had to pay hundred of millions of dollars in legal settlements. Nonetheless, the profits the five companies made not just in the USA but worldwide through their control of tetracycline were enormous, helping to turn them into major pharmaceutical corporations.[16] One can only speculate about how many companies were prevented from entering the competition, and also about the number of people whose lives might have been saved if prices had been allowed to fall earlier.

4   WHO NEEDS PATENTS ANYWAY?

While much of the current debate on pharmaceutical patenting has to do with differences about where to strike the balance to ensure that protection is effective but not excessive, some critics have over the years proposed that we would be better off by dispensing entirely with patents. In the 1960s, Henry Steele argued that the elimination of patents would benefit the public as it would increase price competition and encourage research by non-corporate institutions, where most of the genuinely innovative pharmaceutical research (in his opinion) was carried out anyway.[17]

---

[13]   Sneader, p. 327.

[14]   Braithwaite, J. (1984), *Corporate Crime in the Pharmaceutical Industry*, London: Routledge and Kegan Paul, pp. 184–5.

[15]   Ibid., p. 184.

[16]   Temin, P. (1979), 'Technology, Regulation, and Market Structure in the Modern Pharmaceutical Industry', *The Bell Journal of Economics* **10**, 429–46, 441.

[17]   Steele, H. (1962), 'Monopoly and Competition in the Ethical Drugs Market', *Journal of Law and Economics*, **5**, 131–64, 162. For discussion on gene sequences and

Can this be right? Convincing evidence either way is hard to come by. The experience of Italy during the 1950s and 1960s suggests that lack or absence of patent protection encourages imitative rather than truly innovative pharmaceutical research.[18] However, the introduction of product patent protection there has made little difference in terms of research and development expenditure and the development of innovative new products by domestic firms.[19] Therefore, just as critics who wish to use the Italian case to demonstrate that patents are unnecessary for pharmaceutical innovation need to explain the pre-patent era, those who wish to cite Italy as proof of the opposite must somehow explain the post-1978 situation.

Taylor and Silberston's well-known study on the economic impacts of the patent system on different industrial sectors provides a difference perspective. According to these authors, a weakening of the British patent system would probably result in reduced research and development outlays but massively increased expenditures on advertising and marketing and on the promotion of brand names and minor product differentiation.[20]

Yet things could hardly be worse in this respect than they are now, when the patent system worldwide has never been friendlier to the pharmaceutical industry. The so-called 'research-based industry' is less and less successful in getting new drugs to market. And it has been accused of spending far more on advertising and marketing than on research, of abusing the intellectual property system through tactics referred to as 'evergreening', and overemphasising the development of drugs which are designed for afflictions that are not life-threatening and which are highly similar to existing treatments. Let us consider these issues in some detail.

5 'RESEARCH-BASED' OR 'MARKETING-BASED'?

A study by researchers at Boston University School of Public Health found that the American brand-name drug sector increased its marketing staff from a total of 55 348 people in 1995 to 87 810 in 2000. In the same years the number of researchers actually fell, from 49 409 people to 48 527. One of the authors caustically remarked that

---

patenting see Wallace, H. and Mayer, S. 'Scientific Research Agendas: Controlled and Shaped by the Scope of Patentability', in Chapter 13 of this volume.
[18]   Taylor, C.T. and Silberston, Z.A. (1973), *The Economic Impact of the Patent System: The British Experience*, Cambridge: Cambridge University Press, pp. 262–3.
[19]   Scherer, F.M. and Weisburst, S. (1995), 'Economic Effects of Strengthening Pharmaceutical Patent Protection in Italy', *International Review of Industrial Property and Copyright Law*, **26** (6), 1009–24.
[20]   Taylor and Silberston, p. 266.

these staffing patterns call into question the brand-name drug makers' self-definition as 'research-based' companies ... Since they now employ nearly 40,000 more people in marketing than in research, they might more appropriately call themselves 'America's marketing-based pharmaceutical companies'. Their priority today does not seem to be developing new treatments but defining and selling their brands.[21]

But would a more efficient patent system, or perhaps no patent system at all, encourage the industry to spend less on sales promotion and more on research? Clearly we should be sceptical of claims by industry that they compete purely on the basis of innovation and not also on marketing acumen or advertising expenditure! But there is no easy answer to the question. It is not at all certain that a job created in promotion is a job lost in research, or that, if we discouraged companies from spending so much on advertising, they would simply reallocate the unspent money to research. There again, it is certainly possible that companies would invest more in research the better to differentiate their products from those of rivals if they could not do this through advertising. But how much more depends on a range of factors that go beyond the patent system. Nonetheless, we can hardly be satisfied with a situation whereby the patent incentive fails so badly to induce a greater commitment to research and development than it does when so much money is being spent on marketing. Probably the only way to clarify the patenting–research–marketing connections would be to restrict marketing and advertising and then see where the companies divert their funds to. Somehow it is difficult to imagine the industry agreeing to put this to the test!

6 EVERGREENING

Pharmaceutical companies use patents (and also trade marks) strategically in order to restrict competition, in some cases for several years beyond the 20-year patent duration. 'Evergreening' or 'line extensions' are terms used to refer to the use of intellectual property rights in order to extend the monopoly or at least the market dominance of a drug beyond the life of the original patent protecting it. Since 2001, drugs worth a total of $45 billion a year have been going off patent. It should not be surprising, then, that drug companies will try to stretch out their exclusive rights over blockbuster drugs for as long as possible, especially when they are heavily dependent on a small number of such highly profitable products (or even just one). For example, firms might seek to obtain patents on new delivery methods for the drug, on reduced dosage regimens, or on new versions of the active compound or combinations that are more effective or that produce fewer side-effects than the original substance.[22]

Companies also use trade mark law to extend their market power beyond the patented drug's expiry date. Patented drugs are usually marketed under their brand name rather than the generic name. Since generic producers cannot use this name, it is often very difficult for them to promote their alternative product effectively. Therefore, physicians may continue to prescribe the branded product even if it is more expensive than the generic version. In fact, in many countries, physicians may not even know that alternatives exist. In the case of known compounds whose therapeutic properties were discovered several years after their development, this form of protection may, in the absence of product patent protection, be the most effective one available.[23]

In addition, trade mark law in certain countries can be used to protect the colour and form of the capsules. And to make the legal minefield even more treacherous for generic firms, the original producer of a drug may try to assert copyright over the printed information accompanying the product. According to Abbott, 'despite the apparent overreaching in arguing that "take two tablets every four hours" is the subject of copyright protection, the pharmaceutical manufacturers do not hesitate to delay the introduction of generic drugs with litigation over this question'.[24]

In restricting price competition, the benefits of such tactics for the original producers can be substantial. But it is hardly self-evident that the public benefits, especially considering that so much of the profit goes into marketing rather than further research and development.

---

[22] Correa provides a list of patenting targets chosen by companies to extend their monopolies on drugs. These include polymorphs (crystalline forms of the active compound); pharmaceutical forms (that is, new ways of administering the active compound); selective inventions (elements selected from a group that were not specifically named in earlier patents claiming the group); analogy processes; combinations of known products; optical isomers; active metabolites; prodrugs (inactive compounds that produce active metabolites when introduced into the body); new salts of known substances; variants of existing manufacturing processes; and new uses for old products. Correa, C.M. (2001), *Trends in Drug Patenting: Case Studies*, Buenos Aires: Corregidor, pp. 11–12.

[23] Although the manufacturer may have patents on, for example, production processes and formulations, and these may still provide quite substantial protection.

[24] Abbott, F.M. (2002), 'The TRIPS Agreement, Access to Medicines, and the WTO Doha Ministerial Conference', *Journal of World Intellectual Property*, **5** (1), 15–52, 41.

7   'ME-TOOS' AND THE SKEWING OF RESEARCH PRIORITIES

While vital life-saving drugs continue to be developed and manufactured, it is a fact of economic life that the most profitable medicines are not necessarily the ones that save the most people's lives or even that save *any* lives. Moreover, the pharmaceutical industry is often attacked for investing more in molecular manipulation, or 'me-tooism', than in the development of new chemical substances offering genuine therapeutic advances on existing ones. This strategy can be profitable, but is not very creative (except, one may argue, in the money-making sense) and may not benefit patients very much either. The situation has reached the stage where 65 per cent of 'new' drugs approved by the Food and Drug Administration for sale in the USA from 1989 to 2000 contained active ingredients found in existing products. Of these newly approved drugs, 54 per cent 'differed from the marketed product in dosage form, route of administration, or were combined with another active ingredient', while 11 per cent 'were identical to products already available on the US market'.[25] Patents are implicated. Critics accuse them of failing to stimulate truly original research by encouraging me-tooism, for example by allowing the patenting of new uses of old drugs.

Patents are also alleged to distort research priorities away from lifesavers for the poor who are dying to lifestyle improvers for the rich 'worried well'. Criticisms that industry favours research into treatments for complaints that affect, or are of most interest to, the healthy wealthy are nothing new. In the 1950s, Henry Gadsden, CEO of Merck, Sharp and Dohme, told his researchers in a meeting that 'there are more well people than sick people. We should make products for people who are well.'[26] Examples of such products he mentioned – to the disgust of the scientists present – included a quick-tanning formula and a treatment for straightening hair. Since that time, vast sums have been spent on a range of 'lifestyle drugs' which may admittedly improve the quality of people's lives but in most cases are not exactly lifesavers. Research on treatments for relatively trivial ailments like baldness continues, as well as on dealing with diet-related health concerns of affluent societies such as obesity and high cholesterol, and on chronic problems such as high blood pressure – treatments that do not cure patients but that need to be taken continually for many years. The criticism is not that companies should not do such research at all, but that

---

[25]   Hunt, M. (2002), *Changing Patterns of Pharmaceutical Innovation*, Washington, DC: National Institute of Health Care Management Research and Educational Foundation, p. 3.

[26]   Quoted in Werth, B. (1994), *The Billion-dollar Molecule: One Company's Quest for the Perfect Drug*, New York: Touchstone, p. 131.

there is a severe lack of spending on diseases that disproportionately affect the poor, such as malaria and tuberculosis.

This is not just of academic interest. James Orbinski of Médecins Sans Frontières has pointed out, for example, that while 95 per cent of active TB cases occur in developing countries no new drugs for the disease have been developed since 1967.[27] And the World Health Organization has estimated that only 4.3 per cent of pharmaceutical research and development expenditure is aimed at those health problems mainly concerning low- and middle-income countries.[28]

However, it is fair to point out that 'me-tooism' is not always a bad thing. The critical view, as expressed by Hancher, is that 'the patent system ... can exacerbate these problems [of investing mostly in the development of therapeutically identical products] by sheltering socially worthless but privately profitable research'.[29] On the other hand, as Braithwaite concedes, 'me-too research has occasionally stumbled upon significant therapeutic advances'.[30] Even so, the industry's output in recent years has undeniably been disappointing with respect both to the quantity and quality of new drugs. Between 1969 and 1989 the number of new chemical entities launched per year on the world market fell from over 90 to under 40.[31] The lack of genuinely original products entering the market is a matter for serious concern. But is the patent system responsible? It is difficult to say whether a patent-free world would encourage more original research and less molecular manipulation, or the opposite. Even so, the patent system may be making the situation worse by encouraging too much research in areas that are profitable but not necessarily the most human welfare enhancing.

As for the complaint about skewed research priorities, it is rather difficult to say whether patents are directly responsible for this. With or without patents, the profit motive of capitalism is bound to encourage pharmaceutical research to be aimed at areas where the most money can be made. But this does not let patents completely off the hook. One could argue that, if patents are meant to

---

[27] Orbinski, J. (2001), 'Health, Equity, and Trade: a Failure in Global Governance', in Sampson G.P. (ed.), *The Role of the World Trade Organization in Global Governance*, Tokyo: United Nations University, pp. 230–31.

[28] World Health Organization (1996), *Investing in Health Research and Development: Report of the Ad Hoc Committee on Health Research Relating to Future Intervention Options*, Geneva: WHO.

[29] Hancher, L. (1990), *Regulating for Competition: Government, Law, and the Pharmaceutical Industry in the United Kingdom and France*, Oxford: Clarendon Press, p. 51.

[30] Braithwaite, J. (1984), *Corporate Crime in the Pharmaceutical Industry*, London: Routledge & Kegan Paul, p. 164.

[31] Chartered Institute of Patent Agents (1998), *Briefing Paper – Patenting in the Pharmaceutical Industry – Supplementary Protection Certificates*, London: CIPA.

serve the public interest, they should encourage research where public needs are greatest. And, if they are not, the system should be reformed.

8   IN CONCLUSION ...

Without patents, the therapeutic revolutions discussed above would certainly have happened. Of course, we cannot be certain that as many useful products arising from them would have appeared in the absence of patents. But history, both real and counterfactual, encourages a cautious view on the notion that patents were indispensable.

Nonetheless, bearing in mind the ever mounting costs of developing drugs and getting them to market, it is very difficult to argue convincingly that patents with all their faults should be abolished, at least until we can come up with a better and realistic alternative.[32] But, having said that, it is useful to imagine a world without patents since it leads us to ask – and may help us to answer – a very important question: if we had no patents but agreed that legal rights ought to be created to encourage social-welfare-maximising innovation and investment in pharmaceutical research and development, what form would such rights take? In my view, there is no reason to assume that such rights would look like the patent system.

8.1   From 'Rights versus No Rights' to 'What Kind of Rights Should we Have?'

So *is* a rights-free world workable, and what is the point of it anyway? Apart from the politically challenging (to say the least!) task of achieving a rights-free world, would the world really become a better place if we could just blow away the whole tangly, sticky web of rights in which we are presently enmeshed?

As our discussion on patents and the pharmaceutical industry suggests, legitimate dissatisfaction with the present intellectual property rules does not necessarily lead us to the conclusion that there should be no intellectual property rights. Indeed, even for the most ardently Foucault-inspired anti-rights thinkers,[33] the allure of being regarded as an author, and an author of substance to

---

[32]   Non-governmental organisations led by the Consumer Project on Technology have been drafting a proposed medical research and development treaty. See www.cptech. org/workingdrafts/rndtreaty.html for the most recent draft. See also Hubbard, T. and Love, J. (2004), 'A New Trade Framework for Global Healthcare R&D', *PLoS Biology* **2** (2), 147–50.

[33]   Particularly influential is Foucault, M. (1979), 'What is an author?', in Hariri, J. V. (ed.), *Textual Strategies: Perspectives in Post-Structuralist Criticism*, Ithaca: Cornell

boot, may be irresistible. There is no reason why this point should not apply also to inventors, who are probably just as egotistical as persons of letters. As Mark Rose concluded in a book on what he called 'the invention of copyright' (and which incidentally refers to Foucault and Roland Barthes in its very first line),

> copyright is deeply rooted in our conception of ourselves as individuals with at least a modest grade of singularity, some degree of personality. And it is associated with our sense of privacy and our conviction, at least in theory, that it is essential to limit the power of the state. We are not ready, I think, to give up the sense of who we are.[34]

If Rose is right about this, a rights-free world would diminish us as persons – or at any rate make us writers feel we have lost some of our individuality. But this may be a small price to pay if the material conditions of humanity would be enhanced. At any event we can be certain beyond doubt that the death of patents and copyright will not mean the death of human creativity in all its manifestations. However, as one who considers intellectual property to be neither as good as its most enthusiastic proponents claim it to be nor as bad as its most fervent critics believe it is, I think we should avoid the extreme positions of abolitionism, on the one hand, and the no-such-thing-as-too-many-rights missionary zeal of so many US[35] and European[36] diplomats and trade negotiators, on the other.

In the meantime, let us imagine a rights-free world if in doing so it helps us to conceive a better world of rights than the one we have.

University Press, pp. 141–60; also Barthes, R. (1968), 'The Death of the Author', reprinted in *Image, Music, Text*, London: HarperCollins, pp. 142–8.

[34] Rose, M. (1993), *Authors and Owners: the Invention of Copyright*, Cambridge, MA: Harvard University Press, p. 142.

[35] With the exception of geographical indications, concerning which the USA finds itself in the intellectual property sceptics camp. Doubtless, this is due to a perception that the country has nothing to gain from geographical indications as opposed to patents, copyright and trade marks.

[36] With some exceptions, including the extension of patenting to computer programs, business methods and plant varieties. Presumably, the European Commission's view of where the EU's economic interests lie is at least part of the explanation.

16. The priorities, the values, the public

Charlotte Waelde

1 INTRODUCTION

Previous chapters have given insights into a selection of the public domain's many faces. We have had discussion on historical development (Grosheide);[1] ideas as to how we might visualise the boundaries between public and private spaces (Deazley);[2] questions raised as to whether there is any right to the public domain (Cahir);[3] examination of the public domain in the international sphere (Taubman);[4] analysis of the interaction between the public domain and the public interest (Davies);[5] discussion on categories of intellectual space (Macmillan),[6] of making space (Howkins),[7] of constructing space (Bainton)[8] and of using space (Thompson);[9] debates over the development of public spaces within a privatised system (La Manna,[10] Susskind[11]) and of particular spaces (Gibson);[12]

---

[1]   Grosheide, F.W., 'In Search of the Public Domain during the Prehistory of Copyright Law', Chapter 1 (hereafter Grosheide).

[2]   Deazley, R., 'Copyright's Public Domain', Chapter 2 (hereafter Deazley).

[3]   Cahir, J., 'The Public Domain: Right or Liberty?', Chapter 3 (hereafter Cahir).

[4]   Taubman, A., 'The Public Domain and International Intellectual Property Lay Treaties', Chapter 4 (hereafter Taubman).

[5]   Davies, G., 'The Public Domain and the Public Interest', Chapter 5 (hereafter Davies).

[6]   Macmillan, F., 'Altering the Contours of the Public Domain', Chapter 6 (hereafter Macmillan).

[7]   Howkins, J., 'Creativity, Innovation and Intellectual Property: A New Approach for the 21st Century', Chapter 7 (hereafter Howkins).

[8]   Bainton, T., 'The Public Domain and the Librarian', Chapter 8 (hereafter Bainton).

[9]   Thompson, B., 'The Public Domain and the Creative Author', Chapter 9 (hereafter Thompson).

[10]   La Manna, M.M.A., 'The Public Domain and the Economist', Chapter 10 (hereafter La Manna).

[11]   Susskind, R., 'The Public Domain and Public Sector Information', Chapter 11 (hereafter Susskind).

[12]   Gibson, J., 'Audiences in Tradition: Traditional Knowledge and the Public Domain', Chapter 12 (hereafter Gibson).

concerns voiced over the diminution of public spaces (Wallace and Mayer);[13] and varied views of the public (Bruce).[14] Finally it has been asked whether we really need rights at all (Dutfield),[15] or whether all spaces should be public.

Critically during these discussions not one author has called for doing away with the property rights within intellectual property, not even when challenged to think of a rights-free world.[16] But the majority do seem dissatisfied with the process of determining the boundaries between the public and the private and the consequent impact within the field. The reader has been invited to think about how the boundaries are or might be conceived, how the various spaces might relate to each other, and how and why any changes might be effected.

The purpose of this chapter is to draw together a number of the themes that have emerged. It is in particular to question where and how values (drawing on the discussion by Bruce[17]) that we place within the policy of intellectual property and the intellectual property system are incorporated, and to suggest that, if intellectual property touches the majority of the public, it is for the public to debate the values they would like to see reflected in the priorities set by the policy process.[18] It will be suggested that the categorisation discussed by Macmillan[19] might be a most useful starting point, albeit that in order to engage the public the terminology might have to be changed and contemporised. The question to be addressed is thus: how can the public be engaged in determining the values which should be reflected in the priorities within the intellectual property system?

2 THE PROCESS

The intellectual property development process is relentless. Whether at international, European or domestic level not a day passes without a judgement from a court,[20] a policy proposal, the announcement of an investigation into current

---

[13]   Wallace, H. and Mayer, S., 'Scientific Research Agendas: Controlled and Shaped by the Scope of Patentability', Chapter 13 (hereafter Wallace and Mayer).

[14]   Bruce, A., 'The Public Domain: Ideology vs. Interest', Chapter 14 (hereafter Bruce).

[15]   Dutfield, G., 'A Rights-Free World – Is it Workable, and What is the Point?', Chapter 15 (hereafter Dutfield).

[16]   Dutfield, p. 293.

[17]   Bruce, p. 280.

[18]   Taubman, p. 77.

[19]   Macmillan, p. 139.

[20]   Prince Charles recently won his case for summary judgement against *The Mail on Sunday* to restrain the newspaper from printing further extracts from one of his diaries, but the matter of other diaries was left over for a full trial, *HRH Prince of Wales v Associ-*

practices,[21] a legislative enactment, the publication of a commentary[22] or a set
of principles,[23] or any manner of other communication that comments on, challenges, alters or in some way impacts upon the intellectual property construct.
A casual observer may easily conclude that these initiatives seem piecemeal,
reactive, lacking in clear or even articulated rationales, and based on interest
claims and counter-claims rather than values held by the public.[24] Nonetheless

---

ated Newspapers Ltd [2006] EWHC 522 (Ch). And so the boundary between
confidentiality, freedom of expression, copyright, fair dealing, publication and the public
interest has shifted. For an indication of how regularly intellectual property cases are
referred to the ECJ, see www.patent.gov.uk/about/ippd/ecj/index.htm.

[21]   For a list of recent and current UK and European consultations in the IP sphere
see www.patent.gov.uk/about/consultations/writtenconsult.htm.

[22]   A glance at the following list illustrates how prolific the contributors to this book
are: Deazley, R. (2004), *On the Origin of the Right to Copy: Charting the Movement of
Copyright Law in Eighteenth Century Britain (1695–1775)*, Oxford: Hart Publishing;
Cahir, J. (2004), 'The Withering away of Property: the Rise of the Internet Information
Commons', *Oxford Journal of Legal Studies* **24** (4), 619–41; Grosheide, W. and Brinkhof,
J. (eds) (2005), *Intellectual Property Law: Crossing Borders Between Traditional and
Actual*, Molengrafica Series, Intersentia; Taubman, A. (2005), 'Saving the Village: Con-
serving Jurisprudential Diversity in the International Protection of Traditional Knowledge',
in Maskus, K. and Reichman, J. (eds), *International Public Goods and Transfer of Tech-
nology Under a Globalized Intellectual Property Regime*, Cambridge: Cambridge
University Press, pp. 521–64; Macmillan, F. (ed.) (2006), *New Directions in Copyright
Law, Vol. 2*, Cheltenham, UK and Northampton, MA, USA: Edward Elgar; Howkins, J.
(2002), *The Creative Economy: How People Make Money from Ideas*, London: Penguin
Books Ltd. For Toby Bainton's work in the library field see www.sconul.ac.uk/; and for
Bill Thompson's Weblog and links to his work see www.andfinally.com/index.html and
www.thebillblog.com. See also La Manna, M. and Bennett, J. (2001), 'Reversing The
Keynesian Asymmetry', *American Economic Review*, **91** (5), 1556–63; Susskind, R.
(1998), *The Future of Law: Facing the Challenges of Information Technology*, Oxford:
Oxford University Press; Gibson, J. (2005), *Community Resources: Intellectual Property,
International Trade and Protection of Traditional Knowledge*, Aldershot: Ashgate; Wal-
lace, A. (2003), 'UK Biobank: Good for Public Health?', *Open Democracy* 2003 at www.
opendemocracy.net/theme_9-genes/article_1381.jsp; Mayer, S. and Stirling, A. (2004),
'GM Crops: Good or Bad? Those Who Choose the Questions Determine the Answers',
EMBO Reports, **5** (11); Bruce, A. and Tait, J. (2004), 'Interests, Values and Genetic Da-
tabases in Blood and Data – Ethical, Legal and Social Aspects of Human Genetic
Databases', in Arnason, A., Nordal, S. and Arnason, V. (eds), *ELSAGEN Conference*,
University of Iceland, Reykjavik, pp. 25–28; Dutfield, G. (2004), *Intellectual Property,
Biogenetic Resources and Traditional Knowledge*, Earthscan Publications Ltd.

[23]   Howkins (Chapter 7) has discussed the Adelphi Charter. At a recent expert meeting hosted by the AHRC Research Centre for Studies in Intellectual Property and
Technology Law on comparative approaches to the protection of personality, it was
agreed that a set of Principles for the Protection of Personality should be developed. For
details of the project see www.law.ed.ac.uk/ahrb/personality/.

[24]   Others would of course argue that they are the result of the democratic process:
Cahir, p. 65.

this activity has an impact, sometimes profound, on the spaces within the intellectual property sector domestically, regionally and internationally.

A survey of some of the recent developments in the intellectual property sphere (some of which have been touched upon by other contributors to this volume) serves to highlight the piecemeal approach to intellectual property development and illustrates just some of the tensions that underlie this ad hoc reform.

3 MAKING POLICY

A starting point might be to consider the process through which policy-making is crafted in today's climate. As Taubman says, 'The policy-maker's task is … to craft the optimal dynamic interplay between public domains and forms of legal exclusion, so as to optimise the production of those public goods which the policy process sets as priorities.'[25]

The process for crafting this dynamic interplay is well documented, at least as regards what happens at the international level. A body of literature exists, giving insightful analysis of the ways in which powers and interests negotiate in the development of treaties and other international agreements, and cataloguing the relationships between policy-makers and others as priorities ebb and flow, through which the boundaries between the public and the private are wrought.[26] Less commented upon, at least with the level of intensity of the studies at international level, is how regional and domestic legislation is formulated to optimise the production of public goods.[27] That the process is at least nominally 'open' to participation by anyone who might have an interest is without question. Calls for evidence, discussions on proposals, policy papers and other initiatives bombard the intellectual property interest.[28] But whether this process achieves the results we might wish, or whether it actually reflects what many might like, is a moot point. The process that allows voices to be heard engages the public, but seldom, it would seem, at the point at which the

---

[25]   Taubman, p. 84.

[26]   Braithwaite, J. and Drabos, P. (2000), *Global Business Regulation,* Cambridge: Cambridge University Press; Drahos, P. and Braithwaite, J. (2002), *Information Feudalism: Who Owns the Knowledge Economy?*, Earthscan Publications Ltd; Sell, S. (2003), *Private Power, Public Law: The Globalization of Intellectual Property Rights*, Cambridge: Cambridge University Press.

[27]   Litman, J. (2001), *Digital Copyright*, Prometheus Books.

[28]   I have no fewer than six sitting in my email inbox at the time of writing. And as I wrote another dropped into my email box accompanied by a rather anguished note from the secretary to the relevant committee: 'YET ANOTHER CONSULTATION PAPER'. Yes, the note was in capitals.

policy priorities are set. Instead comment is invited once initiatives appear not to be operating in the way anticipated. In addition, public consultation is not an end in itself (one would not expect it to be) but merely a pause for further reflection by the policy-makers intent on pursuing elusive priorities.

3.1   Policy-makers at Work – How do they Craft the Optimal Dynamic Interplay?

One example can be given from the Commission on Intellectual Property Rights.[29] This body was established in 2001 as a result of a recommendation made in the UK Government's White Paper on International Development, 'Eliminating World Poverty: Making Globalisation Work for the Poor'.[30] The Commission was specifically asked to look at the intellectual property rights interface between developed and developing countries and how it could be designed to benefit developing countries. As was highlighted in the introduction to the final report published in 2002:

> When there is so much uncertainty and controversy about the global impact of IPRs, we believe it is incumbent on policy makers to consider the available evidence, imperfect as it may be, before further extending property rights in scope or territorial extent.[31]

The report also acknowledged the imbalance that can occur in this process:

> Too often the interests of the 'producer' dominate in the evolution of IP policy, and that of the ultimate consumer is neither heard nor heeded. So policy tends to be determined more by the interests of the commercial users of the system, than by an impartial conception of the greater public good.[32]

But even when expression of these interests gathered through an investigative process such as that used by the CIPR might be considered to be representative of those that should be heard, there is no guarantee that what is called for will be acted upon. In one recommendation the CIPR called for commitments to ensure open access to scientific databases. In response the Government agreed 'that the results of publicly-funded research should as a general rule be made publicly available…'.[33]

---

[29]   For general information on the Commission on Intellectual Property Rights (hereafter CIPR) see www.iprcommission.org.

[30]   Cm 5006.

[31]   CIPR Final Report: Integrating Intellectual Property Rights and Development Policy', London, p. 7, available at www.iprcommission.org/home.html.

[32]   Ibid.

[33]   Ibid., p. 4, point 5.

Now there might have been a failing by the CIPR to define precisely what was meant by 'open access';[34] but the results since the report probably fall far short of what the Commission, and indeed those who were consulted, had in mind. Although the CIPR was directed specifically towards developing countries, even within the UK there is no clear policy as to the availability or otherwise, or at what price, of the contents of scientific databases. This is a theme that is reflected in Susskind's contribution to the present volume. As he explains, the Re-use of Public Sector Information Regulations 2005[35] are intended to free up public sector information and make it available for re-use by the community. However, this initiative is set within a mêlée of governmental policies pulling in contrary directions.[36] Some publicly funded collators of public sector information are set up as trading funds and thus need to make a return to the Government.[37] In addition, a number of these compete with their private sector counterparts. Whereas their behaviour might be shaped by the shadow of competition law[38] and OFT investigations,[39] the core governmental strategy as played out in the intellectual property field hardly seems consistent, either within the UK or at the interface with developing countries. The process for crafting the necessary dynamic interplay as it impacts on the intellectual property field seems flawed.

Remaining with the theme of databases, the process which resulted in the Directive for the Legal Protection of Databases[40] serves graphically to illustrate the relentless machinery of policy-makers intent upon a certain prioritised policy path, but says much less about balanced dynamic interplay.

In 1988 the European Commission published a proposal for a Directive on the protection of databases.[41] In this the Commission observed that copyright might be inadequate for protecting database producers. At a hearing in Brussels in April 1990 interested parties were given the opportunity to express their views. As the Commission itself reported, no support at all emerged for a *sui*

---

[34] Open access can have many meanings. For discussion in this volume see La Manna, Chapter 10.

[35] The Re-use of Public Sector Information Regulations 2005, SI 2005 No. 1515.

[36] Susskind, p. 237–40.

[37] For example, the Ordnance Survey (www.ordnancesurvey.co.uk).

[38] *Attheraces Ltd v British Horseracing Board* [2005], EWHC 3015 (Ch).

[39] The Office of Fair Trading is currently (June 2006) conducting an investigation into the interfaces between public sector bodies and public sector information, www.oft. gov.uk/Business/Market+studies/commercial.htm.

[40] Directive 96/9/EC of the European Parliament and of the Council of 11 March 1996 on the Legal Protection of Databases (hereafter Database Directive).

[41] Commission of the European Communities (1988), *Green Paper on Copyright and the Challenge of Technology: Copyright Issues Requiring Immediate Action*, COM (88) 172 final, Brussels, 7 June.

generis approach to protection.[42] Undeterred, and bolstered by findings in a number of cases from various courts within the EU[43] and beyond,[44] holding that fact-based databases were not protected by copyright,[45] the Commission pressed ahead with its idea. In 1992 a further proposal was presented by the Commission to the Council. A common position was adopted in 1995,[46] differing markedly from the original proposal but still containing the *sui generis* right. This was finally accepted by the European Parliament, in 1995.[47] Along the way, while database-makers became enthused with the idea (who would say no to more protection, however uncertain its boundaries?), the dissenting voices became louder; in particular, those from the scientific domain where the advancement of science depends upon the examination and re-use of information held within databases. How would the measure impact on this sector? No one was quite sure and so it appears the question was passed over by the policy-makers.

It took nine years and much spilled ink[48] from the enactment of the measure for it to be emasculated by the European Court of Justice in a series of cases dealing with horseracing and football fixture lists.[49] Subsequently, in a scheduled but late review of the measure, the Commission acknowledged that the Directive had failed to stimulate investment in the database industry (its *raison d'être*).[50] So what should be done? Should the Directive be retained? Who better to consult

---

[42]   European Commission (1990), *Follow-up to the Green Paper*, COM (90) 584 final, Brussels, 5 December.

[43]   Supreme Court of the Netherlands, 4 January 1991, *Van Dale Lexicografie B.V. v Rudolf Jan Romme*, noted in English in Dommering, E.J. and Hugenholtz, P.B. (eds) (1991), *Protecting Works of Fact*, Kluwer Law International, p. 93.

[44]   *Feist Publications, Inc. v Rural Telephone Service Co. Inc.* 111 S.Ct. 1282 (1991).

[45]   The Commission also drew on figures supplied by publishers detailing the size and importance of the publishing industry.

[46]   Common position adopted by the Council on 10 July 1995, OJ C 288/14.

[47]   OJ C 17 of 22 January 1996.

[48]   Reichman, J.H. and Samuelson, P. (1997), 'Intellectual Property Rights in Data?', 50 *Vanderbilt Law Review* 51; Cornish, W.R. and Llewellyn, D. (2003), *Intellectual Property Rights*, 5th edn, London: Sweet & Maxwell, para 19.42; Freedman, C.D. (2002), 'Should Canada Enact a New Sui Generis Database Right?', 13 *Fordham Intellectual Property Media & Entertainment LJ* 35; Lipton, J. (2003), 'Balancing Private Rights and Public Policies: Reconceptualizing Property in Databases', *Berkeley Technology LJ*, 773.

[49]   *British Horseracing Board v William Hill* C-203/02 (from the Court of Appeal, England and Wales); *Fixtures Marketing Ltd. v Svenska Spel AB* C-338/02 (from the Hogsta Domstol, Sweden); *Fixtures Marketing Ltd v OY Veikkaus Ab* C-46/02 (from the Vantaan Darajaoikeus, Finland); and *Fixtures Marketing Ltd. v Organismoa Prognostikon Agnon Podosfairou* (OPAP) C-444/02) (from the Monomeles Protodikio Athinion, Greece); [2004] ECR I-10365, 10415, 10497, 10549.

[50]   First evaluation of Directive 96/9/EC on the legal protection of databases, Brussels, 12 December 2005.

(as the Commission did) than the players in the database industry? Yes, the measure should be retained. The review, together with the results of the consultation, is currently out for public comment.[51] Is this the most suitable way in which to forge dynamic interplay? Interest and counter interest were expressed during the process. But where and of whom was the deeper and value-laden question asked: why do we want this measure?[52] There appeared to be limited public engagement in setting the *priorities* for the policy process.

3.2 Responses that were Heard

An area in which space was made to hear voices was in relation to the proposal for a Directive on the Patentability of Computer Programs.[53] A product of European priorities, the protracted process resulted in a 'no' vote in the European Parliament, and the scrapping of the measure on 6 July 2005. But even here, in the speech acknowledging that this particular proposal would go no further, there were hints that the matter would re-emerge in another guise.[54] Why? Because without it there will remain inconsistencies in approach to protection as between Member States which are not subject to review by the ECJ. That is certainly a consideration, but is it a factor that should be given much weight in setting policy priorities in the intellectual sphere? If voices had been heard at the point of setting the priorities, might the argument have been for less, rather than more, protection (for example, from the point of enactment computer programs could not be patented – more intellectual space). The voices were heard but only once the priorities had been set.

3.3 Will Other Responses be Heard?

Yet another example of public engagement in assessing the impact of already enacted measures is the enquiry into digital rights management (DRM) by the UK All Party Parliamentary Internet Group (APIG).[55] Cahir argues that there is no right to the public domain in the common law,[56] and relatedly that deploying DRM to protect content is merely exercising a liberty.[57] But even here that

---

[51]   Ibid.

[52]   For a series of similar questions see Howkins, p. 170.

[53]   Proposal for a Directive of the European Parliament and of the Council on the patentability of computer-implemented inventions, COM(2002) 92 final 2002/0047.

[54]   europa.eu.int/comm/internal_market/indprop/comp/index_en.htm.

[55]   www.apig.org.uk/current-activities/apig-inquiry-into-digital-rights-management. html.

[56]   Cahir, p. 60.

[57]   Cahir, p. 65.

author acknowledges that there may be room for improving the legislative framework. What effect do DRM and the rules against circumvention have on the spaces within the intellectual property framework? – something presumably the APIG seeks to answer. The legislation, developed during negotiations within WIPO resulting in the WIPO Copyright Treaty, followed by rounds of negotiations at European level when being translated into a Directive[58] and finally implemented domestically,[59] has thus already been the subject of an enquiry which seeks to establish how consumers, artists and distribution companies should be protected in a continually evolving market. The consultation was open: over 90 written submissions were received. The Final Report[60] makes a number of recommendations. Notable for present purposes is the recommendation that the Government consider granting a much wider-ranging exemption to the anti-circumvention measures in the Copyright, Designs and Patents Act 1988 for genuine academic research.[61] One wonders whether this will be acted upon – in the limited space the UK legislature might have to do so within its European and international obligations.

4   VALUES

This discussion on the process begs a prior question hinted at above but explicitly raised in the contribution by Bruce. Many of the processes described above are reacting to initiatives and decisions that have already been made somewhere by someone in response to something. Once those decisions have been made, the relentless machinery starts, carving out the propertised from the public domain. The rather murky beginning of the Database Directive is a case in point. What or who was driving the original agenda is far from clear.

At what stage are the values identified by Bruce in relation to the progress of science (what sort of science do we want?)[62] incorporated into the decision-making process in the sphere of intellectual property? In other words, at what stage can or do we consider what sort of intellectual property system we want (a question also asked by Howkins[63])? Where, by whom and according

---

[58]   Directive 2001/29/EC on the harmonisation of certain aspects of copyright and related rights in the information society (Infosoc Directive).

[59]   In the UK, implemented in the Copyright and Related Rights Regulations 2003, SI 2003 No. 2498.

[60]   'Digital Rights Management: Report of an enquiry by the All Party Internet Group', June 2006, available at www.apig.org.uk/current-activities/apig-inquiry-into-digital-rights-management/DRMreport.pdf.

[61]   Ibid., para 65.

[62]   Bruce, p. 284.

[63]   Howkins, p. 170.

to what evidence are the *priorities* (the value questions) set in the policy process?[64]

In the domain of science, there has been much concern to engage the public in the setting of the scientific priorities. Why should the public not also be engaged in setting the value priorities for the intellectual property system? It is, after all, a system which touches upon the daily lives of the majority. And if the public should be involved, how then can that be done?

4.1 How can we Engage the Public in Determining the Spaces of Value in our Intellectual Property System?

Historical discussion on where and how our current public spaces have developed is vital to our understanding of where and why we are where we are now.[65] The majority of the authors in this volume have expressed dissatisfaction with the current configuration, so knowing how we arrived where we are is essential if we are not to repeat past mistakes.[66]

Armed with this understanding, we can move forward. But if we are to do so on a basis upon which the public can be engaged, and which will engage the public, then perhaps it is time to develop a different conceptual framework from which to think about reconfiguring our boundaries. Such a reconfiguration is hinted at in the present volume by Taubman[67] and more fully articulated and developed by Macmillan.[68] Here there was appeal to Roman law in thinking about spaces as *res communes*, *res publicae*, *res divini juris* and *res universitatis*. Would moving in this direction help to engage the public and give the tools through which the values of the intellectual spaces might be expressed?[69]

4.1.1 *Res communes*
If the ideas–expression dichotomy is valued within the domain of *res communes*, Thompson makes some interesting observations on the resultant parameters of

---

[64] See Wallace and Mayer, Chapter 13, for a discussion on the propertisation of science.

[65] Grosheide, Chapter 1.

[66] We must learn from history or we will be 'doomed to repeat it' (George Santayana, 1863–1952).

[67] Taubman, pp. 87–8.

[68] Macmillan, p. 141. For a different suggested configuration see Howkins, p. 173.

[69] Taubman argues that there would be a 'loss of policy context in setting these concepts in bare opposition to one another' as it would lack 'sufficient inductive basis to guide policy-making overall' (p. 88). That is understood. It is not suggested here that the categories be set against one another, but rather that they do or should encompass values through which the public can be engaged and by virtue of which values can be expressed which can in turn be taken into account in setting the priorities.

the space. Seeking too much clarity may not be of benefit to the creative author.[70] But the boundary between property rights and *res communes* is, as Macmillan notes, constantly tested.[71] A high-profile case was recently conducted in the English courts.[72] The publisher, Random House, was sued over allegations that one of their best-selling authors, Dan Brown, infringed the 'ideas' in an earlier book, *The Holy Blood and the Holy Grail*, by Michael Baigent, Richard Leigh and Henry Lincoln. Now although these issues have been explored in court before,[73] some argued that this particular case would serve to illuminate a rather murky area. But is this type of forum, where one suspects that money rather than values mattered most, really the most appropriate for deciding on the boundaries between the appropriable and the properly non-appropriable? Granted, any spaces are always going to be tested in court, and boundaries will shift as a result. But the more fundamental question is about any public engagement in setting the priorities for these boundaries, which themselves can in turn be fought over. Players in a system which valued greater room for intellectual manoeuvre might not feel so threatened by a case which pushed at the edges. It is only where the room for manoeuvre is so constrained that any clarity which may further erode the freedoms becomes worrisome. Ironies also arise. The publishers (in this case Random House) find themselves aligned with an interest grouping different from the one that they might normally be associated with. In this case they are firmly within the values incorporated by *res communes*. In other scuffles, in particular the open access debate noted below, they are firmly aligned on the property side.

4.1.2   The environment of *res publicae*
There are worthy initiatives which implicate *res publicae*. While *res publicae* in intellectual space refers to the lanes and means of communication,[74] libraries are concerned with *populating* this space, as discussed by Bainton in his contribution.[75] A topical example is that of Google and its Print Library project. Under this initiative Google is scanning materials from Harvard, Stanford,

---

[70]   Thompson, p. 201.

[71]   Macmillan, p. 142.

[72]   *Baigent and Leigh v The Random House Group Limited* [2006] EWHC 719 (Ch).

[73]   *Harman Pictures, N. V. v Osborne and Others* [1967] 1 WLR 723 (Ch); *Ravenscroft v Herbert and New English Library Limited* [1980] RPC 193 (Ch D).

[74]   Rose argues that 'the closest analogy to *res publicae* in intellectual space seems to be to the lanes and means of communication, rather than to the content of communication' in Rose, C. (2003), 'Romans, Roads, and Romantic Creators: Traditions of Public Property in the Information Age', 66 *Law & Contemporary Problems* 89 (Winter/Spring), 104.

[75]   Bainton, Chapter 8.

Oxford and Michigan Universities, and the New York Public Library. Users will be able to browse the full text of works on which the term of copyright has expired.[76] There are of course fears that works still within the term of copyright will be reproduced either under this or another initiative (Google Book Search). As a result Google has been sued in the USA both by authors[77] and publishers.[78] Although details of the claims differ, the motivations are the same. At some stage (for those books still within the term of protection) there is infringement of copyright. Google is appealing to *res communes* (fair use) in its defence. Many commentators believe that part of intellectual space is not sufficiently robust to protect Google under these conditions.

Not to be outdone, the European Commission has embarked on an ambitious programme to digitise European libraries.[79] It is a project 'aimed at making European information resources easier and more interesting to use in an online environment'. The intention is to make at least six million books, documents and other cultural works available to anyone with Internet connection through the European Digital Library.[80]

But here again clashes occur between intellectual property rights and intellectual spaces; accessibility versus ownership. The results of an on-line consultation showed that opinions were sharply divided on copyright issues; in particular, between cultural institutions and right-holders.[81] Whereas the right-holders emphasised that present copyright rules were adequate, cultural institutions stressed that change in the present copyright framework is needed for efficient digitisation and digital preservation.

Within Europe the Commission has said that it will address, in a series of policy documents, the issue of the appropriate framework for intellectual property rights protection in the context of digital libraries.[82] Will the Commission engage the public in a debate on what priorities they (the public) would like to

---

[76] Google Print Library Project, on which more information can be found at print. google.com/googleprint/library.html. See also the contribution by Thompson in this volume.

[77] *The Authors Guild and others v Google Inc.* 2005, US District Court, New York.

[78] *The McGraw-Hill Companies, Inc. and others v Google Inc.* 19 October 2005, US District Court, New York.

[79] Communication from the Commission to the European Parliament, the Council, the European Economic and Social Committee and the Committee of the Regions, Brussels, i2010: Digital Libraries COM(2005) 465 final.

[80] www.theeuropeanlibrary.org/portal/index.htm.

[81] The results of the consultation can be found at europa.eu.int/information_society/ activities/digital_libraries/doc/communication/results_of_online_consultation_en.pdf.

[82] Statement at europa.eu.int/information_society/activities/digital_libraries/index_ en.htm.

see represented within these policy documents? Will the public be asked whether intellectual space *should* be broad enough to encompass these initiatives? Will the public be asked as to what *value* they would place on these types of spaces and means of communication as compared with, say, the social value underpinning the granting of rights to give the incentive to create more works? Or will the Commission presume to speak on behalf of the public, perhaps on the grounds that the issues are much too complicated to be understood by the lay person?

4.1.3 *Res universitatis*
The open access movement discussed in this collection by La Manna[83] is set largely within the university research environment and expresses the values that might most clearly be encompassed by *res universitatis*. Although works are authored and owned (something not necessarily within *res universitatis*[84]), that would appear to matter less to those who populate this space than the ability to make 'freely' available the results of research upon which others may build. It is a movement that has support from the grass roots (those who work within the space) and is one which is nurtured by intermediaries (the research councils who make the funding available for the research, the librarians who support the endeavours).[85] Much more limited support is given by the legislators.[86]

4.1.3.1 Corrective checks in res universitatis The potential negative consequences for the advancement of science in propertising scientific knowledge through patents are highlighted in this volume by Wallace and Meyer, who note with particular concern the conflicting values at the research/commercialisation interface.[87] How then to free or re-energise the values expressed through *res universitatis* that might be crowded out? As Macmillan has identified, *res uni-*

---

[83] La Manna, Chapter 10.
[84] Macmillan, p. 150.
[85] For the position of the Wellcome Trust, funders of medical research, see www. wellcome.ac.uk/doc_WTD002766.html. For slightly less wholehearted support, see Research Councils UK position statement (June 2005) on access to research outputs: 'Where research is funded by the Research Councils and undertaken by researchers with access to an open access e-print repository (institutional or subject-based), Councils will make it a condition for all grants awarded from 1 October 2005 that a copy of all resultant published journal articles or conference proceedings (but not necessarily the underlying data) should be deposited in and/or accessible through that repository, subject to copyright or licensing arrangements', available at www.rcuk.ac.uk/access/statement.pdf.
[86] See *Scientific Publications: Free for All? The Government's Response*, available at www.publications.parliament.uk/pa/cm200304/cmselect/cmsctech/1200/120002.htm.
[87] Wallace and Mayer, Chapter 13.

versitatis is not necessarily just made up of spaces that are unowned but may also comprise spaces contractually designed to facilitate synergies.[88] Recognising the strictures that can operate where too much is propertised, the OECD has been investigating the field of licensing of genetic inventions relating to human healthcare, and in particular what effect the granting of patents might have for researchers, firms and clinical users regarding legal access to genetic inventions.[89] Although the group found that fewer problems than anticipated were borne out in practice, problems did arise with the numbers and breadth of gene patents when considered alongside the rise of patents with reach-through claims. As a follow-up, the OECD has drafted a series of 'Principles for the licensing of healthcare genetics'.[90] Noting that research thrives on collaboration and that getting the most out of the genetics revolution will rely increasingly on efficient and effective exchange between those researching and developing new innovations, the guidelines are drafted so as to try and facilitate licensing grounded in economic principles and the elimination of excessive transactions costs, on a basis which ultimately will serve the interests of society, shareholders and other stakeholders.[91]

The juxtaposition of the principles is interesting. Principle 1 B states:

- Licensing practices should encourage the rapid dissemination of information concerning genetic inventions.

Principle 1 C states:

- Licensing practices should provide an opportunity for licensors and licensees to obtain returns from their investment with respect to genetic inventions.

The two are obviously not mutually exclusive, but the priority in this list for rapid dissemination over returns from investment suggests that the values within *res universitatis* are considered more pressing than those of the intellectual

---

[88] Macmillan, p. 151. See also Waelde, C. (2005), 'Creating a contractual research commons: practical experience', in *Intellectual Property Law: Crossing Borders Between Traditional and Actual*, Grosheide, F.W. and Brinkhof, J. (eds) Molengrafica Series, Intersentia 2005, pp. 155–86.

[89] To explore these issues, the OECD Working Party on Biotechnology held an expert group meeting, 'Genetic Inventions, Intellectual Property Rights, and Licensing Practices Evidence and Policies', 2002, available at www.oecd.org/pdf/M00038000/M00038462.pdf.

[90] The Principles, 'Licensing genetic information', can be found at www.oecd.org/document/26/0,2340,en_2649_34537_34317658_1_1_1_1,00.html.

[91] Ibid., para 8.

property right-holder: an interesting approach from a body comprising representatives of States committed to a market economy. It is noteworthy that these principles have been developed by policy-makers from those same countries that have developed and expanded intellectual property rights in international, European and domestic fora. One might ask what values policy-makers considered when expanding rights which they now seek to limit when they are exercised within the market.

4.1.4   *Res divini juris?*

As thinking over the boundaries of intellectual property protection matures, so some begin reconsideration of what might be encompassed within the property right. That deeply held values accruing to some traditional communities may not be most appropriately protected within the existing system is discussed in the present collection by Gibson.[92] How then to bring this area within our intellectual spaces, if indeed it should be there at all? Macmillan suggests the domain of *res universitatis*: traditional knowledge can be valued within a bounded community where knowledge is shared by those within.[93] But there is surely a problem. *Res universitatis*, as has been discussed, is constantly pressurised by commercial interests and, indeed, in some circumstances can survive only in collaboration with these stakeholders. What then of *res divini juris*? If the 'Mickeys' and the 'Minnies' could be subsumed within this category as examples of contemporary iconography, why not then intangible cultural heritage? Might an advantage be that it represents a space that cannot be owned because of its somehow higher order? Recent efforts by UNESCO, culminating in the Convention for the Safeguarding of the Intangible Cultural Heritage,[94] suggest a move in this direction.[95] Rather than extending property rights, the Convention talks of safeguarding, ensuring respect for, and raising awareness of intangible cultural heritage.[96] To advance these aims of the initiative, UNESCO has over recent years 'proclaimed' a number of cultural masterpieces, chosen for their outstanding historical, artistic and ethnological importance and their value for the cultural identity of the tradition-bearer communities.[97] The challenge might be to defend these spaces from external commercial incursion. And as Taubman

---

[92]   Gibson, Chapter 12. See also Taubman, pp. 94–5.

[93]   Macmillan, p. 148.

[94]   Convention for the Safeguarding of the Intangible Cultural Heritage (hereafter Convention), available at portal.unesco.org/culture/en/ev.php-URL_ID=2225&URL_DO=DO_TOPIC&URL_SECTION=201.html.

[95]   See also the discussion by Taubman, p. 96.

[96]   Convention Article 1. Note the signatory states to the Convention.

[97]   The proclaimed masterpieces can be found at www.unesco.org/culture/masterpieces.

notes, that would depend upon 'the hierarchy of competing public goods within the public policy process'.[98] But, if the ordering took place within a system that had accepted these values, there might be strength to resist colonisation.

5   TERMINOLOGY

So can the intellectual spaces debated within this book and other similar initiatives be categorised within *res communes, res publicae, res universitatis* and *res divini juris*? The contributions have been offered by a select few. Each however stands within a particular intellectual space populated and used by others. How then to engage the 'others' in the discussion of the values that the spaces represent and, relatedly, the priorities that should be pursued in the policy process?

If we are to develop categories from which the free spaces can be defended and engage the public in debate about the values that should be encompassed within these spaces, then not only does there need to be a shared understanding of what might fall into those spaces but in addition the terminology we use needs to be readily understood by those who might wish to engage in the debate. Those of us who are passionate about boundaries and intellectual space should not be so arrogant as to assume that all are interested in engaging in the discussion. But neither should we obfuscate to such an extent that the public are unable to engage.

That there is much work to be done can be simply illustrated. Take the meaning of the terms 'cultural' and 'creative', central to the creative side of intellectual property but of which there seems to be little shared understanding as to meaning or value in the legal field or beyond.[99] Several plausible suggestions have been made:

Topical: culture consists of everything on a list of topics, or categories, such as social organisation, religion and economy;
Historical: culture is social heritage, or tradition, that is passed on to future generations;
Behavioural: culture is shared, learned human behaviour, a way of life;
Normative: culture is ideals, values, or rules for living;
Symbolic: culture is based on arbitrarily assigned meanings that are shared by a society.[100]

---

[98]   Taubman, p. 96.
[99]   See also discussion by Howkins, pp. 170–72.
[100] Bodley, J.H. (1994), *An Anthropological Perspective. From Cultural Anthropology: Tribes, States, and the Global System*, Mountain View, CA: Mayfield.

But the terminology slips; the economy becomes cultural:

> Major study on Europe's cultural economy – Press Release.[101] Currently there is no
> precise idea of what the economy of culture really means in Europe and what it is
> worth in socio-economic terms. The Study will help fill these gaps to maximise the
> development potential of the cultural and creative industry sectors.

And industries become creative:

> WIPO establishes the Creative Industries Division. WIPO has recently established
> the Creative Industries Division. This has been done in response to the growing inter-
> est and needs of the Member States of WIPO to address the economic developmental
> impact that intellectual property policies and practices have on the creative industries.
> The objective of the Division is to provide a focal point for related policy and industry
> discourse.[102]

The point is to emphasise that there is no agreed or accepted vocabulary of what
it is we value. We need a common starting point from which we can develop a
shared set of values which can in turn be subject to public debate and from
which policy priorities can be developed.

6   ENGAGING THE PUBLIC

But even when starting from an agreed vocabulary it might prove difficult to
reach shared understandings of or consensus about what it is that should be
valued. Bruce explains an example in the scientific domain of the constitution
of a committee to discuss values within science and narrates the deadlock that
subsequently occurred.[103] But never let it be said that such an exercise is impossible. Howkins notes a recent initiative, that of drafting the Adelphi Charter.[104]
A team of experts representing the public interest joined together to produce a
statement of principles the group considered should be reflected in intellectual
property law making. Article 9 of the Adelphi Charter provides:

> In making decisions about intellectual property law, governments should adhere to
> these rules:

---

[101]   Study on the cultural economy in Europe (EAC/03/05) information available at
europa.eu.int/comm/culture/eac/sources_info/studies/studies_en.html.

[102]   Information available on the UNESCO website at portal.unesco.org/culture/en/
ev.php-URL_ID=29862&URL_DO=DO_TOPIC&URL_SECTION=201.html. For the
WIPO site (on which there is less information) see www.wipo.int/sme/en/documents/
email_updates/contact_creative_industries_division.htm.

[103]   Bruce, Chapter 14.

[104]   Howkins, p. 175.

- There must be an automatic presumption against creating new areas of intellectual property protection, extending existing privileges or extending the duration of rights.
- The burden of proof in such cases must lie on the advocates of change.
- Change must be allowed only if a rigorous analysis clearly demonstrates that it will promote people's basic rights and economic well-being.
- Throughout, there should be wide public consultation and a comprehensive, objective and transparent assessment of public benefits and detriments.[105]

The public has also been involved in endorsing a call to WIPO – the Geneva Declaration on the Future of WIPO. The plea is that WIPO should consider 'changes of direction, new priorities, and better outcomes for humanity' in setting priorities for the future direction of intellectual property development.[106]

Indeed, a thought experiment in a similar vein was carried out by the AHRC Research Centre for Studies in Intellectual Property and Technology Law at the University of Edinburgh in September 2004. Representatives of a number of diverse interest groups (publishers, academic authors, intellectual property lawyers and organisations, academic libraries, funding bodies and those involved in technology transfer, industry and government) were invited to consider 'an IP-free world in higher education'. The purpose was to reflect on how a system might develop if starting from scratch. A fascinating dialogue took place over the course of two days, during which delegates were invited to swap roles to consider different points of view. Much discussion revolved around the open access debate, which at the time was highly topical. Although no firm consensus was attained (none was sought), the majority of delegates left with a deeper understanding of the values held by others.[107]

These examples illustrate that it is possible to engage in debates over values and that there is value in engaging in the debate. However, to the observer it would appear that these possibilities are not (yet) being heeded by legislators.

---

[105] For examples in the database area, see 'Access to Databases: Principles for Science in the Internet Era', prepared by the ICSU/CODATA Ad Hoc Group on Data and Information, available at www.codata.org/data_access/principles.html. Principles include: 'Science is an investment in the public interest; Scientific advances rely on full and open access to data; A market model for access to data is unsuitable for research and education; Publication of data is essential to scientific research and the dissemination of knowledge; The interests of database owners must be balanced with society's need for open exchange of ideas; Legislators should take into account the impact intellectual property laws may have on research and education'. Each principle is accompanied by an explanatory text.

[106] The Declaration can be found at www.cptech.org/ip/wipo/genevadeclaration. html.

[107] Had we closeted our partners for a week, we might have a new system! An edited note of the meeting can be found at www.law.ed.ac.uk/ahrc/projects/files.aspx?id=1.

Expansive property rights are continually pursued that few (but the most interested) seem to want,[108] only to be followed by corrective checks implemented by those same legislative representatives when exercise of those same property rights appear one-sided. These are complemented by endless public consultations, mostly reactive and too targeted to deal with the prior value issues.[109] One grass-roots response to this has of course been the emergence of alternative systems within the framework – of which the open access movement is an example. But, as these alternative mechanisms develop, is there a danger that the whole system will get even more out of balance? One response from the intellectual property maximalists might be that the very existence of these alternative methods means that property rights can expand. Anyone who wants to join an alternative movement can do so. But that of course is unrealistic. The majority of these movements pit those in favour of the property right against those who would defend the spaces: the effort required is extraordinary and the result in danger of becoming ever more confused.

7   CONCLUSION AND A NEW START?

It seems that, if we are to try to engage the public in a discussion on the values that should be expressed in the intellectual property system, and most particularly as to what it is that is valued in the intellectual spaces in the system, then the categorisations of *res communes*, *res publicae*, *res universitatis* and *res divini juris* are a good starting point. Drawing on historical experience, these categories are at least in part populated by ideas and values which can be understood and thus debated by the interested public. It goes without saying that they need to be elaborated upon as the debate matures. However there is one caveat. By remaining with Latin maxims to hold the values together, are we likely to exclude

---

[108]   See the discussion on the proposal for the Directive on the patentability of computer software above. Note also the discussions in WIPO relating to a proposed broadcasting treaty: Second Revised consolidated text for a Treaty on the Protection of Broadcasting Organisations, available on the WIPO website, paper SCCR/12/2 Rev.2, May 2005, and the controversy it has spawned (e.g. Naughton, J., 'A law unto themselves', *The Guardian*, Sunday 13 June 2004).

[109]   Note the Gowers Review of Intellectual Property, which states in part: 'While it has been suggested that the present UK system strikes broadly the right balance between consumers and rights-holders, it also appears that there are a variety of practical issues with the existing framework. The Review will look at both the instruments (patents, copyright, designs etc.) that are provided by government to protect creative endeavour, and also at the operations: how IP is awarded, how it is licensed in the market, and how it is enforced. The Review will examine whether improvements could be made and, as appropriate, make targeted and practical policy recommendations.'

sections of the potentially interested public by being seen as elitist and exclusionary, fencing the debate from those who might be interested, and corralling only those who share some form of understanding as to what they think these terms actually mean? Populist appeal may be anathema to some, and however populist not everyone will engage, but the attempt should at least be made. Naming has perhaps contributed a good deal to the engagement of the public with other initiatives in recent years. 'Access to medicines' might be one example; 'creative commons' another. The challenge is to find words that would express the values encompassed by *res communes, res publicae, res divini juris* and *res universitatis* through which the public can be engaged, by virtue of which intellectual spaces can represent what is valued, and the result of which can have real impact in setting policy priorities.

Index